Tourist Clusters, Destinations and Competitiveness

Tourism has become one of the largest and fastest growing sectors in the world economy. Increasingly, research on tourism destinations has been at the centre of debates concerning destination competitiveness, governance, policies and destination management and marketing.

This book investigates tourist destinations from two different perspectives. First, it approaches destinations using the concept of tourist clusters and investigates their role in competitiveness and firm performances. The second perspective studies the development of models of competitiveness and governance. The book also develops an international benchmarking system of EU-15 countries, with a specific focus on Italy, the UK and the United States.

The book will appeal to academics, scholars and practitioners in tourism studies, management, urban and regional studies and economic geography.

Francesco Capone is Assistant Professor at the Department of Economics and Management, University of Florence, Italy.

Routledge Advances in Regional Economics, Science and Policy

Tourist Clusters, Destinations and Competitiveness

Theoretical issues and empirical evidences

Edited by
Francesco Capone

Routledge
Taylor & Francis Group

LONDON AND NEW YORK

First published 2016 by Routledge

2 Park Square, Milton Park, Abingdon, Oxfordshire OX14 4RN
52 Vanderbilt Avenue, New York, NY 10017

*Routledge is an imprint of the Taylor & Francis Group,
an informa business*

First issued in paperback 2019

British Library Cataloguing in Publication Data
A catalogue record for this book is available from the British Library

Library of Congress Cataloging-in-Publication Data
A catalog record for this book has been requested

ISBN: 978-1-138-89169-2 (hbk)
ISBN: 978-0-367-87288-5 (pbk)

Typeset in Times New Roman
by Apex CoVantage, LLC

To Elena, Lorenzo and Viola

Contents

PART II
**Tourist clusters and performance, creative and
experience economy**   101

Figures

Tables

Contributors

Rafael Boix, PhD, is Associate Professor at the Department of Economic Structure, University of Valencia. He has been an external advisor for the Organisation for Economic Co-operation and Development (OECD) and other national and local organizations. His most recent research has been published in *Land Use Policy, Papers in Regional Science, European Planning Studies, European Urban and Regional Studies*, and *Service Business*.

Francesco Capone, PhD, is Assistant Professor in Management at the Department of Economics and Management, University of Florence. He is member of the Doctorate Programme 'Developing Economics and Local Systems' at the University of Trento and University of Florence. His research interests deal with firm, network and cluster competitiveness, particularly in tourism, Made in Italy and cultural and creative industries. He recently published in *European Planning Studies, Industry and Innovation, City Culture and Society, Tourism Geographies, European Urban and Regional Research, Annals of Regional Science*, and *Maritime Policy and Management*.

Lisa De Propris is Professor of Regional Economic Development in the Birmingham Business School at the University of Birmingham (UK). Her main research interests are competitiveness in clusters and industrial districts, innovation and knowledge economy, global value chains and creative and cultural industries. In parallel, she has been concerned with the role of the government and institutions, and has looked at policy implications. Her research has been published among others in *Regional Studies, Journal of Economic Geography, Creative Industries Journal, Policy Studies, European Urban and Regional Research*, and others journals.

Niccolò Innocenti, PhD, is Research Fellow at the Department of Economics and Management at the University of Florence. His research interests deal with economic development, growth and competitiveness according to Evolutionary Economic Geography. He spent a visiting period at Utrecht University. He has recently published in *International Review on Public and Nonprofit Marketing* and *Paper in Evolutionary Economics*.

Luciana Lazzeretti is Full Professor of Management and Economics, and Founding Director of the Post-graduate Programme in 'Economics and Management of Cultural Goods and Museums', University of Florence. She is also the vice-coordinator of the Doctorate Programme 'Developing Economics and Local Systems' at the University of Trento and University of Florence, and an Associate Professor at the Institute of Applied Physics CNR-IFAC, Florence. She recently published *Creative Industries and Innovation in Europe* with Routledge (2013), as well as *Creative Cities, Cultural Clusters and Local Economic Development* with Edward Elgar in 2008 (with Phil Cooke) and *Tourism Local Systems and Networking* with Elsevier in 2006 (with Clara S. Petrillo).

Angel Peiró-Signes, PhD, holds a PhD in business and BS degrees in industrial engineering and mechanical engineering. He is Assistant Professor in Analytical Accounting and Strategic Management at the School of Management at the Polytechnic University of Valencia (Spain) and has been a Research Associate of the Center for Hospitality Research, CHR, Cornell University (USA) from 2011–2014. He has published several articles in high impact journals such as *Cornell Hospitality Quarterly, Innovation: Management, Policy & Practice*, and *European Planning Studies*.

Marival Segarra-Oña, PhD, is Associate Professor of Innovation and Competitiveness at the Management School at the Polytechnic University of Valencia (Spain). She holds a PhD in management and BS degrees in industrial engineering and mechanical engineering. She was a Research Associate of the Center for Hospitality Research, CHR, Cornell University (USA) from 2011–2014 and now is the Academic Director of the Master's degree on Management of the Business School in her university. She is the author of several papers and articles. Her research has been published in *Science and Engineering Ethics, Corporate Social Responsibility and Environmental Management*, and *Cornell Hospitality Quarterly*.

Rohit Verma is the Singapore Tourism Board Distinguished Professor and Asian Hospitality Management Professor of Service Operations Management at the School of Hotel Administration (SHA) at Cornell University (USA). He is the Executive Director of the Cornell Institute for Healthy Futures and also served as the Executive Director of the Cornell Center for Hospitality Research (CHR) in 2009–2012. He is currently the director of SHA's Executive Master Program Development Project. Prof. Verma has published over 60 articles in prestigious journals including *Decision Sciences, Journal of Operations Management, Journal of Product Innovation Management, Journal of Service Research, MIT Sloan Management Review*, and *Production and Operations Management*.

Tourist destinations, clusters and competitiveness

An introduction

Francesco Capone

The relevance of tourism and tourist destinations

Tourism has become one of the largest and fastest growing sectors in the world economy. In the last few years, it has demonstrated a remarkable resilience and proved to be strategic in the attempt to exit the present global economic crisis (OECD 2014a; Ritchie 2009).

On average, tourism directly contributes around 4.7% of GDP, 6% of employment and 21% of service exports in the Organisation for Economic Co-operation Development (OECD) member countries (OECD 2014a). Over the period from 2010–30, international tourist arrivals are envisaged to see a 3.3% growth, which means an estimated total of more than 1.8 billion by 2030 (UNTWO 2011). Given these premises, the tourism sector of the industrialised economies still plays a leadership role at international level, differently from manufacturing, which is facing an ever increasing competition from developing countries, especially Brazil, Russia, India and China. In 2012, the tourism sector of the industrialised economies represented 57% of global arrivals (OECD 2014a) and, according to *The Travel and Tourism Competitiveness Report 2015* (WEF 2015), Spain, France, Germany, the USA, the UK, Italy and Australia are keeping the first seven positions.

In recent years, a central focus has been increasingly devoted to tourist destinations, with several studies that dealt with the issues related to competitiveness, governance, policies and destination management and marketing (Kozak and Baloglu 2011; Laws *et al*. 2011; Morrison 2013; Viken and Granas 2014; Halkier, Kozak and Svensson 2015). Even if the study of tourist destinations represents a fairly recent strand of research, having taken root with some contributions written during the 1990s (Laws 1995; Leiper 1995; and others), it has acquired an increasing importance due to globalisation, the heightened competition and the rise of destinations from developing countries.

From this perspective, the study of competitiveness in tourism has widened its reach, having started with a focus on firms and networks and then shifting to include the intra and inter-destinations levels (Capone 2006; Pearce 2013). What seems fundamental for tourism competitiveness is to adopt and develop an approach on destinations aimed at building a sustainable competitive advantage for both the tourist firms and networks, and the tourist places and regions.

This book approaches the study of tourist destinations from two integrated perspectives. The first one focuses on the analysis of tourist clusters in destinations, while the second one regards the governance, destination competitiveness and its management. The next section describes the relevance of these two approaches for the study of destinations.

The relevance of tourist clusters, destination management and competitiveness

The application of the cluster theory to tourism has long been of unquestionable interest, at first in association with problems of competitiveness and later as a means for fostering innovation (Nordin 2003). Research literature reveals that cluster theory has been suitably adapted to the peculiarities of the tourism sector and provides a spatial and organisational model that promotes competitiveness, innovation and local economic development (Jackson and Murphy 2006; Lazzeretti and Petrillo 2006; Novelli, Schmitz and Spencer 2006; Michael 2007; Santos, Almeida and Teixeira 2008).

However, a preliminary question is to define what is then a 'tourist cluster'. Porter (1998) defines clusters as geographical concentrations of interconnected companies, specialised suppliers, service providers, firms in related industries and associated institutions in particular industries that compete, but also co-operate. Porter had already discussed the idea of a tourist cluster while analysing the anatomy of the California wine and tourist cluster, pointing out that:

> A host of linkages among cluster members result in a whole greater than the sum of its part. In a typical tourism cluster, for example, the quality of a visitor's experience depends not only on the appeal of the primary attraction but also on the quality and efficiency of complementary businesses such as hotels, restaurants, shopping outlets and transportation facilities. Because members of the cluster are mutually dependent, good performance by one can boost the success of the others.
>
> (1998: 77)

Clusters are not just only composed of interrelated firms, but they benefit from the presence of local institutions and meta-governance organisation. The cluster concept focuses on the linkages and interdependencies among actors in the value chain of products, services and innovations (OECD 2009). In addition, recalling the concept of industrial districts (Becattini, Bellandi and De Propris 2009), clusters are based on social values that foster trust and encourage reciprocity (Nordin 2003).

Literature on clusters, despite criticism (Martin and Sunley 2003), has widely recognised that the concentration of firms in a specific area promotes the competitiveness of local enterprises and their innovation capabilities (Baptista 2000; Porter 2003; Tallman *et al.* 2004; and others).

The clustering in a territory as a determinant of firms' competitiveness has been extended some time ago to the tourism industry and cultural and creative industries, which led to the coining of terms such as *tourist cluster* and *district*

(Hjalager 2000; Lazzeretti and Petrillo 2006), *cultural cluster* and *district* (Santagata 2002; Lazzeretti 2003) and *creative cluster* (De Propris *et al.* 2009).

Despite the importance of the cluster concept in the field of tourism studies, because much literature has focused on the agglomeration of manufacturing firms in a territory, the effect of tourist clusters on competitiveness and firm performance is often taken for granted, and early contributions have investigated them mainly in terms of case studies in specific destinations (Jackson and Murphy 2006; Novelli, Schmitz and Spencer 2006; Santos, Almeida and Teixeira 2008). In this respect, the present book intends to partly cover some research issues that were not sufficiently discussed until now.

Next to the research branch on tourist clusters, another macro-issue within the study of destinations has powerfully emerged, that of destination management and destination competitiveness. The studies of destination management (and marketing) have in fact recorded an exponential growth in the field of tourism studies (Morgan, Pritchard and Pride 2011; Morrison 2013; Halkier, Kozak and Svensson 2015). The results of a Scopus citation search found more than 1,000 contributions on these topics, most of which had been made during the last decade.[1] In this area of studies, an increasing weight has been placed on destination competitiveness, starting from the contribution of Crouch and Ritchie (1999), up to the more recent works of these and other authors (Dwyer and Kim 2003; Ritchie and Crouch 2003; Enright and Newton 2004).

The competitiveness of tourist destinations is more and more at the centre of the debate on tourism, and the amplification of the economic crisis has certainly been a strong factor in emphasising its significance (Laesser and Beritelli 2013).

Consequently, the analysis of competitiveness turned out to be a multi-level investigation, combining the examination of firms, networks and destinations (Pearce 2013). This is because it is recognised that visitors' satisfaction for a destination is closely linked to local firms – composing the overall visitors' experience – and that the competitiveness of destinations necessarily goes through the configuration and governance of the local tourist supply. Given this background, the analysis of destination competitiveness takes up a fundamental role in terms of the competitiveness not only of territories, but also of firms.

In this light, management studies may provide a useful support, considering how the governance of destination has gained a more and more central position in the analysis of destination competitiveness (Laws *et al.* 2011; Bramwell and Lane 2012; Svensson, Nordin and Flagestad 2005). For this reason, the study of tourism competitiveness must necessarily include also the examination of governance of local tourist supply, and destinations' competitiveness.

Structure, aim and research questions of this book

Considering the above-described general setting, this book investigates tourist destinations from two different perspectives: the tourist supply built by destinations, and their governance as a mean to enhance their competitiveness. The first perspective referring to the study of a destination's supply applies to firms, *filières* and networks of firms, and aims at the identification of the determinants for their competitiveness. In this field, tourist destinations are approached using the concept of tourist cluster, and they are considered as places that develop, along with artistic, cultural and environmental attractions, clusters of firms operating in the tourism sector (either narrowly or broadly defined), cooperating and competing together in view of the system's overall competitiveness.

The second perspective undertakes the study of destinations developing models of competitiveness and governance, starting from the contributions of destination management (Pechlaner and Weiermair 2000; Franch 2002; Howie, 2003; World Tourism Organisation (WTO) 2007; Sciarelli, 2007; Kozak and Baloglu 2011; Morrison 2013; Halkier, Kozak and Svensson 2015; Pencarelli, 2015) and destination competitiveness (Ritchie and Crouch 2003; Bornhorst, Ritchie and Sheehan 2010).

The bibliometric analysis on tourist destination research presented in Chapter 1 proves that the main analytical models of tourist destinations match these two perspectives. The present volume adopts these two approaches, and is aimed at taking into account the competitiveness of destinations and of their firms in a way that fits into an integrated multi-level framework for the analysis of destinations (Pearce 2013).

The focus of this book is in line with literature and, following the previous contributions tries to compose the different strands of research by adopting a multi-level approach and cross-fertilize the strand of research on destination management and marketing with the local development approach. Specifically, the main issues that will be dealt with are presented in Figure I.1, which illustrates the various research branches involved.

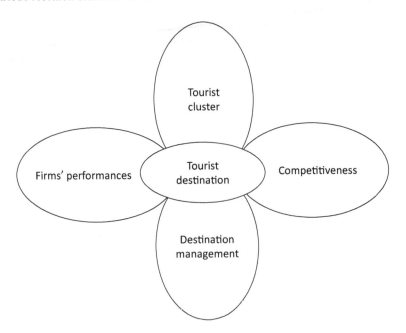

Figure I.1 Intersection of the book's different branches of research

Source: our elaboration.

The key, transversal issue in this book is that of tourist destinations, which are discussed all through its pages, and examined in-depth for what concern their competitiveness as well as that of the firms belonging to them. Hence, the first branch of research pertains to tourist destinations and their competitiveness.

The second branch of research approaches destinations in terms of the possible presence of tourist clusters, which can be defined by a reinterpretation of Porter's (1998) words, like concentrations of interrelated firms and institutions operating in the (more or less broad) tourism sector and cooperating and competing together for the system's overall competitiveness.[2] This area of study echoes the multifarious contributions on tourist clusters and destinations (e.g. Nordin 2003; Lazzeretti and Petrillo 2006; Michael 2007).

The third branch of research recalls the concept of business performance and looks at how tourist destinations and clusters can affect the competitiveness of firms, and thus their performance (Canina, Enz and Harrison 2005; Enz, Canina and Liu 2008; Peiró-Signes *et al*. 2015). In particular, in this book the attention is primarily directed to the firms that operate in one of the most important tourism sectors, i.e. the hotel industry.

The last branch of research concerns destination management and destination competitiveness, and examines how tourist destinations may become more competitive and tourist firms improve their performance with the help of enhanced analytical models, a better governance and an efficient destination management at the local level. In this respect, a special consideration is given to the growing trend in literature of issues like the destination management, the destination marketing and branding (Ashworth and Kavaratzis, 2010; Go and Govers, 2000; 2012; Bellini, Loffredo, Pasquinelli, 2010) and the destination management organisation (Pike 2007; Kozak and Baloglu 2011; Morrison 2013).

An increasing interest in tourist destination, cluster and competitiveness has been shown in several disciplines. In particular, the study of tourist destination, which has always been typical of tourism studies, has recently gained success in other fields. Also, the possible contribution of management studies to the analysis of destination turns quite significant, not only from the viewpoint of governance, but also in terms of the management of the destination's supply system, which fuels much literature on competitiveness. A strong interest was also shown in other disciplines for what concerns the configuration of local supply, the clustering phenomenon, and the development and competitiveness of destinations, cities and regions. This research strand has in fact received important contributions from scholars of economic geography (Brouder and Eriksson 2013; Sanz-Ibáñez and Anton Clavé 2014), and urban and regional studies (Ioannides 2006; Cruz and Teixeira 2010; Estevão and Ferreira 2012; Halkier, Kozak and Svensson 2015), a fact that illustrates the necessary multidisciplinarity of tourist clusters and stands as proof that this book may appeal to different research communities.

This volume fits into this context of evolving literature and of transformations in the tourism phenomenon and seeks to suggest robust and quantitative analysis on tourist destinations, tourist clusters and their competitiveness, through the collaboration of a group of international researchers, including scholars from Europe (Italy, Spain, UK, etc.), and the USA – which makes it a multidisciplinary contribution.

The book is the result of the development of a research branch started about 10 years ago (Capone, 2005; Capone and Boix 2008; Lazzeretti and Capone 2008). The work is developed from this stream of research and allows us to constitute a group of researchers at the international level. The first event that marked this research path was the International Workshop on 'Tourist clusters, destinations and competitiveness in tourism' – organised at the University of Florence on 27 March 2015 in the Master's degree in 'Design of Sustainable Tourism Systems' and in the Postgraduate Course in 'Economics and Management of Museums and Cultural Goods' – where we had our first discussion on the early works and results, and provide some comments and opinions about the project's development.

It seems now useful to recall the main questions that guided our discussion to investigate tourist destinations, which are the following:

- Which are the main analytical models to study tourist destinations? How can we analyse their governance and improve their competitiveness?
- Which role do tourist clusters play in the competitiveness of destination? How can they be defined and then identified?
- Which role do clusters play in the performance of tourist firms? How do we increase the performance of local firms?
- What are the connections between tourism, creativity and experience economy in regard to the future of destination competitiveness?

The first part of this book attempts to answer the first two groups of questions, while the second part is focuses on the following two. We propose a set of quantitative methodologies for the analysis of tourist destinations and of their competitiveness that is easily extendable to other industries, territories and contexts. Following this introduction, the volume is divided into two parts and eight chapters.

The first part, 'Tourist destinations, destination management, cluster and competitiveness', starting from the investigation of tourist destinations focuses on two main themes of great significance in literature: tourist clusters and destination management. In summary, the corresponding approaches turn to represent the main research branches on tourist destinations, and thus deserve a precise, in-depth examination in terms of an analysis of firm and destination competitiveness.

The reader is introduced to the book in Chapter 1, which presents a bibliometric analysis of literature on tourist destination research. The chapter surveys the main contributions on tourist destinations and outlines the main approaches of research: the destination management, which has chiefly developed in the area of management and governance studies on destinations, and the tourist cluster, which stands in the middle between management studies and industrial economics, and is mainly focused on the configuration of tourist supply in a specific destination and on the benefits obtained from firm clustering.

After having examined tourist destination research, the first part moves on to the issues of destination management and marketing, with a chapter devoted to the review of literature and then to the study of destination competitiveness.

Next, an analysis of tourist destinations is carried out under the lens of the concept of the tourist cluster, which focuses on the crucial presence of synergies among the tourism activities of destinations using the related-variety approach.

This part concludes with an analysis that defines and identifies tourist clusters in Europe using firm data so as to derive a first mapping of the tourist destinations in the continent. Chapter 4 underlines the importance of recognising clusters in the territory, seen as crucial for suggesting governance implications and improve the tourism competitiveness in Europe. The chapter puts forward an examination of the main tourist clusters in the 15-EU countries and offers a wide, original set of data. This study, among others, may be extended and applied to different contexts and territories.

The second part, 'Tourist cluster and performances, creativity and experience economy', especially in what concerns the first two chapters, is centred on the macro-issue of firm performance in tourist destinations and clusters, and specifically presents two studies on this subject. The first two chapters in this part illustrate two cases, one for Italy and the other for the USA, of firm performances in the hotel industry, considered one of the main industries in the tourism sector. Both chapters seek to underline the cluster effect in the performance of tourist firms, and the importance of localisation for the business strategies of tourist firms.

In the last chapters, the book aims to widen the debate over tourism, also reflecting on the recent development trends of tourism studies, like creative economy (Florida, 2002; Lazzeretti, 2013), creative tourism and creative industries (Richards and Wilson 2007; Richards 2011; 2013; OECD 2014b), and the experience and event economy (Lorentzen and Hansen 2009; Lorentzen 2013). In fact, Chapter 7 is focused on the interrelations between tourism and creativity, particularly in the creative industries (DCMS 2001; 2013; Lazzeretti 2013), and evaluates their contribution to the generation of new entrepreneurship and firm formation. Finally, Chapter 8 concerns an enlarged analysis of tourism that concentrates on the new trend of the experience economy. This final chapter investigates key features of the experience-related industries in order to appreciate how they compare with the new trend of the creative economy and creative industries.

In the following section, the single chapters are presented with a brief description of the methodologies adopted and the results achieved.

Chapter organisation

Chapter 1 aims to analyse the academic research on tourist destinations and its evolution in tourism studies, through a bibliometric co-citations analysis on the Thomson Reuters Web of Science database. *Capone* elaborates a database of journal articles on the Thomson Reuters Web of Science database. The birth and evolution of research on tourist destinations and clusters is investigated through the analysis of almost 1,000 publications appearing over the course of 15 years, and its most interesting trajectories are highlighted. The results show that the dissemination of the cluster concept has fast developed from the initial years of its rise and constantly grown until recent years, whereas today its use in tourism studies has declined as compared to the rising branch of research on destination management and destination marketing.

Chapter 2 discusses how in recent years competitiveness in tourism has intensified because of both the economic crisis and the process of globalisation, so that the study of competitiveness has shifted from the focus on firms and networks of firms to that on competitiveness for destinations and among destinations. The aim of Chapter 2 is twofold. On the one hand, the first part presents the state of the art and evolution of the literature on destination management and marketing, until dealing with the studies on destination competitiveness, seen as a prominent topic in recent research. On the other hand, the second part develops an analytical model of destination competitiveness that combines the most relevant contributions on this issue and investigates a specific case of competitiveness in an Italian tourist destination, Maremma.

Chapter 3 aims to measure the impact of related tourism activities in the competitiveness of tourist destinations, according to the concept of related variety. The purpose of this chapter is to explore the factors behind the clustering of tourist firms. Recent studies exploring the growth of destinations have suggested that the presence of clusters is the main reason for their competitiveness. *Lazzeretti, Capone* and *Innocenti* contribute to this line of research by applying an analytical model to the factors underlying the clustering of firms in Italian tourist destinations. The study analyses the evolution of tourist destinations over a decade using spatial analysis and applying the related-variety approach to the phenomenon of clustering. The results show that related variety is an important factor in the clustering of tourist firms, emphasising that the existence of groups of related tourism activities in a particular destination is essential for the destination's development and competitiveness.

How many clusters of tourist firms are there in Europe and where are they located? Although it seems an elementary question, so far there is not any geography of tourist clusters in Europe. In Chapter 4, *Capone* and *Boix* provide basic stylised facts about the spatial patterns of clustering of tourist firms in Europe. The authors propose a novel methodology which minimises statistical information requirements and allows to identify the number and spatial boundaries of tourist clusters. The methodology is based on a geo-statistical algorithm and firm-based micro-data. The procedure is applied to a continuous space of 15 European countries and a basic chain of tourism activities in 2013. The investigation reveals that tourist firms are highly clustered, and that clusters are concentrated in a 'belt' stretching from the south of Europe to the northern European countries. The chapter provides a first analysis of tourist clusters in Europe that it is original and was not developed before.

Capone in Chapter 5 points out that despite the relevance of the cluster concept in tourism studies, the contribution of the agglomeration of firms to their performance is often taken for granted. This chapter aims to test and measure the effects of clustering in the tourism industry, in particular whether hotels have a better performance if they are located inside clusters. In order to investigate this aspect, Capone analyses the performances of more than 11,000 hotels located in the Italian territory in the last five years as drawn from the Amadeus database (2008–12). The results demonstrate substantially better performances of firms located inside clusters as compared to firms located outside. However, the results differ depending on some variables, like the structural characteristics of hotels and the typology of the local clusters. The implications deal with the role of location choices of hotels in clusters and the relevance for small and medium hotels to develop networks and improve the competitiveness of the overall systems.

In Chapter 6, *Segarra, Peiró* and *Verma* identify geographical concentrations in the tourism, travel and leisure industry in the United States, using the location quotient. After developing this classification, they locate hotels inside and outside these agglomerations in order to see whether the cluster effect can be identified in this particular industry and, if so, how it affects the different types of establishments segmented by price. They use panel data from 2006–11 retrieved from PKF Consulting's Hotel Horizons database. The results show that the upper-priced and lower-priced segments inside and outside the cluster do not evolve in the same way. Clustered markets grow more slowly than other markets, but are significantly more efficient in growing their occupancy than the corresponding markets outside the cluster, if they are in the upper-priced segment.

In Chapter 7, *Lazzeretti* and *Capone* discuss the relevance of the creative economy, which is continuing to grow in recent years, and find that important synergies with tourism are emerging, offering considerable potential for increasing demand and developing new products, experiences and markets. According to the authors, this contemporary debate focuses on the shift from conventional models of cultural tourism to new models of creative tourism based on intangible culture and contemporary creativity. The aim of Chapter 7 is to examine the relationship between tourism and creativity, with a specific focus on cultural and creative industries. The study investigates the contribution to new firm creation and entrepreneurship in tourism and in the cultural and creative industries, analysing also their patterns of clustering and co-locations, through a case study of Tuscany.

Chapter 8 presents an analysis of the experience economy in the UK context. *Boix* and *De Propris* propose an analytical framework where the key features of the experience-related industries are identified in order to appreciate how they compare with creative industries. The authors present a map of the British experience economy providing a better understanding of its spatial patterns. Key findings are that in the UK experience-related industries tend to concentrate in rural and peripheral areas; besides, the correlation analysis shows that such industries tend to co-locate and in particular, places that show a high degree of specialisation of experience activities also host a critical mass of hospitality activities.

Acknowledgements

I would like to thank all the contributors of this book, and especially to Rossella Lazzeretti, for their collaboration, support and help in getting to the end of this long road. I express my gratitude also to Robert Langham for his interest in this project and to Lisa Thompson for her support and always kind help. This volume would not have been possible without the editing assistance of Alessandra Pini.

Notes

1   On this point, see Chapter 2.
2   In this definition the role of interrelations among firms is underlined so as to avoid an overemphasis on 'pure agglomerations'. See Chapters 3, 4 and 5 in this book for a discussion of the different aspects of firms' interrelations, like trust and cooperation relationships, which are of fundamental importance for the competitiveness of clustered firms.

References

Ashworth G. and Kavaratzis M. (2010) (eds.) *Towards Effective Place Brand Management. Branding European Cities and Regions*, Cheltenham, UK: Edward Elgar Publishing.

Baptista, R. (2000) 'Do innovations diffuse faster within geographical clusters?' *International Journal of Industrial Organization*, 18(3): 515–35.

Becattini, G., Bellandi, M. and De Propris, L. (eds) (2009) *Handbook of Industrial Districts*, Cheltenham, UK: Edward Elgar.

Bellini, N., Loffredo A. and Pasquinelli C., (2010) 'Managing Otherness: The Political Economy of Place Images in the Case of Tuscany' in Ashworth G. and Kavaratzis M. (2010) (eds.) *Towards Effective Place Brand Management. Branding European Cities and Regions*, Cheltenham: Edward Elgar, pp. 89–115.

Bornhorst, T., Ritchie, J.R.B. and Sheehan, L. (2010) 'Determinants of tourism success for DMOs and destinations: An empirical examination of stakeholders' perspectives', *Tourism Management*, 31(5): 572–89.

Bramwell, B. and Lane, B. (2012) *Tourism Governance. Critical Perspectives on Governance and Sustainability*, Abingdon: Routledge.

Brouder, P. and Eriksson, R. H. (2013) 'Tourism evolution: On the synergies of tourism studies and evolutionary economic geography', *Annals of Tourism Research*, 43 (October): 370–89.

Canina, L., Enz, C. A. and Harrison, J. (2005) 'Agglomeration effects and strategic orientations: Evidence from the US lodging industry', *Academy of Management Journal*, 48(4): 565–81.

Capone, F. (2005) *I Sistemi Locali Turistici in Italia. Identificazione, analisi e misurazione delle fonti di competitività*, Firenze University Press, Firenze.

Capone, F. (2006) 'Systemic approaches for the analysis of tourism destination: Towards the tourist local systems', in L. Lazzeretti and C. S. Petrillo (eds), *Tourism Local Systems and Networking*, Amsterdam: Elsevier, pp. 7–23.

Capone, F. and Boix, R. (2008) 'Sources of growth and competitiveness of local tourist production systems: An application to Italy (1991–2001)', *The Annals of Regional Science*, 42(1): 209–24.

Crouch, G. I. and Ritchie, J.R.B. (1999) 'Tourism, competitiveness, and societal prosperity', *Journal of Business Research*, 44(3): 137–52.

Cruz, S. and Teixeira, A. (2010) 'The evolution of the cluster literature: Shedding light on the regional studies', *Regional Studies*, 44(9): 1263–88.

DCMS – Department for Culture, Media and Sport (2001) *Creative Industries Mapping Document*, London: DCMS.

DCMS – Department for Culture, Media and Sport (2013) *Classifying and Measuring the Creative Industries*, London: DCMS.

De Propris, L., Chapain, C., Cooke, P., MacNeill, S. and Mateos-Garcia, J. (2009) *The Geography of Creativity*, London: NESTA.

Dwyer, L. and Kim, C. (2003) 'Destination competitiveness: Determinants and indicators', *Current Issues in Tourism*, 6(5): 369–414.

Enright, M. J. and Newton, J. (2004) 'Tourism destination competitiveness: A quantitative approach', *Tourism Management*, 25(6): 777–88.

Enz, C., Canina, L. and Liu, Z. (2008) 'Competitive dynamics and pricing behavior in US hotels: The role of co-location', *Scandinavian Journal of Hospitality and Tourism*, 8(3): 230–50.

Estevão, C. and Ferreira, J. M. (2012) 'How to identify regional specialization measurement of clusters in tourism industry?' *Management and Business Economics*, 287(2): 347–60.

Florida, R. (2002) *The Rise of the Creative Class*, New York: Basic Books.

Franch, M. (2002) *Destination Management: Governare il Turismo Tra Locale e Globale*, Torino: Giappichelli.

Go, F. and Govers, R. (2000) 'Integrated quality management for tourist destinations: A European perspective on achieving competitiveness', *Tourism Management*, 21(1): 79–88.

Go, F. and Govers, R. (2012) *The International Place Branding Yearbook 2012: Managing Smart Growth and Sustainability*, Basingstoke: Palgrave Macmillan.

Halkier, H., Kozak, M. and Svensson, B. (2015) *Innovation and Tourism Destination Development*, Abingdon: Routledge.

Hjalager, A. (2000) 'Tourism destinations and the concept of industrial districts', *Tourism and Hospitality Research*, 2(3): 199–213.

Howie, F. (2003) *Managing the Tourist Destination*, London: Continuum.

Ioannides, D. (2006) 'The economic geography of the tourist industry: Ten years of progress in research and an agenda for the future', *Tourism Geographies*, 8(1): 76–86.

Jackson, J. and Murphy, P. (2006) 'Clusters in regional tourism An Australian case', *Annals of Tourism Research*, 33(4): 1018–35.

Kozak, M. and Baloglu, S. (2011) *Managing and Marketing Tourist Destinations: Strategies to Gain a Competitive Edge*, Abingdon: Routledge.

Laesser, C. and Beritelli, P. (2013) 'St Gallen consensus on destination management', *Journal of Destination Marketing and Management*, 2(1): 46–49.

Laws, E. (1995) *Tourist Destination Management*, Edinburgh: Napier University.

Laws, E., Richins, H., Agrusa, J. and Scott, N. (eds) (2011) *Tourist Destination Governance: Practice, Theory and Issues*, Cambridge, USA: CABI.

Lazzeretti, L. (2003) 'City of art as a high culture local system and cultural districtualization processes: The cluster of art restoration in Florence', *International Journal of Urban and Regional Research*, 27(3): 635–48.

Lazzeretti, L. (ed.) (2013) *Creative Industries and Innovation in Europe*, London: Routledge.

Lazzeretti, L. and Capone, F. (2008) 'Mapping and analysing local tourism systems in Italy, 1991–2001', *Tourism Geographies*, 10(2): 214–32.

Lazzeretti, L. and Petrillo, C. S. (eds) (2006) *Tourism Local Systems and Networking*, Amsterdam: Elsevier.

Leiper, N. (1995) *Tourism Management*, Melbourne: RMIT Press.

Lorentzen, A. (2013) 'Post-industrial growth: Experience, culture or creative economies?', in J. Sundbo and F. Sorensen (eds), *Handbook on the Experience Economy*, Cheltenham, UK: Edward Elgar, pp. 45–65.

Lorentzen, A. and Hansen, C.J. (2009) 'The role and transformation of the city in the experience economy: Identifying and exploring research challenges', *European Planning Studies*, 17(6): 817–27.

Martin, R. and Sunley, P. (2003) 'Deconstructing clusters: Chaotic concept or policy panacea?' *Journal of Economic Geography*, 3(1): 5–35.

Michael, E. (ed.) (2007) *Micro-clusters and Networks: The Growth of Tourism*, Amsterdam: Elsevier.

Morgan, N., Pritchard, A. and Pride, R. (2011) *Destination Brands*, Abingdon: Routledge.

Morrison, A.M. (2013) *Marketing and Managing Tourism Destinations*, Abingdon: Routledge.

Nordin, S. (2003) *Tourism Clustering and Innovation*, Östersund, Sweden: Etour.

Novelli, M., Schmitz, B. and Spencer, T. (2006) 'Networks, clusters and innovation in tourism: A UK experience', *Tourism Management*, 27(6): 1141–52.

OECD – Organization for Economic Cooperation and Development (2009) *Clusters, Innovation and Entrepreneurship*, Paris: OECD Publishing.

OECD – Organization for Economic Cooperation and Development (2014a) *OECD Tourism Trends and Policies 2014*, Paris: OECD Publishing.

OECD – Organization for Economic Cooperation and Development (2014b) *Tourism and the Creative Economy*, OECD Studies on Tourism, Paris: OECD Publishing.

Pearce, D.G. (2013) 'Toward an integrative conceptual framework of destinations', *Journal of Travel Research*, 53(2): 141–53.

Pechlaner, H. and Weiermair, K. (eds) (2000) *Destination management: fondamenti di marketing e gestione delle destinazioni turistiche*, Milan: Touring Club Italiano.

Peiró-Signes, Á., Segarra-Oña, M., Miret-Pastor, L. and Verma, R. (2015) 'The effect of tourism clusters on US Hotel Performance', *Cornell Hospitality Quarterly*, 56(2): 155–67.

Pencarelli T., (2015) (eds) *Comunicare le destinazioni balneari*, Milano: Franco Angeli.

Pike, S. (2007) *Destination Marketing Organisations*, London: Routledge.

Porter, M.E. (1998) *On Competition*, Boston, MA: Harvard Business School Press.

Porter, M.E. (2003) 'The economic performance of regions', *Regional Studies*, 37(6–7): 549–78.

Richards, G. (2011) 'Creativity and tourism. The state of the art', *Annals of Tourism Research*, 38(4): 1225–53.

Richards, G. (2013) 'Tourism development trajectories: From culture to creativity?' in M. Smith and G. Richards, *Handbook of Cultural Tourism*, London: Routledge, pp. 9–16.

Richards, G. and Wilson, J. (2007) *Tourism, Creativity and Development*, Abingdon: Routledge.

Ritchie, B.W. (2009) *Crisis and Disaster Management for Tourism*, Bristol: Channel View.

Ritchie, J.R.B. and Crouch, G.I. (2003) *The Competitive Destination: A Sustainable Tourism Perspective*, Trowbridge, UK: Cromwell Press.

Santagata, W. (2002) 'Cultural districts, property rights and sustainable economic growth', *International Journal of Urban and Regional Research*, 26(1): 9–23.

Santos, C., Almeida, A. and Teixeira, A. (2008) *Searching for Clusters in Tourism: A Quantitative Methodological Proposal*, FEP Working Papers no. 293, Oporto University, Portugal.

Sanz-Ibáñez, C. and Anton Clavé, S. (2014) 'The evolution of destinations: Towards an evolutionary and relational economic geography approach', *Tourism Geographies*, 16(4): 563–79.

Sciarelli S., (2007) *Il management dei sistemi turistici locali*, Torino: Giappichelli.

Segarra-Oña, M., Miret-Pastor, L., Peiró-Signes, A. and Verma, R. (2012) 'The effects of localization on economic performance: Analysis of Spanish tourism clusters', *European Planning Studies*, 20(8): 1319–34.

Svensson, B., Nordin, S. and Flagestad, A. (2005) 'A governance perspective on destination development. Exploring partnership, clusters and innovation systems', *Tourism Review*, 60(2): 32–37.

Tallman, S., Jenkins, M., Henry, N. and Pinch, S. (2004) 'Knowledge, clusters and competitive advantage', *Academy of Management Review*, 29(2): 258–71.

UNWTO – United Nations World Tourism Organization (2011) *Tourism Towards 2030. Global Overview*, http://e-unwto.org/doi/pdf/10.18111/9789284414024.

Viken, A. and Granas, B. (2014) *Tourism Destination Development: Turns and Tactics*, Burlington, VT: Ashgate.

WEF – World Economic Forum (2015) *The Travel and Tourism Competitiveness Report 2015*, http://reports.weforum.org/travel-and-tourism-competitiveness-report-2015.

WTO – World Tourism Organization (2007) *A Practical Guide to Tourism Destination Management*, Madrid: World Tourism Organization.

Part I
Tourist destinations, destination management, clusters and competitiveness

1 A bibliometric analysis on tourist destinations research

Focus on destination management and tourist cluster

Francesco Capone

1 Introduction: the tourist destinations research

In the tourism field, the focus on the tourist destination has emerged about 20 years ago with some seminal contributions (Laws 1995; Leiper 1995). In this context, the issues of destination management and marketing have been given special attention in the specialised studies on tourism, and have indeed developed as independent branches for the study of tourist destinations (Morrison 2013; Wang and Pizam 2011; Kozak and Baloglu 2011).[1] The concept of destination management (DM) has been developed from the works of Laws (1995), Buhalis and Spada (2000), Howie (2003), Ritchie and Crouch (2003) and the members of the International Association of Scientific Experts in Tourism (AIEST) (Pechlaner and Weiermair 2000). The focus has then shifted from the issue of management to that of marketing, with destination marketing (Baloglu and McCleary 1999; Buhalis 2000) and destination image (Echtner and Ritchie 1993; Bigne, Sanchez and Sanchez 2001; Morgan, Pritchard and Pride 2011).

The DM approach has been growingly employed in Italy as well, with several significant contributions (Franch 2002; 2010; Martini 2005; Sciarelli 2007; Trunfio 2008; Della Corte 2009).

The study of destinations has taken different and varied approaches over time, depending on the original discipline taken into account or the special issue developed in the analysis.

Some contributors have reviewed the literature on the various approaches to the study of destinations. Pearce (2013) identifies a series of analytical models of tourist destinations among the systemic approaches to tourism, such as the tourist clusters, districts and destination networks. Trunfio (2008) widens the analysis to the local system of tourist supply and the paradigm of vital system. Capone (2006) distinguishes the studies carried out with an economic-industrial vs a managerial viewpoint, separating the analyses of *milieu*, tourist district, cluster and DM and marketing.

In international literature of economic-industrial derivation, a stronger emphasis has been placed on different types of approach, such as the tourist *milieu* or the tourist district (Stansfield and Richert 1970; Jansen-Verbeke and Ashworth 1990; Getz 1993; Pearce 1998a; Hjalager 2000, Antonioli Corigliano 1999), with contributions that in fact did not gain much support, at least in the journals specialising in the field of tourism.

Given this background, the most appealing model of study for destinations has turned out to be the *tourist cluster*, an extension of Porter's well-known work (1998) on clusters, competitiveness and localisation of the tourism industry. In this article, the scholar introduced the notion that the competitive advantages deriving from the presence of a cluster of firms could be gained as well by the tourism sector.

Later on, one of the first studies on tourist clusters was led by Nordin (2003), who underlined the question of competitiveness, looking at it as a means of fostering innovation, even in the developing countries.

The international literature on the tourist cluster has grown considerably, producing a stronger and stronger impact on tourism studies. Several contributions reveal that the cluster concept has been suitably adapted to the peculiarities of the tourism sector and provides a spatial and organisational model that promotes competitiveness, innovation and local development (Jackson and Murphy 2002; 2006; Lazzeretti and Petrillo 2006; Novelli, Schmitz and Spencer 2006; Michael 2007; Shaw and Williams 2009). Consequently, the concept of cluster has been widely used also for the tourism industry.

In spite of this, among the approaches to the study of destinations, many are much too fragmented still today (Goeldner 2011; Crouch and Perdue 2014), and the factual development of these concepts in a comparative perspective is still unclear. The aim of this chapter is to analyse the evolution of these approaches over time, and to investigate their multidisciplinary provenance as well as their impact on tourism studies. In other terms, it will examine the birth and evolution of research on tourist destinations, focusing on two of the most relevant issues: the tourist clusters and DM. The privileged contributions are those keeping a systemic approach to tourism and tourist destinations, and emphasising the territory, tourism and destinations' competitiveness.

Specifically, the research is guided by the following research questions:

- Which have been the most addressed issues in the analysis of destinations?
- What has been the evolution over time of the concepts under analysis?
- Who have been the authors and communities that investigated and disseminated them?
- Which are the original theories for these concepts?

In the first part of the work, the examined publications are those gathered from the ISI database which deal with tourist destinations, starting from the end of the 1990s from the initial contributions on destination (Leiper, 1995; Laws, 1995, etc.) and from the contribution of Porter (1998) on 'Clusters and the new economics of competition' up to those published in 2014. The survey of the most important journals and most relevant authors is aimed at analysing the birth and evolution of the concepts under study.

In the second part, a textual analysis is developed on the most cited abstracts, using Semantria, a textual data mining software. This is a valuable tool for text-mining research as it identifies the most frequently used concepts within a body of text and can also be employed for sentiment analysis (Aston, Liddle and Hu 2014; Lawrence 2014).

Finally, in the concluding part of the work, an assessment is made of the 64 most important publications (pivotal publications), that is those having received 44% of total citations, and thus considered as the essential publications on research of tourist destinations. A relational perspective is adopted to look at the evolution of the scientific concepts, and to investigate the backward citations of the pivotal publications, given that the dissemination of concepts is primarily a product of the way other authors quote and use these concepts in their subsequent works (Lazzeretti, Sedita and Caloffi 2014).

The chapter is subdivided as follows. After this introduction, section 2 illustrates the state of the art of bibliometric analyses of tourism, giving a special attention to those with a relational perspective, to co-citations and the use of social network analysis (SNA). Section 3 introduces the methodological approach and the data sources employed. Subsection 4.1 discusses the weight of the issues under study, focusing on the principal journals involved; subsection 4.2 deals with the examination of the evolution of concepts over time; subsection 4.3 makes a textual analysis of the different publications and attempts a separation of communities with similar contributions; finally, subsection 4.4 identifies who are the founders for such concepts, while underlining the multidisciplinarity and thematic fragmentation of the contributions under exam. The chapters ends with some conclusive remarks.

2 Bibliometric analysis in tourism studies

Bibliometric analysis in tourism literature has been applied in a large amount of contributions in recent years (Jogaratnam *et al.* 2005; Hall 2010; 2011; Tribe 2010; Tokic 2012), starting from the seminal work of Garfield (1972). Most of this research has been devoted to journals' evaluation, development and rankings (McKercher 2005; 2008). Pechlaner *et al.* (2004) define a rating system of tourism and hospitality journals using the journals' readership frequency, their scientific and practical relevance, overall reputation, and the importance of being published in the journals for the academic career of the respondents. Howey *et al.* (1999) wrote one of the first articles to analyse cross-citations among research communities in tourism journals. Law *et al.* (2009) proposed a different approach that makes use of Google Scholar citations to survey the most influential articles on tourism for the period 2000–07.

Given that tourism has been largely viewed as a fragmented field, some contributors tried and analysed the most important disciplines in tourism studies, or managed to disentangle the approaches to tourism sciences (Goeldner 2011; Crouch and Perdue 2014). Cheng *et al.* (2011) analysed the development of tourism knowledge from the reconstruction of trends in tourism journals, evaluating 59 tourism-related journals.

Other contributions are more focused on the research methodologies of tourism studies. Palmer, Sesé and Montaño (2004) carry out a bibliometric analysis on the use of statistical methods in tourism research, surveying 1,790 articles in 12 tourism journals for the period of 1998–2002, while Baloglu and Assante (1999) present an analysis of qualitative methodologies and research methods for five tourism journals.

The latest research contributions are centred on the use of SNA as a method to survey tourism literature (Hu and Racherla 2008; Benckendorff and Zehrer 2013; Ye, Li and Law 2013). In this context, SNA (Wasserman and Faust 1994; Hanneman and Riddle 2005) is employed to find out co-citations and co-authorships, and also as a method for visualising the analysis's results.

However, there are few contributions that scrutinise specific tourism-related issues. An example is offered by the work of Stepchenkova and Mills (2010), who analyse the concept of 'destination image', and perform a meta-analysis of 152 articles for the period of 2000–07, presenting current and emerging trends in the area. Another one is Lazzeretti, Capone and Innocenti (2014), who investigate the research on creative economy from 2001–14, using the ISI Web of Science; or Chuluunbaatar *et al.* (2013), who study academic research on cultural and creative industries, both involving cultural tourism and related themes.

2.1 Social network analysis and bibliometrics in tourism studies

Benckendorff (2009) and Hall (2011) classify bibliometric studies in two macro-typologies: evaluative and relational.

Evaluative researches are, on their turn, subdivided into three categories. The first group includes productivity measures such as the number of (cited) papers, per year or per author; the second one comprises impact metrics such as the total number of citations, number of citations per year and per author, the third group consists of hybrid metrics such as average number of citations per paper or various other indices aiming to capture both productivity and impact.

Relational researches are based on the analysis of co-citation and co-authorship, using the technologies of SNA applied to bibliometric analyses. The most common techniques used in relational analyses, though, are co-authorship and co-citation (Benckendorff and Zehrer 2013).

There has been an increasing use of SNA for tourism studies, which is mainly applied as a methodology to study destinations or networks of tourist firms (Scott, Cooper and Baggio 2008; Baggio, Scott and Cooper 2010; Baggio 2011), and particularly through the bibliometric analysis of co-citations and academic research (Ahmed 2012; Dwyer, Gill and Seetaram 2012).

In this branch of studies we find some rather interesting works. For example, Benckendorff (2009) presents a bibliometric analysis of tourism literature, examining papers authored by Australian and New Zealand researchers and published in the *Annals of Tourism Research* (*ATR*) and in *Tourism Management* (*TM*) during the period of 1994–2007. He analyses the keywords, the most cited authors and works, as well as co-citation patterns, using SNA to explore the links between keywords and influential works in the field.

Benckendorff and Zehrer (2013) use the network analysis to identify the pioneering scholars and seminal works which have influenced recent papers in leading tourism journals, developing a co-citation analysis. Ye, Li and Law (2013) applied SNA to research collaborations among tourism and hospitality researchers. They analysed six tourism journals during the period of 1991–2010, and provided an overview of research collaborations in this field in terms of co-authorship networks, using degree centrality and betweenness.

In two recent contributions, Hu and Racherla (Hu and Racherla 2008; Racherla and Hu 2010) investigate the patterns of collaborations in the tourism research community, applying SNA to the co-authorship data obtained from three top tourism journals (*TM, ATR* and the *Journal of Travel Research*). They find out how large and heterogeneous is the tourism research community, which is mainly composed of closed and small networks. Tribe (2010) applied the actor–network methodology to explore the nature and structure of the tourism academia.

Outside the field of tourism studies, other contributors analysed the literature on clusters and districts and its evolution over time, applying SNA to the analysis of co-citations. Hervas-Oliver, Gonzalez and Caja (2014) analyse the fairly fragmented literature on industrial districts and clusters applying bibliometric methods to explore prospective research priorities through the method of bibliographic coupling.

Lazzeretti, Sedita and Caloffi (2014) analyse the development of cluster research and the increasing relevance of peripheral themes in recent years, investigating the birth and evolution of Porter's 'cluster' research. They identify disseminators and founders of this concept by examining more than 1,500 articles from several disciplines.

Cruz and Teixeira (2010) investigate the rising importance of cluster literature in regional sciences and studies, carrying out an empirical study on its precise magnitude and evolution; their conclusion is that research on clusters is still fragmented and multidisciplinary.

3 Research design and methodological approach

Our data come from the Thomson Reuters Web of Science database (ISI). The choice of ISI as the referring database is motivated by its internationally widespread use for rating the research output of scientists for all disciplines. However, this database has some limitations; it is worth recalling that it collects only the contributions published in ISI journals – which are mainly in English – leaving out other languages, and it omits most of the contributions published in books.[2]

The publications collected from the ISI database were those available from 1998, the year of the seminal contribution by Porter (1998). Using the Web of Science's search option, all publications whose topic contains the terms 'cluster', 'destination' and 'tourism' were distinguished.

Several contributors underline that the research on tourist destinations is still fragmented and identifies a series of different approaches to study tourist destinations, such as the tourist cluster, milieu, district, local systems and so on (Capone 2006; Lazzeretti and Petrillo 2006; Pearce 2013). Therefore, we decide to broaden the keywords underpinning the bibliometric analysis, in order also to consider other approaches and evaluate them in a comparison. The following keywords were also included in the query: 'tourist district', 'tourist local system', 'tourist local production system', 'destination management', 'destination marketing', 'location choices', 'localisation strategy' and 'tourism' (both in their singular and plural forms).

The publications selected were either articles, book chapters or conference proceedings collected among the social sciences subjects in the ISI database. In particular, a selection was made of the journals specialised in business economics, economic geography, urban studies and other social sciences. From a first search, a total of about 1,400 contributions was obtained, spanning from 1998–2014. More than 90% of these were journal articles, whereas 5% were represented by the chapters in books included in the database through the ISI Web's Book Citation Index, and the remaining 2.5% concerned the proceedings of international conferences.

After an initial analysis of topics, a skimming of data was made through the reading of the articles' abstracts, which led to the removal of duplications, since, at a first approximation, an article might have been highlighted in more search queries.[3]

The final database contained about 900 works published in the period of 1998–2014, for an overall total of 9,000 citations. The following step has been to investigate the evolution in these publications and related topics, by means of descriptive analyses.

In the second part of the research (section 4.2), a textual analysis was developed on the 500 most-cited abstracts using the Semantria software. Text mining helps provide detailed conceptual insights by shifting the level of analysis from authors and their citations to the actual texts/words used by the authors for a content-driven review of literature (Feldman and Sanger 2006).

The 500 most cited articles reach a cumulative percentage of 97% of overall citations. Consequently, the restriction of analysis to 500 articles allowed to reduce the time of elaborations and analyses, and also to consider all the most important contributions on the themes. With the help of SNA and UCINET/Netdraw software package (Borgatti, Everett and Freeman 2002), it is possible to graphically represent the links among the contributions and the foremost topics identified in the textual analysis.

Finally, the concluding part of the analysis (Section 4.3) applied to the 64 most important publications (from now on, 'pivotal publications'), that is those having received 44% of total citations, and hence the most representative of researches on tourist destinations (see Appendix 1.1).

A relational perspective was adopted to examine the evolution of scientific concepts, and a co-citation analysis was carried out, given that the dissemination of concepts is primarily a product of the way other authors quote and use these concepts in their following works.

Accordingly, the theoretical background of pivotal publications was investigated by downloading from the ISI database their backward citations. The result was a database containing 605 references cited in the 64 pivotal publications, called the *founders* of research on tourist clusters and destinations. The analysis of backward citations refers to all the articles, books and book chapters that have been cited in the articles under observation. The web of relations between cited and backward-cited works, as well as that among backward-cited works, is analysed with the help of the SNA tool.

4 Bibliometric analysis

4.1 Relevance of the theme and journals involved

Figure 1.1 presents the evolution of citations in the last 20 years, which confirms the increasing importance of research on clusters and destinations in tourism studies.

As it can be seen, contributions began to increase by the end of the 1990s, following the celebrated article by Porter about clusters (1998) and the first works on tourist destinations (Laws 1995; and others). From 2000 on, the articles reach the amount of 10 per year, and by the end of the decade 20 per year; citations as well follow an upward trend.

The main journals concerned are listed in Table 1.1. Obviously, the ones that stand out are those related to tourism, like *TM, Journal of Travel and Tourism Marketing* and *ATR*. Also present, although less significant, are journals from different disciplinary areas, such as *European Planning Studies, Regional Studies*

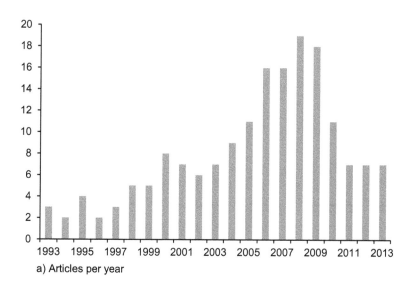

a) Articles per year

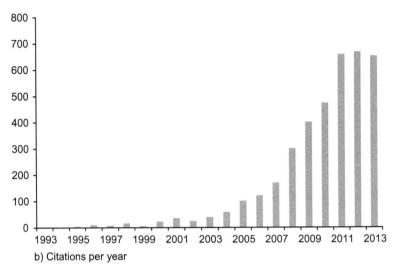

b) Citations per year

Figure 1.1 Publications and citations on tourist destination research

Source: ISI Web of Science.

Table 1.1 Most involved journals on tourist destination research

Journals	Percentage of contributions	Percentage of citations
Tourism Management (TM)	16	34
Journal of Travel & Tourism Marketing (JTTM)	6	1
Annals of Tourism Research (ATR)	6	18
Journal of Travel Research	6	3
International Journal of Tourism Research	4	2
Journal of Sustainable Tourism	4	2
Current Issues in Tourism	3	1
Tourism Geographies	3	1
International Journal of Hospitality Management	2	1
Tourism Economics	2	0
Asia Pacific Journal of Tourism Research	2	0
European Planning Studies (EPS)	2	1
Scandinavian Journal of Hospitality and Tourism	2	1
Journal of Hospitality & Tourism Research	2	1
International Journal of Contemporary Hospitality Management	1	1
Cornell Hospitality Quarterly	1	1
Journal of Business Research (JBR)	1	0
Quantitative Methods in Tourism: A Handbook	1	0
Service Industries Journal	1	1
Environmental Management	1	0
Strategic Management Journal (SMJ)	1	6
Sustainability	1	0
Urban Geography (UG)	1	0
Urban Studies (US)	1	1

Source: Our elaboration.

and others, which denote the multidisciplinarity of the analysed issues. These were also familiar to non-tourism journals, specialised in local, regional or urban development or management publications like the *Journal of Business Research* or *Strategic Management Journal (SMJ)*. The journals falling in the area of tourism studies prove to be the most relevant in their specific scientific field (Hall 2011; Au, Law and Lee 2012; and others), thus highlighting the importance of the issue of tourism.

A striking result is that, even though *TM* and *ATR* receive, respectively, 34% and 18% of citations, the third journal as to the amount of citations is *SMJ*, which collects only 1% of total contributions. This fact evidences the significance of the issues also in terms of strategic management.[4]

4.2 The evolution of the concepts

Figure 1.2 illustrates the subdivision of the selected articles by topic. As discussed below, the main issues in terms of number of contributions are 'destination management' and 'destination marketing', which total a 38% share. This result will take a particular significance in the analysis of the evolution of issues over time. The 'tourist cluster' registers 27% and, if taken together with 'district', 39% of total contributions, thus proving the significance of tourism issues. All the other

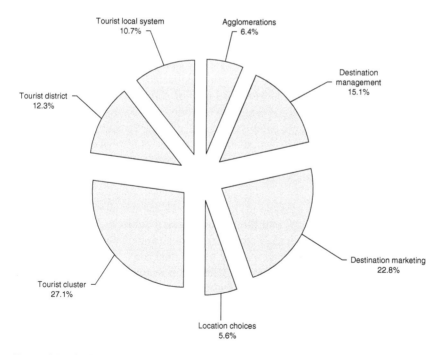

Figure 1.2 Distribution of articles per researched topic

Source: Our elaboration.

issues are only residual. Based on these first data, in the literature on tourist destinations it is possible to distinguish a demarcation between two macro-subjects: DM and marketing, and the tourist cluster.

Regarding the evolution in the period under exam (1998–2014), Figure 1.3 presents the contributions classified by topic for the whole period, with the number of both publications (Figure 1.3a) and citations received (Figure 1.3b).

It is worthwhile to notice that the 'tourist cluster' issue had initially registered a great amount of contributions, but in the final part of the period suffers a decline in the number of contributions and citations. In point of fact, this topic has gradually turned into a specialised concept in the field of tourism studies, mainly used in the economic-business disciplines of management, regional studies, economic geography, etc. At the end of the period, in fact, the topics of DM and marketing are gaining more success, while the relevance of cluster seems to slow down.

It should finally be noted that DM and marketing can be either viewed as two distinct topics or as a comprehensive issue. In the latter case, their prevalence over the tourist cluster is even higher. However, in my opinion, it seems better to separate the two topics, given that whereas cluster and DM are more focused on the analysis of supply at local level, the one of destination marketing is more inclined to portray the visitors' demand of destinations, and the corresponding communication strategy.

At all events, 20 years after its ascent, the concept of cluster seems to be decreasingly used by the international academic community, as already evidenced in other works (Lazzeretti, Sedita and Caloffi 2014).

4.3 A textual analysis of the articles: a focus on keywords

The aim of this subsection is to analyse the collected publications and identify the major issues dealt with, presenting a *map of connections* among topics and publications. A textual analysis (Feldman and Sanger 2006; Lawrence 2014) was conducted on the 500 most-cited abstracts, using the Semantria software. The corresponding articles reach a cumulative percentage of 97% of overall citations. Limiting the analysis of these 500 contributions reduces the time of elaboration and, at the same time, takes into account the most significant contributions on the issues under exam.

Consequently, it was possible to find out which are the most-cited keywords associated to the abstracts, and the most-addressed subjects. With the help of SNA, it is possible to graphically represent the links among contributions and the most important topics identified with the textual analysis.

The Semantria software helped register the potential presence of the most recurring and significant words in the abstracts' text. Figure 1.4 represents the classification results for most relevant keywords.

The subject matter of competitiveness proves to be the most relevant, being found in 30% of contributions. The hotel industry is the most-debated sector, reaching 9% of contributions. The two issues of marketing and destination marketing total 20%, and DM, 7%. All the other are residual issues.[5]

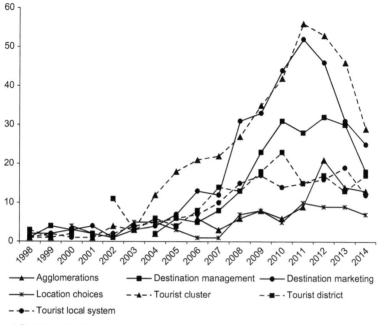

a) Evolution of publications per topic, 1998–2014

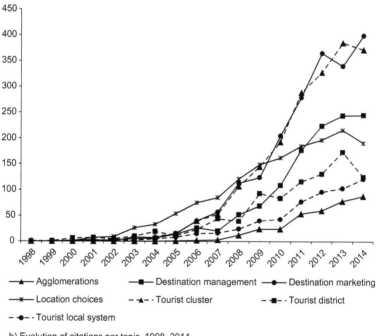

b) Evolution of citations per topic, 1998–2014

Figure 1.3 The evolution of research on tourist destination

Source: Our elaboration.

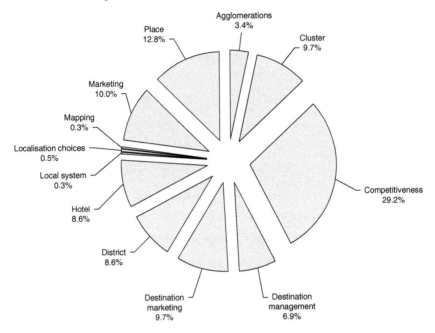

Figure 1.4 The distribution of the most relevant keywords in the abstracts

Source: Our elaboration.

A matrix publications-keywords was then built in order to create a map of knowledge, and it was then transformed into a graph using SNA. The resulting picture is shown in Figure 1.5. The squared nodes correspond to the most relevant keywords, and the rounded ones to publications, while the connecting line designates a citation of the keyword in the abstract. The size of nodes quantifies relevance, measured by the number of citations received in the contributions.

In this figure, it is possible to spot a few significant groups of contributions. The business areas dealing with destination marketing and management are recognisable in the left section of the graph; they are connected to the network by the issues of performance and competitiveness. The most-cited contributions are: Tosun (2002); Bornhorst, Ritchie and Sheehan (2010) on destination competitiveness; Mihalič (2000) on destination management; Lew and McKercher (2006) on the analysis of destinations; Buhalis (2000) on destination marketing; Bigne, Sanchez and Sanchez (2001) on the image of destinations and purchase behaviours; Kozak (2001) on the multiple relationships among tourist satisfaction and behavioural intention to revisit; Pritchard and Morgan (2001) on destination branding and marketing; and so on.

The central section of the graph collects all the contributions associated to the issue of competitiveness, starting from the work of Crouch and Ritchie (1999),[6]

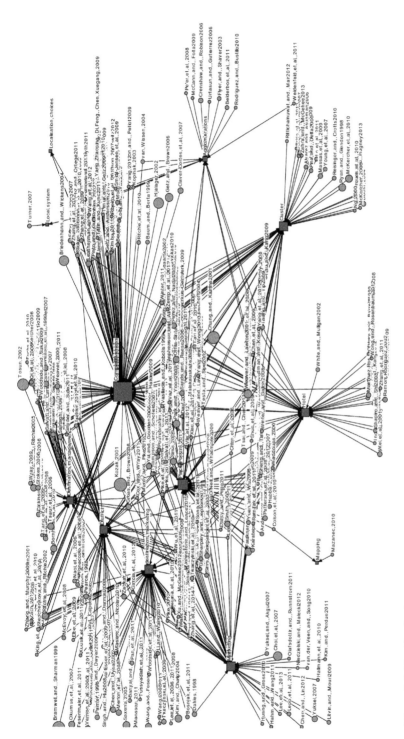

Figure 1.5 The distribution of authors per keyword

Source: Our elaboration.

Legend: Node's size: degree of total citations in articles; Square node: main topics; circle node: contributions.

which must be seen as one of the main themes, being capable of linking all the subject matters concerning destinations.

In the lower-right section is the network of authors of tourist clusters. The most important contributions in this respect are Canina, Enz and Harrison (2005), Jackson and Murphy (2006), Novelli, Schmitz and Spencer (2006), plus some others. They are all connected by way of competitiveness among places and firms.

The main sector analysed in these contributions is the hotel industry, with the noteworthy works of Baum and collaborators (Baum and Mezia 1992; Ingram and Baum 1997; Baum, Barnett and Carroll 2000), Getz and Carlsen (2000), Chung and Kalnins (2001) and Canina, Enz and Harrison (2005).

The issues tackling agglomerations and local systems have a residual impact in terms of citations, but have a strong connection with various networks. Some of the main studies in this field are McCann and Folta (2008) on location matters, or Urtasun and Gutierrez (2006), on location choices. However, they represent about 3% of the overall networks of contributions.

The issues related to tourist districts are secondary; among the related contributions, the renowned works by Pearce (1998a) and Sainaghi (2006) deserve notice. At all events, in the majority of these contributions the term 'district' is merely employed to identify a territorial unit (e.g. urban district, park district), with the exception of Lazzeretti and Capone (2006; 2008), who survey Italy's tourist districts and the seminal work of Antonioli Corigliano (1999).

The network for localisation choices and strategy has strong links with competitiveness (upper right of the graph). In this field, reference must be made to the much cited works of Baum and Mezias (1992), and Baum and Ingram (1998), and some others. They received several citations and many were published in notable management journals (like *SMJ* and *Management Science*), even though they only represent 1% of total contributions.

In conclusion, this analysis allowed not only to identify the foremost contributions on the research issue, but also to draw a map of connections among the various subjects and publications. Furthermore, it made possible to highlight the issues shared by several contributions and, consequently, the multidisciplinarity of the object of study.

4.4 Social network analysis of backward citations

This subsection goes into details about the 64 most important publications (pivotal publications), the ones having received 44% of total citations and thus representing the disseminators of research on destinations in the tourism field (Appendix 1.1). To explore the theoretical ground on which the most-cited articles are based, their backward citations were downloaded from the ISI database. A database was then created, containing 605 references cited by the most significant publications. Similarly to other contributions (Lazzeretti, Sedita and Caloffi 2014), these 605 references are called the *founders* of research on destinations.

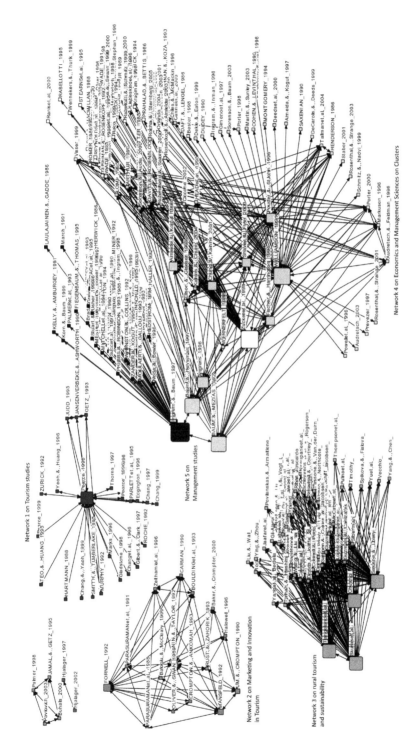

Figure 1.6 Founders with more than two co-citations

Source: Our elaboration.

Legend: Node's size: degree of total citations in articles.

With the investigation through co-citations, the contributions frequently cited together are considered to belong to the same disciplinary area or be grounded on the same theories, being the founders of future developments of research.

Figure 1.6 presents the 64 founders which had at least two co-citations. The resulting graphical representation of the network has a reduced number of nodes (as compared to those among the 605 references) and produces a more readable picture. Each node in the graph identifies a publication, while the line that links two nodes indicates a co-citation.

The most remarkable result we find is the constitution of five sub-networks, which validates the idea of fragmentation and multidisciplinarity of the issues under exam. Network 1, at the upper centre of the graph, represents the contributions from tourism studies, the most part of which were published in *ATR* and *TM*. They are works tackling tourism in cities, urban tourism and urban districts, starting with the work of Pearce (1996; 1998a; 1998b) on urban tourism in particular in Paris, of Judd (1995) on tourism in the American cities, and of Jansen-Verbeke and Ashworth (1990), and Murphy (1992).

Network 2 stems from studies of marketing and innovation in tourism, and management of services. The contributions found here are those of Jamal and Getz (1995), Buhalis (2000), Hjalager (2002), and all of them published in the chief journals focused on tourism-related issues. The main subject matters are: marketing of destinations, analysis of supply, research on tourists' motivations (Mansfeld 1992), and analysis of customer satisfaction and quality of services (Parasuraman, Zeithaml and Berry 1988; 1991).

Network 3 is a much smaller complex, with contributions published in journals of less renown and dealing with secondary themes, such as rural tourism, sustainable tourism and peripheries. In particular, there are some specific case studies, like the works of Tangeland and others (Tangeland and Aas 2011; Tangeland, Vennesland and Nybakk 2013) on the nature-based and outdoor tourism of Saxena and Ilbery (Saxena *et al.* 2007; Saxena and Ilbery 2008) and Iorio and Corsale (2010), on rural tourism, and so on.

Networks 4 and 5 are instead centred not on tourism issues, but on economic and management sciences, and represent the conceptual founders of the tourist cluster. Network 4 is of a most distinct economic nature, and collects the founding works of cluster research, that is in economics, or urban and economic geography. They comprise the writings of Krugman (1991), Williamson (1991) and Porter (1998) on the new economic geography, of Rabellotti (1995), Markusen (1996), Schimtz and Nadvi (1999), and others supporting the idea of a growing significance of the developing countries.

Network 5 is comprised of relevant contributions in management studies, published in the *Academy of Management Review*, *SMJ* and *Research Policy*, for example: Wernerfelt (1988) on the umbrella branding; Prahalad and Hamel (1990) on core competencies and dynamic capabilities; Almeida and Kogut (1997; 1999) on localisation choices and strategy; Audretsch and Feldman (1996), and Baptista and Swan (1998; 1999) on clustering; Ellison and Glaeser (1999), and Tallman *et al.* (2004) on agglomeration economies and clusters. In connection with them, are the works of Baum and Mezias (1992), Ingram and Baum (1997), and others, tackling the issue of hotel and location strategy.

A striking outcome is that the sub-networks that are separated one from the other. Their corresponding communities that study and work on these issues seem to be cut off from the outside and very closed and united inside. The results of the analysis show that the topics under exam are even more fragmented than expected, and highlight the multidisciplinary feature of tourism studies, which also impacts on the issues of destination competitiveness and clusters of firms.

5 Conclusions

The aim of this chapter was to develop an analysis of research on tourist destinations, focusing on two specific issues: the tourist cluster and DM. This choice was justified by the importance attached to them in tourism studies, and their increasing diffusion at international level.

The research was guided by the following research questions:

- Which have been the most addressed issues in the analysis of destinations in tourism studies?
- What has been their evolution over time?
- Who have been the authors and communities that investigated and disseminated them?
- On which theories are they founded?

We have elaborated a database of journal articles and book chapters drawn from the ISI Web of Science database. Through the analysis of almost 1,000 publications appeared during the last fifteen years, the birth and evolution of research on tourist destinations was investigated. Based on a selection of those that were recognised as pivotal publications, an analysis was carried out on the backward citations so as to identify the theories on which they are founded.

The analysis's results showed that the most relevant topics, i.e. those which obtained the most citations and contributions, were the tourist cluster and DM (and marketing), whereas other subject matters like the tourist district or the tourism system appeared to be residual.

As to the evolution of these concepts over time, the tourist cluster concept has been widespread during the first years of its emergence, but has recently experienced a slight decline, in terms of both contributions and numbers of citations, to the advantage of the issues of DM and marketing. Consequently, the question is to understand whether or not, at about 16 years from its foundation (Porter 1998), the concept of tourist cluster has entered a stage of decline, but a clear answer is not yet available. What is clear is that the issues of DM and marketing have been increasingly employed, particularly in the field of tourism studies, while the issue of tourist cluster is in point of fact decreasing, maybe because it is still a specialised concept.

The main authors and communities having dealt with tourist destinations were also explored, and a map was drawn of the connections between authors and research issues, built on the textual analysis of abstracts. The resulting map of knowledge turns to be an original tool, which draws attention to the multidisciplinarity concern over these issues, as well as to the variety of interconnections among authors and disciplines. Consistently with other examinations of tourism research, this feature proves the fragmentation of the subject of destinations, which has been considered from different approaches and points of view. In this regard, one of the main results has come from the analysis of pivotal publications. The survey of the number of citations, which involved an extensive elaboration for the building of a large database of contributions, allowed us to have a deeper view of the interlaced issues tackled in the study of tourist destinations, and to identify the most exploited in recent years (think, for example of the import of rural tourism, the destination image and so on).

The last part of the research was centred on the analysis of backward citations in the pivotal publications, which was aimed at recognising the theories in which the various issues had taken root. In this regard, the survey brought to light the different disciplinary areas and the main authors and publications from which these issues were derived. The most striking result was to find rather unrelated sub-networks of communities, working in isolation but as very cohesive groups. In this study, the issues under exam prove to be even more fragmented than expected, a finding that corroborates the multidisciplinarity of the related literature.

To conclude, the present analysis was meant to reach challenging goals and, at a first approximation, it does provide relevant and useful information for an initial broadening and deepening of research on tourist destinations. There are certainly some limitations that need to be considered. First of all, the use of the ISI Web of Science database entailed the exclusion of a number of worthy studies, books that are not listed in the Book Citation Index, or articles in low impact factor journals (hence, not written in English). This restriction has been partly corrected by the analysis of backward citations, which allowed the inclusion of contributions cited by the most influential authors (which were either books, research reports or conference proceedings). A second limitation is that the whole effort was based on the analysis of citations (and co-citations), in the assumption that the most important contributions are those that receive the highest number of citations. On this supposition, the oldest contributions (an earlier date of publication generally involves more citations as compared to recent literature) are rewarded, and much more emphasis is placed on the mainstream contributions, which in time have become more and more successful. However, at the moment there seems to be no alternative way of measuring the weight or the diffusion of a publication, to that of totaling the citations it received.

Notwithstanding the limits of research, the results obtained are remarkable and provide a knowledge basis to guide future investigations.

Appendix 1.1 The 64 most-cited *founders* among 40 pivotal publications

Founders	Times cited	Founders	Times cited
Almeida & Kogut_1999	3	Kalnins & Chung_2004	2
Anderson & Sullivan_1993	2	Lomi_1995	2
Arthur_1990	2	Mansfeld_1992	3
Audretsch & Feldman_1996	2	Markusen_1996	2
Baker & Crompton_2000	2	Murphy_1992	2
Baloglu & McCleary_1999	2	Novelli et al._2006	2
Baum & Haveman_1997	4	Oliver & Swan_1989	2
Baum & Mezias_1992	4	Palmer_1998	2
Boulding et al._1993	2	Parasuraman et al._1988	2
Buhalis_2000	2	Parasuraman et al._1991	2
Canina et al._2005	2	Pavlovich_2003	2
Carman_1990	2	Pearce_1998	2
Chung & Kalnins_2001	3	Porter_1998	2
Cooper & Jackson_1989	2	Porter_2000	2
Crompton & Ankomah_1993	2	Pouder & St John_1996	3
Cronin & Taylor_1992	3	Rust & Zahorik_1993	2
David & Rosenbloom_1990	2	Saxena & Ilbery_2008	2
Ellison & Glaeser_1999	2	Saxena_2005	2
Fischer & Harrington_1996	3	Selin & Beason_1991	2
Fornell_1992	3	Shaver & Flyer_2000	3
Getz_1993	2	Silver_1993	2
Granovetter_1985	3	Skuras et al._2006	2
Hallowell_1996	2	Sorenson & Audia_2000	2
Head et al._1995	2	Tallman et al._2004	2
Henderson_1986	2	Tangeland et al._2013	2
Hjalager_1997	2	Um & Crompton_1990	3
Hjalager_2002	2	Visser_1999	2
Ingram & Baum_1997	3	Wernerfelt_1988	2
Ingram_1996	3	Williamson_1991	2
Jamal & Getz_1995	2	Zeithaml et al._1996	2
Jansen-V. & Ashworth_1990	2	Zucker et al._1998	3
Judd_1995	2		

Source: Our elaboration.

Notes

1 For a wider discussion of destination management and marketing, see Chapter 2 in this volume.
2 Recently, ISI has also taken into account the books and book chapters included in the Book Citation Index.
3 88% of contributions were about only one topic, while 11% were about two topics, and only 1% were about more than two topics. This already underlines the separation of issues, which will be discussed further on.
4 The specific reference is to a niche literature on location choices and strategies involving a group of scholars whose leading figures are Baum, Mezias and others.

5   The 'district' is covered by 9% of publications, but most of them use the term only as
     a territorial unit of analysis, like urban district or the like.
6   The competitiveness of destinations is discussed in Chapter 2 in this volume.

References

Ahmed, E. (2012) 'Network analysis', in L. Dwyer, A. Gill and N. Seetaram (eds), *Hand-book or Research Method in Tourism: Quantitative and Qualitative Approaches*, Cheltenham, UK: Edward Elgar, pp. 472–95.

Almeida, P., and Kogut, B. (1997) 'The exploration of technological diversity and geographic localization in innovation: Start-up firms in the semiconductor industry', *Small Business Economics*, 9(1): 21–31.

Almeida, P., and Kogut, B. (1999) 'Localization of knowledge and the mobility of engineers in regional networks', *Management Science*, 45(7): 907–17.

Antonioli Corigliano M. (1999), "*Strade del vino ed enoturismo. Distretti turistici e vie di comunicazione*", Milano, Franco Angeli.

Aston, N., Liddle, J. and Hu, W. (2014) 'Twitter sentiment in data streams with Perceptron', *Journal of Computer and Communications*, 2(3): 11–16.

Au, N., Law, R. and Lee, A. (2012) 'Source analysis of citations and self-citations of leading hospitality and tourism journals', *Journal of Hospitality and Tourism*, 10(2): 66–80.

Audretsch, D. and Feldman, M. (1996) 'Knowledge spillovers and the geography of innovation and production', *American Economic Review*, 86(3): 630–40.

Baggio, J. A. (2011) 'Agent-based modeling and simulations', in R. Baggio and J. Klobas (eds), *Quantitative Methods in Tourism: A Handbook*, Bristol, UK: Channel View, pp. 199–219.

Baggio, R., Scott, N. and Cooper, C. (2010) 'Network science. A review focused on tourism', *Annals of Tourism Research*, 37(3): 802–27

Baloglu, S. and Assante, L. (1999) 'A content analysis of subject areas and research methods used in five hospitality management journals', *Journal of Hospitality & Tourism Research*, 23(1): 53–70.

Baloglu, S. and McCleary, K. W. (1999) 'A model of destination image formation', *Annals of Tourism Research*, 26(4): 868–97.

Baptista, R. and Swan, P. (1998) 'Do firms in clusters innovate more?', *Research Policy*, 27(5): 525–40.

Baptista, R. and Swan, P. (1999) 'The diffusion of process innovations: A selective review', *International Journal of the Economics of Business*, 6(1): 107–29.

Baum, J. and Ingram, P. (1998) 'Survival-enhancing learning in the Manhattan hotel industry, 1898–1980', *Management Science*, 44(7): 996–1016.

Baum, J. and Mezias, S. (1992) 'Localized competition and organizational failure in the Manhattan hotel industry, 1898–1990', *Administrative Science Quarterly*, 37(4): 580–604.

Baum, J., Barnett, W. P. and Carroll, G. R. (2000) 'Competition and mutualism among early telephone companies', *Administrative Science Quarterly*, 32(3): 400–21.

Benckendorff, P. (2009) 'Themes and trends in Australian and New Zealand tourism research: A social network analysis of citations in two leading journals (1994–2007)', *Journal of Hospitality and Tourism Management*, 16(1): 1–15.

Benckendorff, P. and Zahrer, A. (2013) 'A network analysis of Tourism research', *Annals of Tourism Research*, 43(October): 121–49.

Bigne, J. E., Sanchez, M. I. and Sanchez, J. (2001) 'Tourism image, evaluation variables and after purchase behaviour: Inter-relationship', *Tourism Management*, 22(6): 607–16.

Borgatti, S. P., Everett, M. G. and Freeman, L. C. (2002) *Ucinet for Windows: Software for Social Network Analysis*, Harvard, MA: Analytic Technologies.

Bornhorst, T., Ritchie, J.R.B. and Sheehan, L. (2010) 'Determinants of tourism success for DMOs and destinations: An empirical examination of stakeholders' perspectives', *Tourism Management*, 31(5): 572–89.

Buhalis, D. (2000) 'Marketing the competitive destination of the future', *Tourism Management*, 21(1): 97–116.

Buhalis, D. and Spada, A. (2000) 'Destination management systems: Criteria for success. An exploratory research', *Information Technology and Tourism*, 3(1): 41–58.

Canina, L., Enz, K. and Harrison, J. (2005) 'Agglomeration effects and strategic orientations: Evidence from the US lodging industry', *Academy of Management Journal*, 48(4): 565–81.

Capone, F. (2006) 'Systemic approaches for the analysis of tourism destination: Towards the tourist local systems', in L. Lazzeretti and C.S. Petrillo (eds), *Tourism Local Systems and Networking*, Amsterdam: Elsevier, pp. 7–23.

Cheng, C., Li, X. R., Petrick, J. F. and O'Leary, J. T. (2011) 'An examination of tourism journal development', *Tourism Management*, 32(1): 53–61.

Chuluunbaatar, E., Ottavia, Luh, D. and Kung, S. (2013) 'The development of academic research in cultural and creative industries', *International Journal of Cultural and Creative Industries*, 1(1): 4–15.

Chung, W. and Kalnins, A. (2001) 'Agglomeration effects and performance: A test of the Texas lodging industry', *Strategic Management Journal*, 22(10): 969–88.

Crouch, G. I. and Perdue, R. R. (2014) 'Tourism foundations and conceptual articles: The disciplinary foundations of tourism research, 1980–2010', *Journal of Travel Research*, published online 20 November 2014.

Crouch, G. I. and Ritchie, J.R.B. (1999) 'Tourism, competitiveness, and societal prosperity', *Journal of Business Research*, 44(3): 137–52.

Cruz, S. and Teixeira, A. (2010) 'The evolution of the cluster literature: Shedding light on the regional studies', *Regional Studies*, 44(9): 1263–88.

Della Corte, V. (2009) *Imprese e sistemi turistici*, Milano: Egea.

Dwyer, L., Gill, A. and Seetaram, J. (eds) (2012) *Handbook or Research Method in Tourism: Quantitative and Qualitative Approaches*, Cheltenham, UK: Edward Elgar.

Echtner, C. M. and Ritchie, J.R.B. (1993) 'The measurement of destination image: An empirical assessment', *Journal of Travel Research*, 31(4): 3–13.

Ellison, G. and Glaeser, E. (1999) 'The geographic concentration of an industry: Does natural advantage explain agglomeration?', *American Economic Association Papers and Proceedings*, 89(2): 311–16.

Feldman, R. and Sanger, J. (2006) *The Text Mining Handbook*, New York: Cambridge University Press.

Franch, M. (2002) *Destination management: governare il turismo tra locale e globale*, Torino: Giappichelli.

Franch, M. (2010) *Marketing delle destinazioni turistiche*, Milano: McGraw Hill.

Garfield, E. (1972) 'Citation analysis as a tool in journal evaluation', *Science*, 178(4060): 471–79.

Getz, D. (1993) 'Planning for tourism business districts', *Annals of Tourism Research*, 20(3): 583–600.

Getz, D. and Carlsen, J. (2000) 'Characteristics and goals of family and owner-operated businesses in the rural tourism and hospitality sectors', *Tourism Management*, 21(6): 547–60.

Goeldner, C. R. (2011) 'Reflecting on 50 years of the Journal of Travel Research', *Journal of Travel Research*, 50(6): 583–86.

Hall, C. M. (2010) 'A citation analysis of Tourism Recreation Research', *Tourism Recreation Research*, 35(3): 305–9.

Hall, C. M. (2011) 'Publish or perish? Bibliometric analysis, journal ranking and the assessment of research quality in tourism', *Tourism Management*, 32(1): 16–27.

Hanneman, R. A. and Riddle, M. (2005) *Introduction to Social Network Methods*, Riverside, CA: University of California.

Hervas-Oliver, J. L., Gonzalez, G. and Caja, P. (2014) *Clusters and Industrial Districts: Where is the Literature Going? Identifying Emerging Sub-fields of Research*, INGENIO (CSIC-UPV) Working Paper Series no. 9, Universidad de Valencia.

Hjalager, A. (2000) 'Tourism destinations and the concept of industrial districts', *Tourism and Hospitality Research*, 2(3): 199–213.

Hjalager, A. (2002) 'Repairing innovation defectiveness in tourism', *Tourism Management*, 23(5): 465–74.

Howey, R. M., Savage, K., Verbeeten, M. J. and Van Hoof, H. B. (1999) 'Tourism and hospitality research journals: Cross-citations among research communities', *Tourism Management*, 20(1): 133–39.

Howie, F. (2003) *Managing the Tourist Destination*, London: Continuum.

Hu, C. and Racherla, P. (2008) 'Visual representation of knowledge networks: A social network analysis of hospitality research domain', *International Journal of Hospitality Management*, 27(2): 302–12.

Ingram, P. and Baum, J. (1997) 'Chain affiliation and the failure of Manhattan hotels, 1898–1980', *Administrative Science Quarterly*, 42(1): 68–102.

Iorio, M. and Corsale, A. (2010) 'Rural tourism and livelihood strategies in Romania', *Journal of Rural Studies*, 26(2): 152–62.

Jackson, J. and Murphy, P. (2002) 'Tourism destinations as clusters: Analytical experiences from the New World', *Tourism and Hospitality Research*, 4(1): 36–52.

Jackson, J. and Murphy, P. (2006) 'Clusters in regional tourism: An Australian case', *Annals of Tourism Research*, 33(4): 1018–35.

Jamal, T. B. and Getz, D. (1995) 'Collaboration theory and community tourism planning', *Annals of Tourism Research*, 22(1): 186–204.

Jansen-Verbeke, M. C. and Ashworth, G. (1990) 'Environmental integration of recreation and tourism', *Annals of Tourism Research*, 17(4): 618–22.

Jogaratnam, G., Chon, K., McCleary, K., Mena, M. and Yoo, J. (2005) 'An analysis of institutional contributors to three major academic tourism journals: 1992–2001', *Tourism Management*, 26(5): 641–48.

Judd, D. R. (1995) 'Promoting tourism in US cities', *Tourism Management*, 16(3): 175–87.

Kozak, M. (2001) 'Repeaters' behaviour at two distinct destinations', *Annals of Tourism Research*, 28(3): 784–807.

Kozak M. and Baloglu S., (2011) *Managing and Marketing Tourist Destinations. Strategie to Gain a competitive edge*, Routledge: Abingdon.

Krugman, P. (1991) *Geography and Trade*, Cambridge, MA: MIT Press.

Law, R., Ye, Q., Chen, W. and Leung, R. (2009) 'An analysis of the most influential articles published in tourism journals from 2000 to 2007: A Google Scholar approach', *Journal of Travel and Tourism Marketing*, 26(7): 735–46.

Lawrence, L. (2014) *Reliability of Sentiment Mining Tools: A Comparison of Semantria and Social Mention*, PhD Thesis, Enschede: University of Twente.

Laws, E. (1995) *Tourist Destination Management*, Edinburgh: Napier University.

Laws, E., Richins H., Agrusa J. and Scott N., (2011) (eds) *Tourist Destination Governance: Practice, Theory and Issues*, CABI, Cambridge, USA.

Lazzeretti, L. and Capone, F. (2006) 'Identification and analysis of tourist local systems: An application to Italy (1996–2001)', in L. Lazzeretti and C.S. Petrillo (eds), *Tourism Local Systems and Networking*, Amsterdam: Elsevier, pp. 25–40.

Lazzeretti, L. and Capone, F. (2008) 'Mapping and analysing local tourism systems in Italy, 1991–2001', *Tourism Geographies*, 10(2): 214–32.

Lazzeretti, L. and Petrillo, C. S. (eds) (2006) *Tourism Local Systems and Networking*, Amsterdam: Elsevier.

Lazzeretti, L., Capone, F. and Innocenti, N. (2014) 'The evolution of creative economy research', paper presented at the AISRE Conference, Padua, Italy, 11–13 September.

Lazzeretti, L., Sedita, S. and Caloffi, A. (2014) 'Founders and disseminators of cluster research', *Journal of Economic Geography*, 14(1): 21–43.

Leiper, N. (1995) *Tourism Management*, Melbourne: RMIT Press.

Lew, A.A. and McKercher, B. (2006) 'Modeling tourist movements: A local destination analysis', *Annals of Tourism Research*, 33(2): 402–23.

Mansfeld, Y. (1992) 'From motivation to actual travel', *Annals of Tourism Research*, 19(3): 399–419.

Markusen, A. (1996) 'Sticky places in slippery space: A typology of industrial districts', *Economic Geography*, 72(3): 293–313.

Martini, U. (eds) (2005) *Management dei sistemi territoriali. Gestione e marketing delle destinazione turistiche*, Torino: Giappichelli.

McCann, B. T. and Folta, T. B. (2008) 'Location matters: Where we have been and where we might go in agglomeration research', *Journal of Management*, 34(3): 532–65.

McKercher, B. (2005) 'A case for ranking tourism journals', *Tourism Management*, 26(5): 649–51.

McKercher, B. (2008) 'A citation analysis of tourism scholars', *Tourism Management*, 29(6): 1226–32.

Michael, E. (eds) (2007) *Micro-clusters and Networks: The Growth of Tourism*, Amsterdam: Elsevier.

Mihalič, T. (2000) 'Environmental management of a tourist destination: A factor of tourism competitiveness', *Tourism Management*, 21(1): 65–78.

Morrison A. M. (2013) *Marketing and Managing Tourism Destinations*, Abingdon, UK: Routledge.

Morgan, N., Pritchard, A. and Pride R. (2011) *Destination Brands*, Abingdon, UK: Routledge.

Murphy, P.E. (1992) 'Urban tourism and visitor behavior', *American Behavioral Scientist*, 36(2): 200–11.

Nordin, S. (2003) *Tourism Clustering and Innovation*, Östersund, Sweden: Etour.

Novelli, M., Schmitz, B. and Spencer, T. (2006) 'Networks, clusters and innovation in tourism: A UK experience', *Tourism Management*, 27(6): 1141–52.

Palmer, A., Sesé, A. and Montaño, J. (2004) 'Tourism and statistics: Bibliometric study 1998–2002', *Annals of Tourism Research*, 32(1): 167–78.

Parasuraman, A., Zeithaml, V. and Berry, L. L. (1988) 'SERVQUAL: A multiple-item scale for measuring consumer perceptions of service quality', *Journal of Retailing*, 64(1): 12–40.

Parasuraman, A., Zeithaml, V. and Berry, L. L. (1991) 'Refinement and reassessment of the SERVQUAL scale', *Journal of Retailing*, 67(4): 420–50.

Pearce, D. G. (1996) 'Tourist organizations in Sweden', *Tourism Management*, 17(6): 413–24.

Pearce, D. G. (1998a) 'Tourist districts in Paris: Structure and functions', *Tourism Management*, 19(1): 49–65.

Pearce, D. G. (1998b) 'Tourism development in Paris: Public intervention', *Annals of Tourism Research*, 25(2): 457–76.

Pearce, D. G. (2013) 'Toward an integrative conceptual framework of destinations', *Journal of Travel Research*, 53(2): 141–53.

Pechlaner, H. and Weiermair, K. (eds) (2000) *Destination management: fondamenti di marketing e gestione delle destinazioni turistiche*, Milano: TCI.

Pechlaner, H., Zehrer, A., Matzler, K. and Abfalter, D. (2004) 'A ranking of international tourism and hospitality journals', *Journal of Travel Research*, 42(4): 328–32.

Porter, M. E. (1998) 'Clusters and the new economics of competition', *Harvard Business Review*, 76(6): 77–90.

Prahalad, C. K. and Hamel, G. (1990) 'The core competence of the corporation', *Harvard Business Review*, 68(3): 79–91.

Pritchard, A. and Morgan, N. J. (2001) 'Culture, identity and tourism representation: Marketing Cymru or Wales?', *Tourism Management*, 22(2): 167–79.

Rabellotti, R. (1995) 'Is there an "industrial district model"? Footwear districts in Italy and Mexico compared', *World Development*, 23(1): 29–41.

Racherla, R. and Hu, C. (2010) 'A social network perspective of tourism research collaborations', *Annals of Tourism Research*, 37(4): 1012–34.

Ritchie, J.R.B. and Crouch, G. I. (2003) *The Competitive Destination. A Sustainable Tourism Perspective*, Trowbridge, UK: Cromwell Press.

Sainaghi, R. (2006) 'From contents to processes: Versus a dynamic destination management model (DDMM)', *Tourism Management*, 27(5): 1053–63.

Saxena, G. and Ilbery, B. (2008) 'Integrated rural tourism a border case study', *Annals of Tourism Research*, 35(1): 233–54.

Saxena, G., Clark, G., Oliver, T. and Ilbery, B. (2007) 'Conceptualising integrated rural tourism', *Tourism Geographies*, 9(4): 347–70.

Schmitz, H. and Nadvi, K. (1999) 'Clustering and industrialization: Introduction', *World Development*, 27(9): 1503–14.

Sciarelli, S. (eds) (2007) *Il management dei sistemi turistici locale. Strategie e strumenti per la governance*, Torino: Giappichelli.

Scott, N., Cooper, N. and Baggio, R. (2008) *Network Analysis and Tourism: From Theory to Practice*, Clevedon, UK: Channel View.

Shaw, G. and Williams, A. (2009) 'Knowledge transfer and management in tourism organisations: An emerging research agenda', *Tourism Management*, 30(3): 325–35.

Stansfield, C. Richert, J. E. (1970) 'The recreational business district', *Journal of Leisure Research*, 2(4): 238–51.

Stepchenkova, S. and Mills, J. (2010) 'Destination image: A meta-analysis of 2000–2007 research', *Journal of Hospitality Marketing & Management*, 19(6): 575–609.

Tallman, S., Jenkins, M., Henry, N. and Pinch, S. (2004) 'Knowledge, clusters and competitive advantage', *Academy of Management Review*, 29(2): 258–71.

Tangeland, T. and Aas, Ø. (2011) 'Household composition affect the importance of experience attributes of nature based tourism activity products. A Norwegian case study of outdoor recreationists', *Tourism Management*, 32(4): 822–32.

Tangeland, T., Vennesland, B. and Nybakk, E. (2013) 'Second-home owners' intention to purchase nature-based tourism activity products. A Norwegian case study', *Tourism Management*, 36(June): 364–76.

Tokic, K. (2012) 'Citation analysis of the journal Tourism', *Tourism*, 60(4): 447–55.

Tosun, C. (2002) 'Host perceptions of impacts: A comparative tourism study', *Annals of Tourism Research*, 29(1): 231–53.

Tribe, J. (2010) 'Tribes, territories and networks in tourism academy', *Annals of Tourism Research*, 37(1): 7–33.Trunfio, M. (2008) *Governance turistica e sistemi turistici locali. Modelli teorici ed evidenze empiriche in Italia*, Torino: Giappichelli.

Urtasun, A. and Gutierrez, I. (2006) 'Hotel location in tourism cities. Madrid 1936–1998', *Annals of Tourism Research*, 33(2): 382–402.

Wang Y., and Pizam A., (2011) (eds) *Destination marketing and management. Theories and Applications*, CABI, Cambridge, USA.

Wasserman, S. and Faust, K. (eds) (1994) *Social Network Analysis: Methods and Applications*, New York: Cambridge University Press.

Wernerfelt, B. (1988) 'The resource-based view of the firm', *Strategic Management Journal*, 5(2): 171–80.

Williamson, O. E. (1991) 'Comparative economic-organization. The analysis of discrete structural alternatives', *Administrative Science Quarterly*, 36(2): 269–99.

Ye, Q., Li, T. and Law, R. (2013) 'A coauthorship network analysis of tourism and hospitality research collaboration', *Journal of Hospitality & Tourism Research*, 37(1): 51–76.

2 Destination management and competitiveness

Literature review and a destination competitiveness analysis

Francesco Capone

1 Introduction

In the course of the last decade, the issues related to destination management and marketing have seen an exponential growth (Morgan, Pritchard and Pride 2011; Morrison 2013; Halkier, Kozak and Svensson 2015). A search on Scopus for 'destination management' and 'destination marketing' records more than 1,000 articles.[1] Such increasing importance also led to the foundation of a new specialised journal, the *Journal of Destination Marketing and Management*, which denotes the attention paid to these issues in the field of tourism studies.

The focus on destinations has been made about two decades ago, with the seminal contributions of Leiper (1979; 1995), Laws (1995) and others. Later on, a specific interest was developed for destination management, following the contributions of relevant scholars all around the world (Howie 2003; Ritchie and Crouch 2003; Godfrey and Clarke 2000, etc.) and in particular thanks to the contribution of the International Association of Scientific Experts in Tourism (AIEST) (Pechlaner and Weiermair 2000).[2] The issue of destination marketing has followed a similar course, although it had developed a little time before, with the works tackling the subjects of place branding and city marketing (Kotler, Haider and Rein 1993). As compared to destination management, the marketing of destinations has always constituted a more widely and deeply analysed issue, extensively related to the studies of marketing scholars (Buhalis 2000; Go and Govers 2012; and others).

In what concerns Italy, the study of tourist destinations has been highly successful and gained much relevance in the field of management (Della Corte 2000; Tamma 2000; Franch 2002; Pencarelli 2003; Martini 2005; Casarin 2006; Sciarelli 2007).

The researches on destination management and marketing have initially focused on the strategies of governance, marketing and communication of destinations (Howie, 2003; Kozak and Baloglu 2011; Pike and Page 2014), whereas in the last few years more and more studies have drawn attention to destination development and competitiveness (Laws *et al.* 2011; Viken and Granas 2014). In fact, destination competitiveness has actually become a significant part of the tourism literature (Heath 2003; Bornhorst, Ritchie and Sheehan 2010).

In recent years, competitiveness in tourism has further intensified because of both the economic crisis and the process of globalization (Laesser and Beritelli 2013), so the exploration of this phenomenon has shifted from the study of firms and networks of firms to that of competitiveness of destinations and among destinations (Pearce 2013). Given this background, the analysis of destination competitiveness takes up a fundamental role not only in terms of the territories' competitiveness, but also from the point of view of companies, which can benefit from management studies. In this context, with regard to the debate on destination and competitiveness, Laesser and Beritelli (2013) underline that there are still some under-researched factors, as there are no appropriate causal models to describe and explain the phenomenon.

The aim of this chapter is twofold. On the one hand, the first part presents the state of the art and evolution of the literature on destination management and marketing, until dealing with the studies on destination competitiveness, seen as a prominent topic in recent research on tourism. On the other hand, the second part develops an analytical model of destination competitiveness that combines the most relevant contributions on this issue (Crouch and Ritchie 1999; Dwyer and Kim 2003; Ritchie and Crouch 2003; Enright and Newton 2004) and investigates a specific case of competitiveness in an Italian tourist destination, Maremma, finally suggesting some implications of destination management.

In order to investigate the competitiveness of the destination, a questionnaire was administered to entrepreneurs in the tourism sector at large operating in the destination, during the months of February and March 2015. According to earlier studies, Maremma comes out like a tourist destination having a fairly high level of competitiveness (Becheri 2011; Bimonte and Faralla 2012; Lazzeretti and Capone 2015) and therefore a rather representative case study on which to test our model.

This chapter is organised as follows. After this introduction, section 2 reviews the wide literature on the tourist destination, illustrating the development of the main lines of research on destination management (DM), destination marketing and destination management organisation (DMO). Section 3 presents the state of the art on the models of destination competitiveness and summarises them into an analytical model to investigate the competitiveness determinants of a destination. Section 4 describes the research design and the survey. Section 5 illustrates the application of the model to a case study in Maremma, Tuscany. The work ends with some conclusive considerations and managerial implications.

2 Literature review on destination, destination management and marketing

2.1 Destination and destination management

The initial analyses of tourist destinations have focused, in the first place, on the definition of the concept of destination and the different analytical perspectives on this research area. According to Buhalis (2000), destinations are amalgams of tourism products, offering an integrated experience to consumers. Leiper (1995) explains that destinations are places towards which people travel and where they choose to stay for a while in order to experience certain features or characteristics – perceived attractions of some sort.

The geographical delimitation of a destination varies according to the visitor's provenance, his knowledge and information about it. Laesser and Beritelli (2013) define a destination like a geographic entity, a cluster, a (latent) network of suppliers or additionally, a network of suppliers activated by visitors' demand; in other words, a productive social system with specific business and related non-business goals.

Some authors (Pearce 1998; Leiper 1995; Pechlaner and Weiermair 2000) focused on the demand side of destinations and defined them as a set of products, services and natural resources capable of attracting the visitor. Other scholars, instead (Rispoli and Tamma 1995; Michael 2003) circumscribed destinations taking a supply-side perspective, and focused on how firms concentrate in a specific place which, by way of coordination mechanisms, constitute the destination's supply capability.

The study of destinations as a subject of analysis in tourism studies has also been crucial for the development of the research branches of DM and marketing. According to the World Tourism Organisation (WTO 2007), DM is concerned with all the activities and processes aimed at matching buyers and sellers by providing answers to consumers' demands so as to gain a competitive position.

The study of tourist destinations has been highly successful and gained much relevance also in Italy, particularly in the field of management (Franch 2002; Pencarelli 2003; Martini 2005; Casarin 2006). The explanation can be found not only in the relevant role of tourism for the Italian economy, but also in the difficulties of managing and governing destinations in such a context, with its mixture of public–private provision, and its industry characterised by small and medium-sized firms.

The main studies have dealt originally with DM and marketing (Pechlaner and Weiermair 2000; Franch 2002) and then a relevant strand of research dealt with the concept of the tourist local system and its governance (Della Corte 2000; Capone 2006; Sciarelli 2007; Trunfio 2008), given also the relevance of an Italian law on this concept (no. 135/2001). Following this, the marketing and management of tourist destinations have received a wide numbers of contributions (Martini 2005; Casarin 2006; Franch 2010), all aimed at increasing the competitiveness of Italian tourist destinations and the performances of local firms.

A relevant attention has also been devoted to the territorial identification of tourist clusters and destinations (Lazzeretti and Capone 2006; Della Lucia 2010), and finally to the analysis of the sources of competitiveness (Capone and Boix 2008). Some recent contributions have underlined how the identification of systems of firms in the territory constitutes a first necessary step to identify a tourist destination (Laesser and Beritelli 2013). This must involve the existence in the area of a shared project, a typical product, a governance system, a legislative framework of reference and, finally, some system performances (Della Lucia *et al.* 2007). In this context, Sciarelli (2007) puts forward a model for the identification of a tourist destination which is composed of three variables, and called 'project-product-territory'.[3] Lazzeretti and Capone (2008) start the analysis of a destination's competitiveness from the identification of tourist clusters in the territory.

The different research approaches to destinations have recommended management models that have become more and more complex depending on the tourist destination or system under analysis (Mill and Morrison 1992; Laws 1995; Leiper 1995). For example, some authors (Rispoli and Tamma 1995; Tamma 2000) put forward a taxonomy of destinations on which to build different strategies: package, fragmented and network destinations. Flagestad and Hope (2001) suggest that there are two typologies of destinations, the corporate and the community. Fragmented destinations are the most difficult to manage because the offer is spread out and there is no particular subject to assemble and supervise the single products supplied by different local stakeholders. Many European destinations have this sort of arrangement, and they definitely must find new modalities of integration and cooperation among actors in order to develop a medium-long-term project and establish a local governance (Svensson, Nordin and Flagestad 2006).

2.2 Destination marketing

Destination marketing is widely recognised today as a pillar of the literature on tourist destinations, and its field of research has a 40-year tradition, having started in the 1970s (Leiper 1979; and others).

Pike and Page (2014) underline how destination marketing has become a crucial issue of tourism studies since the early 1970s (Wahab, Crampon and Rothfield 1976). They stress the differences between destination marketing and DM, given that many managerial tasks cannot be completed by a DMO, which is predominantly centred on the marketing of resources, the communication of brand identity and similar tasks. Dredge, Jenkins and Taplin (2011) have recently lamented the lack of research relating to DM in comparison to destination marketing. In this respect, Volgger and Pechlaner (2014) also find a lack of research relating to the theme of DM as compared to destination marketing.

Destinations are among the most difficult entities to manage and market, due to the complexity of relationships among local stakeholders. Buhalis (2000) lists the following activities as contributions of marketing research to destinations: (a) formulating the destination's products; (b) pricing destinations; (c) distributing tourist destinations; and (d) promoting destinations.

In this respect, there is also a marked difference between destination marketing and place branding, since the latter takes place where tourism is only one component of local industry (Ashworth and Kavaratzis 2010; Go and Govers 2012; and others).

Pike and Page (2014) stress the importance of destination marketing; they notice that, starting from the 1990s, there have been 11 conferences on this theme, 10 WTO reports, and – including only the years from 1999 –11 journal special issues. All this certainly proves the influence of this subject in mainstream tourism studies.

Within the research on destination marketing (Stepchenkova and Mills 2010), the literature has largely focused on brand identity, image and positioning of destinations (Blain, Levy and Ritchie 2005; Della Corte, Piras and Zamparelli 2010). Some studies have also drawn attention to the network branding of destinations, and to the management of stakeholders' image, seen in association with the destination's general brand (Cox, Gyrd-Jones and Gardiner 2014).

2.3 Destination management organisation

Finally, the last main strand of research on destinations has dealt with the DMO. In these last few years, the number of researches on DMOs has strongly increased, also due to the loss of competitiveness of destinations, the recent economic crises and the rising competition from the developing countries (Pike and Page 2014).

Some authors focused on the analysis of the DMO activities that should be enhanced in order to improve the success and competitiveness of destinations (Crouch and Ritchie 1999; Dwyer and Kim 2003), while others concentrated on the framework and processes that must be improved to manage a destination efficiently (Sainaghi 2006). Still other authors applied to the examination of a destination's stakeholders and how to reconcile their somehow conflicting interests (Bornhorst, Ritchie and Sheehan 2010). Only few contributions have analysed how tourism is actually viewed in the studies of destinations and DMO activities (Pearce and Schänzel 2013).

According to the WTO (2007), the DMO is the organisation responsible for the management and marketing of a destination, with the assignment of promoting the elements existing in a territory and combining their mixture into a single tourist supply, as a condition for increasing the performances and competitive capabilities of that destination. The DMO may be constituted starting from a project of territorial or destination marketing (Pencarelli 2003), which identifies a system of services and resources involved in the implementation and management of an integrated tourist supply for a specific territory.

Laesser and Beritelli (2013) underline four domains of study in the DM strand of research: (a) definition and delimitation of DM; (b) its competitiveness; (c) sustainable development and governance of destinations; and (d) practical implications for DM.

The authors in the DMO strand of research call attention to the dominance in the related literature of the issues of destination marketing and promotion activities, destination stakeholders, critical role of policy and strategy, decision making and behaviours facing tourism and, finally, DMO financial management (Pike 2007).

The following are some of the main activities designed for a DMO (Godfrey and Clarke, 2000): (a) generation of incoming flows of tourists; (b) management of the destination's image and symbolic value; (c) building and keeping of relationships with stakeholders; and (d) impact evaluation of tourism in the local territorial system.

Pike and Page (2014) suggest that an effective DMO should work to improve the management of internal resources, the appropriateness of its own activities, the effectiveness of interventions aimed at achieving a leadership position. To do so, it should support the development of a destination's brand identity, strategic positioning and performance measures.

Traditionally, DMOs have mostly taken a marketing and communication role with regard to destinations, but in the last few years DMOs have also become more involved in their management and development, with the goal of increasing their competitiveness (Presenza, Sheehan and Ritchie, 2005; Minguzzi, 2006).

3 The state of art on the models of destination competitiveness

Destination competitiveness has become a significant part of the tourism litera-ture. The interest in this subject has stimulated a number of research studies all over the world, in Italy (Cracolici and Nijkamp 2008; Angeloni 2012; Goffi and Cucculelli 2012; 2015), East Europe (Mihalič 2000), Canada (Bornhorst, Ritchie and Sheehan 2010), South Africa (Heath 2003) and Asia (Crouch and Ritchie 1999; Enright and Newton 2004). Some influential research has tried to approach destinations' success more indirectly via the construct of destination competi-tiveness. Crouch and Ritchie (1999; 2000) probably offer the most widely cited framework within this line of research, even though a similar model had already been introduced by Laws (1995).

Other researchers have focused on particular aspects of destination competi-tiveness, including destination branding, image and positioning (Pike 2007), DM systems (Buhalis and Spada 2000), destination satisfaction (Fuchs and Weiermair 2004), price competitiveness (Dwyer, Forsyth and Prasada 2000), quality man-agement (Go and Govers 2000), the environment (Mihalič 2000), nature-based tourism (Huybers and Bennett 2003) and so on.

Laesser and Beritelli (2013), regarding the debate on destination and competi-tiveness, underline that there are still several research gaps to fill and there are no appropriate causal models to describe and explain the competitiveness of destina-tions. Volgger and Pechlaner (2014) investigate destinations' success as dependent on DMO's achievements. In particular, they are among the few who develop a net-work approach on destinations' success and stakeholders' influence on DMOs. Sev-eral authors focus on performances from a supply perspective, while others adopt a demand perspective (Ritchie and Crouch 2003; Fuchs and Weiermair 2004).

Crouch and Ritchie (1999) define competitiveness as the ability of a tourist des-tination to contribute to the economic base (prosperity) of a place, i.e. to provide high standards of living both for residents and visitors. Less generally, according to Dwyer and Kim (2003: 375), destination competitiveness is 'the ability of a destination to deliver goods and services that perform better than in other destina-tions on those aspects of the tourism experience considered to be important by tourists'.

One of the main patterns applied to tourism and destination competitiveness is undoubtedly the well-known Porter's (1990) model, describing the structure of national competitiveness as a diamond. Porter's model states that success in a particular industry at international level depends on a set of forces of competitiveness: factor conditions, demand conditions, related and supporting industries, firm strategy, structure and rivalry.

This model has also been applied to tourist destinations, starting from the contribution of Crouch and Ritchie (Crouch and Ritchie 1999; Ritchie and Crouch 2003) and to the more complex model of Enright and Newton (2004; 2005).

Enright, Frances and Scott-Saavedra (1996) proposed an alternative framework that divides the drivers of competitiveness into six categories: (1) inputs, (2) industrial and consumer demand, (3) inter-firm competition and cooperation, (4) industrial and regional clustering, (5) internal organisation and strategy of firms and (6) institutions, social structures and agendas.

Crouch and Ritchie (1999) have incorporated the concepts of Porter's diamond and derived a model that postulates that destination competitiveness is determined by four major components (Figure 2.1): (1) core resources and attractors, (2) supporting factors and resources, (3) destination management and (4) qualifying determinants. The core resources and attractors include the primary elements of a destination's appeal.

Dwyer and Kim's (2003) model of destination competitiveness displays a number of factors considered to impact on tourism competitiveness, including available resources (natural resources, cultural assets and heritage items); created resources (tourism infrastructures, available activities); supporting factors (infrastructure in general, quality of services, access to destinations); and DM factors.

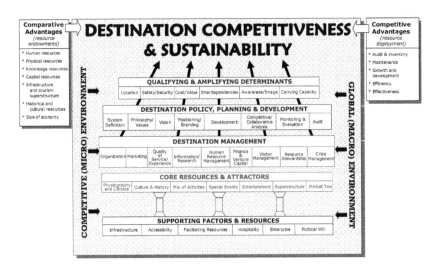

Figure 2.1 The Crouch and Ritchie conceptual model of destination competitiveness

Source: Crouch and Ritchie (2003: 63).

Bornhorst, Ritchie and Sheehan (2010) look into the success of Canadian destinations and present a model of DMO success, with competition based on input, process and performance variables.

Enright and Newton (2004) present a reworking of Porter's model, while Ritchie and Crouch (2003) produce a new model of destination competitiveness, tested for the case of Hong Kong. Six items are included in the set of generic competitiveness factors, which are added to a further set of 31 'business-related' items derived from the generic competitiveness frameworks of Porter (1990), and Enright, Frances and Scott-Saavedra (1996).

Figure 2.2 illustrates the model of tourism competitiveness as drawn up by Porter (1990) and then by Crouch and Ritchie (Crouch and Ritchie 1999; 2000; Ritchie and Crouch 2003), Dwyer and Kim (2003), and finally Enright and Newton (2004). This model was presented at two consecutive meetings,[4] and further revisions deriving from presentations made at national and international conferences have been included.

The model is a development of the one proposed by Crouch and Ritchie (Crouch and Ritchie 1999; Ritchie and Crouch 2003), which recognises some new elements introduced in later models (Dwyer and Kim 2003; Enright and Newton 2004; 2005) and highlights the configuration of Porter's (1990) diamond. At the base, there is a diamond-shaped structure composed of four elements which recalls Porter's

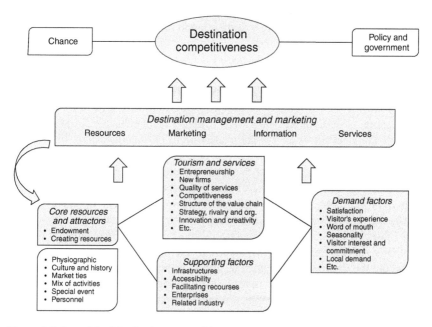

Figure 2.2 A model of destination competitiveness

Source: Our elaboration from Porter (1990), Crouch and Ritchie (1990; 2000), Enright and Newton (2004; 2005), Dwyer and Kim (2003) and Ritchie and Crouch (2003).

representation, but two more components are added: policies and government, and chance. The four main elements of the diamond are constituted by the conditions present in the model of Crouch and Ritchie (1999), which are the following:

- Core resources (and attractors) – condition factors in Porter (1990) – described according to the traditional classification (physiographics, culture and history, etc.). Also valued are the endowments of resources and those possibly created or implemented; in addition, personnel and special events are included.
- Supporting factors (related industries), which correspond to tourism infrastructures, accessibility, and facilitating resources (public services, knowledge and capital resources, etc.).
- Demand factors, which had no corresponding item in the model of Crouch and Ritchie (1999). They take into account the role of demand in stimulating the tourism industry of destinations. The demand satisfaction and positive experience of visitors allow to improve the competitiveness of destinations and establish positive words of mouth. The concern and commitment of visitors can also affect the competitiveness of demand. On its turn, demand can give confidence to local firms and boost competitiveness at the international level, and *vice versa* (Pearce and Schänzel 2013).
- Rivalry and local firms' organisation also constitute a specific item. The presence of a well-organised supply chain supports the competitiveness of destinations. The success of companies and entrepreneurs, as well as new venture developments contribute to a destination in different ways.

A last aspect that should be discussed is the possibility that, based on the elements described above, the level of competitiveness of a destination increases. Important factors in this regard are marketing (Buhalis 2000), image (Stepchenkova and Mills 2010), quality of services (Go and Govers 2000), but also the organisation of destinations and DMOs (Volgger and Pechlaner 2014), as well as whether the local actors accept the leadership of DMOs (just think of corporate and community destinations).

Obviously, the DMO can also work on resources, thus regulate the impact of seasonality, increase tourists' use of tangible resources, and implement a mechanism of proliferation – or at least of conservation and respect – of resources. This is why the link between DMOs and resources is a recursive one.

A Likert scale evaluation of the various items can be implemented on the destination's stakeholders and/or visitors, and the corresponding results will then constitute the framework on which to plan new strategies. These results can also be analysed in a four-quadrant matrix, like in Enright and collaborators (Enright, Frances and Scott-Saavedra 1996; Enright and Newton 2004), which returns a graphic representation, valuable for the analysis of the critical or favourable features of a destination. In the following section, the above-described model will be used for a first investigation of the competitiveness of the tourist destination Maremma in Tuscany.

4 Research design

This aim of the following sections is to present a destination analysis aimed at testing the proposed model, evaluating the competitiveness of the destination under analysis, and suggesting managerial implications for DM.

The survey is based on a questionnaire on tourist destinations, built on the basis of the competitiveness model presented in the previous section. The questionnaire was administered to entrepreneurs in the tourism sector at large, operating in Maremma (Figure 2.3), Tuscany, during the months of February and March 2015. According to earlier studies,[5] Maremma comes out like a tourist destination having a fairly high level of competitiveness (Becheri 2011; Bimonte and Faralla 2012; Lazzeretti and Capone 2015) and thus represents an emblematic case for testing the analytical model of destination competitiveness. In addition, it is a place that has not been extensively studied at the international level, as compared to the more renowned areas of Tuscan tourism (Lazzeretti and Petrillo 2006).

The questionnaire has been tested on few entrepreneurs in Spring 2015, and was then administered online. It was forwarded to 125 tourism entrepreneurs[6] and

Figure 2.3 The destination Maremma in South Tuscany

Source: Our elaboration.

to some policy makers located in the destination. The most part of the managers questioned were first contacted and given information about the survey's goal, and afterwards received the questionnaire via computer.

During the administration period, 41 answers were received, for an overall response rate of 32%, which is in line with similar surveys.[7] Other authors, like Crouch and Ritchie (2000) have instead contacted persons linked to the DMO of destinations, while Dwyer and Kim (2003) interviewed research scholars, experts and entrepreneurs in a face-to-face workshop. The choice of focusing on the supply side, i.e. on tourist firms, is consonant with the main quantitative researches on the issue (Enright and Newton 2004) as well as with this book's train of though.

Table 2.1 lists the specific items of the questionnaire evaluated then on a five-point Likert scale. The first rows in the table comprise the factors derived from the

Table 2.1 Competitiveness factors of tourist destinations

Core resources	*Supporting factors*
• Night life and entertainment	• Quality of local road system
• Daily recreational activities	• Quality of public transport
• Shopping opportunities	• Accessibility
• Local art and cultural heritage	• Telecommunication system (GMS, 3G, etc.)
• Environmental and natural resources	• Accessibility for people with disabilities
• Festivals and other entertainment events	• Medical care facilities
• Gastronomy and typical products	• Waste management and environmental issues
Competitiveness of the local tourist industry	*Competencies and management of tourist firms*
• Amount of hotel accommodation	• Use of Internet in tourist firms
• Amount of non-hotel accommodation	• Management competencies of tourist firms
• Quality of services in hotel accommodation	• High qualification of personnel
• Quality of services in non-hotel accommodation	• Hospitality of residents towards tourists
• Quality and quantity of other tourist firms	
Policy and government	*Demand factors*
• Public commitment to improve the competitiveness of the destination	• Tourist satisfaction
• Public effort to limit environmental impact of tourism	• Level of repeat visits
• Policy for the creation of occupational opportunities	• Tourist's respect for the environment
• Public–private cooperation in the development of tourism	• Seasonality
• Public communication of the destination	• Presence of foreigners
• Policy for the training of highly qualified tourist personnel	

Marketing and management of the destination	Competitiveness of the destination
• Awareness of the destination • Efficacy of communication strategy and marketing • Choice of the right segment of clients • Development of inter-firm collaborations • Existence of a shared project about destination	• Value for money of hotel accommodation • Value for money of non-hotel accommodation (camping sites, and others) • Value for money of restaurant services • Value for money of the tourist's overall experience

Source: Our elaboration from Crouch and Ritchie (1999; 2000); Enright and Newton (2004; 2005); Ritchie and Crouch 2003; Goffi and Cucculelli (2012; 2015); Dwyer and Kim (2003).

Porter's (1990) diamond model, i.e. core resources, supporting factors, and competitiveness of the local tourism industry, plus the management competences of local firms and the role of government. The last section is devoted to the appraisal of management and marketing strategies, and the overall competitiveness of the destination.

The next section is intended to test the suggested model and carry out an experimental investigation on a real destination so as to suggest management strategies and actions for the improvement of the destination's competitiveness.

5 A destination competitiveness analysis: Maremma in Tuscany

The analysis results are presented in Table 2.2, where the answer percentages are ordered in a Likert scale, and rank of importance and average are shown. The rank of importance was computed by sorting the items by average results, like in Enright and Newton (2004).[8] In other words, rank 1 was assigned to the item that the interviewed persons believed the most important for the destination's competitiveness, so that rank 42 corresponds to the less relevant one.

First of all, it is interesting to mark out the most important results on the basis of the items' rank. Core resources turn out to be the most relevant, in particular the natural and environmental ones, together with the typical products, outcome that had already emerged in a previous study of this destination (Bertella 2011). More than 93% of the interviewed assign a great importance to nature and the environment, and 88% of them to gastronomy and typical products. This result is consistent with the image of the analysed tourist destination, a coastal resort with a national natural park, a low level of art and cultural heritage, but a great endowment of natural and environmental resources.

Other important factors are those on the demand side of tourism, which are believed to be of crucial importance for the destination's competitiveness. Seasonality is considered strategic by the entrepreneurs, since Maremma is a seaside place, popular for summer tourism, but also important is the problem related to the difficulty of seizing segments of foreign tourism. More than 55% of respondents

Table 2.2 Results of the survey

No	Item	Percentage					Mean	Rank
		Not important	Slightly important	Neutral	Somewhat important	Very important		
Supporting factors (general infrastructure and access to the destination)								
1	Quality of local road system	6.9	44.8	44.8	3.4	0.0	-0.55	32
2	Quality of public transport	34.5	48.3	17.2	0.0	0.0	-1.17	42
3	Accessibility	10.3	27.6	55.2	6.9	0.0	-0.41	27
4	Telecommunication system	13.8	17.2	44.8	20.7	3.4	-0.21	24
5	Accessibility for people with disabilities	3.4	27.6	58.6	10.3	0.0	-0.24	25
6	Medical care facilities	3.4	27.6	44.8	24.1	0.0	-0.10	19
7	Waste management and environmental issues	6.9	20.7	51.7	13.8	6.9	-0.14	20
Core resources								
8	Night life and entertainment	17.9	42.9	28.6	10.7	0.0	-0.68	36
9	Daily recreational activities	10.3	51.7	34.5	3.4	0.0	-0.69	37
10	Shopping opportunities	10.3	34.5	41.4	10.3	3.4	-0.38	26
11	Local art and cultural heritage	3.4	13.8	31.0	31.0	20.7	0.52	5
12	Environmental and natural resources	0.0	0.0	7.1	39.3	53.6	1.46	1
13	Festivals and other entertainment events	7.1	17.9	46.4	14.3	14.3	0.11	12
14	Gastronomy and typical products	0.0	0.0	13.8	37.9	48.3	1.34	2
Competitiveness of local tourist firms and services								
15	Amount of hotel accommodation	3.4	27.6	44.8	17.2	6.9	-0.03	18
16	Amount of non-hotel accommodation	0.0	0.0	31.0	62.1	6.9	0.76	3
17	Quality of services in hotel accommodation	0.0	24.1	51.7	20.7	3.4	0.03	16
18	Quality of services in non-hotel accommodation	0.0	6.9	65.5	24.1	3.4	0.24	10
19	Quality and quantity of other tourist firms	0.0	17.2	65.5	13.8	3.4	0.03	17

Competencies and management of tourist firms

20	Use of Internet in tourist firms	0.0	25.9	40.7	29.6	3.7	0.11	*13*
21	Management competencies of tourist firms	14.8	44.4	29.6	11.1	0.0	-0.63	*34*
22	High qualification of personnel	18.5	29.6	37.0	14.8	0.0	-0.52	*30*
23	Hospitality of residents towards tourists	7.4	29.6	40.7	14.8	7.4	-0.15	*21*

Marketing and management of the destination

24	Awareness of the destination	0.0	29.6	51.9	14.8	0.0	-0.15	*22*
25	Efficacy of communication strategy and marketing	11.1	37.0	44.4	7.4	0.0	-0.52	*31*
26	Choice of the right segment of clients	14.8	22.2	55.6	3.7	3.7	-0.41	*28*
27	Development of inter-firm collaborations	25.9	40.7	33.3	0.0	0.0	-0.93	*40*

Demand factors

28	Tourist satisfaction	0.0	3.7	66.7	25.9	3.7	0.30	*8*
29	Level of repeat visits	0.0	14.8	48.1	29.6	7.4	0.30	*9*
30	Words to mouth	0.0	7.4	48.1	40.7	3.7	0.41	*7*
31	Seasonality	0.0	7.4	33.3	40.7	14.8	0.65	*4*
32	Difficulty of involving foreign tourists	0.0	14.8	40.7	18.5	22.2	0.50	*6*

Policy and government

33	Public commitment to improve the competitiveness of the destination	14.8	40.7	40.7	3.7	0.0	-0.67	*35*
34	Public effort to limit environmental impact of tourism	7.4	48.1	40.7	0.0	3.7	-0.56	*33*
35	Policy for the creation of occupational opportunities	22.2	63.0	14.8	0.0	0.0	-1.07	*41*
36	Public–private cooperation in the development of tourism	22.2	48.1	25.9	3.7	0.0	-0.89	*39*
37	Public communication of the destination	11.1	33.3	44.4	7.4	0.0	-0.50	*29*
38	Policy for the training of highly qualified tourist personnel	22.2	48.1	22.2	7.4	0.0	-0.85	*38*

(Continued)

Table 2.2 Continued

No	Item	Percentage					Mean	Rank
		Not important	Slightly important	Neutral	Somewhat important	Very important		
	Competitiveness of the destination							
39	Value for money of hotel accommodation	0.0	29.6	55.6	14.8	0.0	-0.15	23
40	Value for money of non-hotel accommodation	0.0	14.8	51.9	33.3	0.0	0.19	11
41	Value for money of restaurant services	3.7	7.4	63.0	25.9	0.0	0.11	14
42	Value for money of the tourist's overall experience	0.0	18.5	55.6	25.9	0.0	0.07	15

Source: Our elaboration of data from questionnaires.

think that seasonality is a hindrance to competitiveness, and 40% of them consider it highly important to reach foreigners.

As for the analysis of competitiveness applied to tourist firms, what comes out is that hotel facilities are not extremely relevant, whereas non-hotel accommodation facilities, due to their great number and high quality, constitute a more relevant factor for the destination. In fact, almost 70% of the interviewed think that the quantity and quality of non-hotel facilities is remarkable. The Maremma area has a strong concentration of non-hotel accommodation facilities, like agritourisms, and the like (Bertella 2011; Fondazione Univerde 2013). From the viewpoint of DM, these features need to be strengthened and improved in order to enhance the destination's competitiveness.

In what concerns the examination of the main crucial problems, the results show that the quality of public transport and accessibility are considered weak points, although the section that receives the poorest ratings is the one concerning policies and state intervention. Many of the interviewed (83%) think the transport infrastructure constitutes a bad contribution to local tourism, and 50% have a very low estimation of the local road system.

As for the local policies, 85% of respondents think that the creation of new employment opportunities is low; all the other related items are judged negatively, in a range of 50–70%. Among these, both the policies for the training of highly qualified tourist personnel, and public–private cooperation indicate points of weakness. Many interviewed entrepreneurs have in fact underlined the weaknesses of the destination from the point of view of human resources, attributed to the low training of tourist personnel compared to other Italian regions – a clear example comes from the great attractiveness of the Adriatic coast (even in off-season periods) and its highly qualified personnel (Figini and Vici 2012).

Another consideration regards the section concerning destination marketing and management, which reveals the tourism managers' lack of competencies (more than 60%) and the personnel's low profile of qualification (more than 50% of the interviewed).

The most crucial problems seem to concern the aspects associated to destination marketing and management. The efficacy of communication strategy and marketing is considered a weak point by almost a 50% of the sample, the choice of the right segment of clients by the 36%, and the lack of collaboration among local firms by the 65%. The awareness of the destination is not considered among the relevant factors.

The latter results seem to establish that the main problem for the destination's competitiveness is the lack of a common strategy, and that the way to solve these problems goes through a more incisive DM and the constitution of a DMO, which might tackle the most common problems and advocate a more effective and well-timed public intervention. Besides, the DMO could intervene in the problems on the side of demand, such as seasonality and difficulty to seize an international segment of tourists, by attempting to position Maremma among the most profitable destinations.

6 Conclusive remarks and managerial implications

Destination competitiveness has become a significant part of the tourism literature, and has stimulated a wide number of research studies. This chapter fits into this strand of research, offering a contribution with the working of a competitiveness model.

First of all, we decided to include this branch of studies in the area of DM and marketing to keep a destination-oriented approach to the competitiveness of tourist firms and accordingly recommend management strategies to tourist localities. This was because, as widely underlined in literature, tourist satisfaction does not depend on the single experience with a specific tourist firm, but on the overall experience made during the trip.

The suggested model of competitiveness draws from significant contributions in this literature topic, and a preliminary study of an Italian destination, Maremma, allows to investigate the destination and provide some methodological and managerial implications. This case study intends to offer an emblematic example of a destination which possesses many strategic tourist attractions (natural and environmental resources, tourist satisfaction, and so on), but lacks the managerial ability to convert them into a long-lasting competitive advantage.

The present analysis brings to light, at a first approximation, the weaknesses and strengths of the destination under exam, and suggests some possible corrective actions to improve its competitiveness. Since a benchmarking analysis of a competitor is not made, it is not possible to suggest some competitive benchmarking. At any rate, this model proves significant at this first level of investigation.

The most crucial problems emerge in the area of the firms' managerial competencies, in the human resources and their level of qualification, and in the low efficacy of DM strategies and actions. Most of these problems might be solved by a collaboration between public and private actors, i.e. economic operators and administration. In fact, one of the issues of strategic relevance is the establishment of public–private collaborations on the government side.

Given these premises, the analysed destination – but the same consideration may be extended to other contexts and destinations – requires the institution of a multi-subject organisation where each component plays a part in the strategic decision-making process. Literature underlines that it is essential to form a DMO constituted by a set of actors which partially forgets about their single-operator rationale and shapes a more composite production and supply, which will in turn be beneficial to each participant.

Below are the summarised main points on which a DMO should focus and operate, which have already been highlighted in literature as crucial problems for destination governance.

In the first place, as many authors have already underlined, it is essential to balance the demand and the supply sides of destinations. This is also true for the case of Maremma and a first step in this direction would be towards a better targeting, a more strategic choice of the destination's segments of clients. However, in the long run, a further step must be taken with a careful analysis and a possible reconfiguration of local supply, in line with the market segments on which the destination is intended to be positioned. This is a crucial point to deal with, since it requires a consistent and strong involvement of the DMO, and consequently must have the approval of the local actors concerned.

This consideration introduces the second important factor, the development of a plan for the destination, shared by the relevant actors. This is of fundamental importance for the implementation of medium-long-term strategies, which must necessarily involve a network of local actors sharing a common vision. The DMO will not take upon itself the task of forming a vision of the destination, but it can stimulate local actors to join in a shared vision.

In this context, the third factor, pertaining to local competencies, collaboration relations and competition at the local level, enters the scene. In fact, it is vital that the input of each firm works as a part of a complex system called destination. Therefore, competition should be perceived especially from the outside and among destinations, rather than internally, among local firms.

The fourth and last factor has to do with the constitution and development of the DMO, an event that in the analysed case study emerges as one of the main crucial issues for the destination's competitiveness. As underlined in literature, at the onset of the development process, it would be sufficient to introduce simple and straightforward organisations, initially maybe of a public–private nature, which can aggregate local demands and reach consensus around the destination's prospects.

Notes

1 The analysis developed on Scopus for the keywords 'destination management' and 'destination marketing' took place in January 2015.
2 A further indication is that three consecutive conferences of AIEST (1996, 1997 and 1998) have dealt with the issues of destination management and marketing.
3 A tourist destinations can be said to exist if at least one out of three of the following conditions are fulfilled (Della Lucia, Franch, Martini and Tamma, 2007): (a) the 'product' dimension, which must conform to and be recognizable as a tourism experience factually offered to/availed by the tourist, relating to a specific territorial area and involving a set of resources and actors; (b) the 'project' dimension, which refers to initiatives or interventions that bear a systemic significance, i.e. imply the enhancement of the area's resources, the activation of public and/or private actors, and the acknowledgement of a governing body; (c) the 'territory' dimension, which concerns the presence of a local tourism industry whose activities are more or less strongly interconnected through the relationships built in the local economic and social setting, together with the existence of tourism-related resources, already exploited or exploitable, as well as a good institutional and administrative setup.
4 AISRE Conference, Padua, 20 September 2014, and International Workshop on 'Tourist cluster, destinations and competitiveness', 27 March 2015, University of Florence. The participants to the conferences and workshops are gratefully acknowledged for offering interesting comments.
5 For details, see also Chapter 8 in this volume.
6 In details, the questionnaire was sent to all the hotel and non-hotel accommodation facilities (hotels and camping sites), travel agencies and tour operators, transport companies and restaurants located in the destination.

7   Enright and Newton have a redemption rate of 16.4%, while Pearce and Schänzel (2013) interviewed 61 entrepreneurs, Volgger and Pechlaner (2014) 41 members of the South Tyrolean Board of Tourism, and Bornhorst, Ritchie and Sheehan (2010) 81 actors.
8   Enright and Newton (2004) also built an importance performance analysis (IPA) matrix on the rank and the weighted average with a competing destination.

References

Angeloni, S. (2012) *Destination Italy. Un approccio manageriale per il sistema turistico italiano*, Milano: Pearson.

Ashworth, G. J. and Kavaratzis, M. (eds) (2010) *Towards Effective Place Brand Management: Branding European Cities and Regions*, Cheltenham, UK: Edward Elgar.

Becheri, E. (ed.) (2011) *XIX rapporto sul turismo italiano*, Firenze: Mercury.

Bertella, G. (2011) 'Knowledge in food tourism: The case of Lofoten and Maremma Toscana', *Current Issues in Tourism*, 14(4): 355–71.

Bimonte, S. and Faralla, V. (2012) 'Tourist types and happiness: A comparative study in Maremma, Italy', *Annals of Tourism Research*, 39(4): 1929–50.

Blain, C., Levy, S. L. and Ritchie, J. R. (2005) 'Destination branding: Insights and practices from destination management organizations', *Journal of Travel Research*, 43(4): 328–38.

Bornhorst, T., Ritchie, J.R.B. and Sheehan, L. (2010) 'Determinants of tourism success for DMOs and destinations: An empirical examination of stakeholders' perspectives', *Tourism Management*, 31(5): 572–89.

Buhalis, D. (2000) 'Marketing the competitive destination of the future', *Tourism Management*, 21(1): 97–116.

Buhalis, D. and Spada, A. (2000) 'Destination management systems: Criteria for success. An exploratory approach', *Information Technology and Tourism*, 3(1): 41–58.

Capone, F. (2006) 'Systemic approaches for the analysis of tourism destination: Towards the tourist local systems', in L. Lazzeretti and C.S. Petrillo (eds), *Tourism Local Systems and Networking*, Amsterdam: Elsevier, pp. 7–23.

Capone, F. and Boix, R. (2008) 'Sources of growth and competitiveness of local tourist production systems: An application to Italy (1991–2001)', *The Annals of Regional Science*, 42(1): 209–24.

Casarin, F. (ed.) (2006) *Il marketing dei prodotti turistici. Specificità e varietà*, Torino: Giappichelli.

Cox, N., Gyrd-Jones, R. and Gardiner, S. (2014) 'Internal brand management of destination brands: Exploring the roles of destination management organisations and operators', *Journal of Destination Marketing and Management*, 3(2): 85–95.

Cracolici, M. F. and Nijkamp, P. (2008) 'The attractiveness and competitiveness of tourist destinations: A study of Southern Italian regions', *Tourism Management*, 30(3): 336–44.

Crouch, G. I. and Ritchie, J.R.B. (1999) 'Tourism, competitiveness, and societal prosperity', *Journal of Business Research*, 44(3): 137–52.

Crouch, G. I. and Ritchie, J.R.B. (2000) 'The competitive destination: A sustainability perspective', *Tourism Management*, 21(1): 1–7.

Della Corte, V. (2000) *La gestione dei sistemi locali di offerta turistica*, Padova: Cedam.

Della Corte, V., Piras, A. and Zamparelli, G. (2010) 'Brand and image: The strategic factors in destination marketing', *International Journal of Leisure and Tourism Marketing*, 1(4): 358–77.

Della Lucia, M. (2010) 'Offerta della destinazione in chiave sistemico-distrettuale', in M. Franch (ed.), *Marketing delle destinazioni turistiche. Metodi, approcci e strumenti*, Milano: McGraw-Hill, pp. 103–50.

Della Lucia, M., Franch, M., Martini, U. and Tamma, M. (2007) 'Metodologia della ricerca', in Sciarelli, S., (2007), *Il management dei sistemi turistici locale. Strategie e strumenti per la governance*, Giappichelli, Torino, pp. 3–26.

Dredge, D., Jenkins, J. and Taplin, J. (2011) 'Destination planning and policy: Process and practice', in Y. Wang and A. Pizam (eds), *Destination Marketing and Management: Theories and Applications*, Cambridge, UK: CAB International, pp. 21–38.

Dwyer, L. and Kim, C. (2003) 'Destination competitiveness: Determinants and indicators', *Current Issues in Tourism*, 6(5): 369–414.

Dwyer, L., Forsyth, P. and Prasada, R. (2000) 'The price competitiveness of travel and tourism: A comparison of 19 destinations', *Tourism Management*, 21(1): 9–22.

Enright, M. J. and Newton, J. (2004) 'Tourism destination competitiveness: A quantitative approach', *Tourism Management*, 25(6): 777–88.

Enright, M. J. and Newton, J. (2005) 'Determinants of tourism destination competitiveness in Asia Pacific: Comprehensiveness and universality', *Journal of Travel Research*, 43(4): 339–50.

Enright, M. J., Frances, A. and Scott-Saavedra, E. (1996) *Venezuela: The Challenge of Competitiveness*, New York: St Martin's Press.

Figini, P. and Vici, L. (2012) 'Off-season tourists and the cultural offer of a mass-tourism destination: The case of Rimini', *Tourism Management*, 33(4): 825–39.

Flagestad, A. and Hope, C.A. (2001) 'Strategic success in winter sports destinations: A sustainable value creation perspective', *Tourism Management*, 22(5): 455–61.

Fondazione Univerde (2013) *III rapporto italiano, turismo sostenibile e ecoturismo*, Rome: IPR Marketing.

Franch, M. (2002) *Destination management: governare il turismo tra locale e globale*, Torino: Giappichelli.

Franch, M. (2010) *Marketing delle destinazioni turistiche. Metodi, approcci e strumenti*, Milano: McGraw-Hill.

Fuchs, M. and Weiermair, K. (2004) 'Destination benchmarking: An indicator-system's potential for exploring guest satisfaction', *Journal of Travel Research*, 42(3): 212–25.

Go, F. and Govers, R. (2000) 'Integrated quality management for tourist destinations: A European perspective on achieving competitiveness', *Tourism Management*, 21(1): 79–88.

Go, F. and Govers, R. (2012) *The International Place Branding Yearbook 2012: Managing Smart Growth and Sustainability*, Basingstoke: Palgrave Macmillan.

Godfrey, K. and Clarke, J. (2000) *The Tourism Development Handbook: A Practical Approach to Planning and Marketing*, London: Continuum.

Goffi, G. and Cucculelli, M. (2012) 'Attributes of destination competitiveness: The case of the Italian destinations of excellence', in *Proceedings of the International Conference on Tourism (ICOT 2012)*, Crete, 23–27 May 2012.

Goffi, G. and Cucculelli, M. (2015) 'Components of destination competitiveness. The case of small tourism destinations in Italy', *International Journal of Tourism Policy*, 5(4): 296–326.

Halkier, H., Kozak, M. and Svensson, B. (2015) *Innovation and Tourism Destination Development*, Abingdon: Routledge.

Heath, E. (2003) 'Towards a model to enhance destination competitiveness: A Southern African perspective', *Journal of Hospitality and Tourism Management*, 10(2): 124–41.

Howie, F. (2003) *Managing the Tourist Destination*, London: Continuum.

Huybers, T. and Bennett, J. (2003) 'Environmental management and the competitiveness of nature-based tourism destinations', *Environmental and Resource Economics*, 24(3): 213–33.

Kotler, P. Haider, D. H. and Rein, I. (1993) *Marketing Places*, New York: Free Press.

Kozak M. and Baloglu S. (2011) *Managing and Marketing Tourist Destinations. Strategie to Gain a competitive edge*, Routledge: Abingdon.

Laesser, C. and Beritelli, P. (2013) 'St Gallen consensus on destination management', *Journal of Destination Marketing and Management*, 2(1): 46–49.

Laws, E. (1995) *Tourist Destination Management*, Edinburgh: Napier University.

Laws, E., Richins, H., Agrusa, J. and Scott, N. (eds) (2011) *Tourist Destination Governance: Practice, Theory and Issues*, Cambridge, USA: CABI.

Lazzeretti, L. and Capone, F. (2006) 'Identification and analysis of tourist local systems: An application to Italy (1996–2001)', in L. Lazzeretti and C.S. Petrillo (eds), *Tourism Local Systems and Networking*, Amsterdam: Elsevier, pp. 25–40.

Lazzeretti, L. and Capone, F. (2008) 'Mapping and analysing local tourism systems in Italy', *Tourism Geographies*, 10(2): 216–34.

Lazzeretti, L. and Capone, F. (2015) 'Narrow or broad definition of cultural and creative industries: Some evidence from Tuscany, Italy', *International Journal of Cultural and Creative Industries*, 2(2): 4–18.

Lazzeretti, L. and Petrillo, C.S. (eds) (2006) *Tourism Local Systems and Networking*, Amsterdam: Elsevier

Leiper, N. (1979) 'The framework of tourism: Towards a definition of tourism, tourist, and the tourist industry', *Annals of Tourism Research*, 6(4): 390–407.

Leiper, N. (1995) *Tourism Management*, Collingwood, Victoria, Australia: RMIT Press.

Martini, U. (2005) *Management dei sistemi territoriali. Gestione e marketing delle destinazione turistiche*, Torino: Giappichelli.

Michael, E. J. (2003) 'Tourism micro-clusters', *Tourism Economics*, 9(2): 133–45.

Mihalič, T. (2000) 'Environmental management of a tourist destination: A factor of tourism competitiveness', *Tourism Management*, 21(1): 65–78.

Mill, R. C. and Morrison, A. M. (1992) *The Tourism System*, London: Prentice Hall.

Minguzzi A., (2006) 'Destination competitiveness and the role of destination management organization (DMO): An Italian experience' in Lazzeretti, L. and Petrillo, C.S. (eds) (2006) *Tourism Local Systems and Networking*, Amsterdam: Elsevier, pp. 197–208.

Morgan, N., Pritchard, A. and Pride, R. (2011) *Destination Brands*, Abingdon: Routledge.

Morrison, A. M. (2013) *Marketing and Managing Tourism Destinations*, Abingdon: Routledge.

Pearce, D. G. (1998) 'Tourist districts in Paris: Structure and functions', *Tourism Management*, 19(1): 49–65.

Pearce, D. G. (2013) 'Toward an integrative conceptual framework of destinations', *Journal of Travel Research*, 53(2): 141–53.

Pearce, D. G. and Schänzel, H. A. (2013) 'Destination management: The tourists' perspective', *Journal of Destination Marketing and Management*, 2(3): 137–45.

Pechlaner, H. and Weiermair, K. (eds) (2000) *Destination management: fondamenti di marketing e gestione delle destinazioni turistiche*, Milano: Touring Club Italiano.

Pencarelli, T. (2003) *Letture di economia e management delle organizzazioni turistiche*, Trieste: Edizioni Goliardiche.

Pike, S. (2007) *Destination Marketing Organisations*, London: Routledge.

Pike, S. and Page, S. (2014) 'Destination marketing organizations and destination market- ing: A narrative analysis of the literature', *Tourism Management*, 41(April): 202–27.

Presenza A., Sheehan L., Ritchie J.R.B (2005) 'Towards a model of the roles and activities of Destination Management Organizations', *Journal of Hospitality, Tourism & Leisure Science*, 3(1): 1–16.

Porter, M. E. (1990) *The Competitive Advantage of Nations*, London: Macmillan.

Rispoli, M. and Tamma, M. (1995) *Risposte strategiche alla complessità: le forme di offerta dei prodotti alberghieri*, Padova: Cedam.

Ritchie, J.R.B. and Crouch, G.I. (2003) *The Competitive Destination: A Sustainable Tour- ism Perspective*. CAB International, Wallingford, UK.

Sainaghi, R. (2006) 'From contents to processes: Versus a dynamic destination manage- ment model (DDMM)', *Tourism Management*, 27(5): 1053–63.

Sciarelli, S. (ed.) (2007) *Il management dei sistemi turistici locale*, Torino: Giappichelli.

Stepchenkova, S. and Mills, J. (2010) 'Destination image: A meta-analysis of 2000–2007 research', *Journal of Hospitality Marketing and Management*, 19(6): 575–609.

Svensson, B., Nordin, S. and Flagestad A., (2006) 'Destination Governance and Contem- porary Development Models', Lazzeretti, L. and Petrillo, C.S. (eds) (2006) *Tourism Local Systems and Networking*, Amsterdam: Elsevier, pp. 83–95.

Tamma, M. (2000) 'Aspetti strategici del destination management', in H. Pechlaner and K. Weiermair (eds), *Destination Management: fondamenti di marketing e gestione delle destinazioni turistiche*, Milano: Touring Club Italiano, pp. 31–55.

Trunfio, M. (2008) *Governance turistica e sistemi turistici locali. Modelli teorici ed evi- denze empiriche in Italia*, Torino: Giappichelli.

Viken, A. and Granas, B. (2014) *Tourism Destination Development: Turns and Tactics*, Burlington, VT: Ashgate.

Volgger, M. and Pechlaner, H. (2014) 'Requirements for destination management organi- zations in destination governance: Understanding DMO success', *Tourism Manage- ment*, 41(April), 64–75.

Wahab, S., Crampon, L. J. and Rothfield, L. M. (1976) *Tourism Marketing*, London: Tour- ism International Press.

WTO – World Tourism Organization (2007) *A Practical Guide to Tourism Destination Management*, Madrid: World Tourism Organization.

3 The impact of related variety on tourist destinations

An analysis of tourist firms clustering

Luciana Lazzeretti, Francesco Capone and Niccolò Innocenti

1 Introduction

The purpose of this chapter is to investigate the factors underlying the clustering of tourist firms in tourist destinations. The increasing attention paid to clusters (Porter 1998a; 1998b) in the international literature on tourism has always focused on the increased competitiveness of tourist destinations (Nordin 2003; Novelli, Schmitz and Spencer 2006; Lazzeretti and Petrillo 2006) and the improved performance of firms in clusters (Enz, Canina and Liu 2008; Shaw and Williams 2009).

Several recent studies have attempted to analyse the growth of tourist destinations (Lazzeretti and Capone 2009; Yang and Wong 2012; 2013; Yang and Fik 2014; and others). All these works have suggested that the presence of clusters of tourist firms in destinations is one of the major reasons for their growth. These studies have analysed the development of destinations in relation to the clustering of firms. However, to date, the reasons why firms cluster in destinations and the factors involved in clustering have not been investigated.

Although there is extensive literature on the reasons for clustering in the manufacturing sector (Baptista 1998; Steinle and Schiele 2002; Tallman *et al.* 2004), few studies have examined the factors that underlie clustering in service sectors, such as the creative and cultural industries (Lorenzen and Frederiksen 2008; Lazzeretti, Boix and Capone 2012; Branzanti 2014). This chapter is innovative in that it extends theories that support clustering as a determinant of local competitiveness and improved business performance to the tourism industry.

The chapter applies an analysis model to the factors that underlie the clustering of tourist firms in an Italian context. It does this by analysing the evolution of tourist destinations over a decade from 2001–11.

In this context, it should be noted that there is a growing emphasis in tourism studies on the related-variety approach (Brouder and Eriksson 2013; Sanz-Ibáñez and Clavé 2014). A related-variety industry is defined in terms of sectors that are related because of shared or complementary competences in a cognitive-based definition. This approach is particularly useful for the analysis of tourist destinations as they are based on activities with high cognitive proximity. Also recently Porter (Delgado, Porter and Stern 2015) reminds us that the cluster strength reflects specialization in an array of related industries, thus, it is conceptually similar to the notion of 'related variety', introduced by Frenken, Van Oort and Verburg (2007).

This chapter therefore seeks to develop an integrated approach based on different fields of study: first, classical studies on tourist destinations and tourist clusters; second, the application of spatial statistics (Anselin 1988; 1992); and, finally, an evaluation of the relevance of activities with high cognitive proximity through the related-variety approach (Frenken *et al.* 2007).

We first consider destinations as closed units. We then go beyond their boundaries to analyse border effects and spillovers between neighbouring destinations, considering the idea of destination networks (Lue, Crompton and Fesenmaier 1993; Stewart and Vogt 1997). With regard to spatial spillovers, the aim is not to consider tourist destinations as isolated places, but to deepen relations and intra-regional ties (Acs *et al.* 2009). Here, the main idea is that geographical proximity facilitates the transmission of ideas and the dissemination of knowledge through imitation and the exchange of knowledge between firms and employees.

Ideas are developed and disseminated among neighbouring firms through knowledge spillovers (Acs *et al.* 2009). The concept of spatial spillovers presupposes diffusion of knowledge at the local level.

The results show that related variety is an important factor in the clustering of tourist firms. It emphasises how the existence of a chain of related activities is essential for the formation of clusters and competitiveness in tourist destinations. The tourist also benefits from the presence of a coordinated system of tourist firms. In addition, this chapter shows that natural resources are another factor (e.g. being a UNESCO world heritage site). In the same way, environmental resources (parks, beaches and skiing resorts) add to the attractiveness of tourist destinations.

The chapter is organised as described below. After this introduction, we explore the theoretical background of clustering and growth in tourist destinations, with a particular emphasis on the related-variety approach. Section 3 presents the research design and methodological approach, while section 4 identifies tourist clusters in Italy. Section 5 presents the results of the classical and spatial analysis models we applied to the factors that underlie clustering. The chapter closes with some concluding remarks.

2 Clustering, growth and related variety in tourist destinations

2.1 Tourist clusters and the growth in tourist destinations

Several recent studies have dealt with tourist destinations as tourist clusters (Michael 2003; Nordin 2003; Novelli, Schmitz and Spencer 2006; Shaw and William 2009). An important element of this research includes quantitative analysis and applied research that focuses on the factors that promote the growth of destinations.

A study by Beatty and Fothergill (2004) gives an in-depth analysis of English seaside towns from 1971–2001. Townsend (1992) analyses tourism-related employment in the UK from 1981–89 in areas that range from coastal resorts to urban tourist destinations including museums and recreational activities. Bull and Church (1994) carried out a similar analysis for employment in the hotel and catering industry in the UK, with particular attention to its evolution during the 1980s.

More recently, Capone and Boix (2008) analysed the growth of the taxonomy of tourist destinations in Italy over a decade. They looked at municipalities and networks of municipalities. Their results confirm that higher levels of development are based on localisation economies in addition to the specialisation of neighbouring tourist destinations. Lazzeretti and Capone (2009) have analysed the factors affecting the long-term occupational dynamics of Italian tourist destinations, taking into consideration the existence of spatial spillovers and applying the spatial model to employment dynamics from 1991–2001.

Yang and Fik (2014) examine two types of spatial effect in tourism growth: spatial spillover and spatial heterogeneity. A spatial growth regression framework is used to model the development of tourism and identify the economic and spatial factors that explain the variability in tourism growth in China from 2002–10. The analysis identifies several important factors, which include local economic development, localisation economies, tourism resources, hotel infrastructure and spatial spillover effects. In the same way, Yang and Wong (2012) analyse spatial spillovers in employment growth in China. Yang and Wong (2013) analyse the spatial distribution of tourist flows to China's cities with spatial models.

Most of the studies referred to above have emphasised that the growth of tourist destinations is closely related to the clustering of tourist firms. However none of these studies have looked in depth at the reasons behind the clustering of tourist firms in specific destinations.

As stated earlier, few studies have focused on clustering in the cultural and creative industries (CCIs). To meet the need for such research, this chapter measures factors that lead to the development of clusters in tourist destinations in Italy using spatial econometric models (Anselin 1988; 1992) and the related-variety approach (Frenken, Van Oort and Verburg 2007).

2.2 *Related variety and tourism*

The dynamics of clustering help us understand how particular areas with a concentration of specific tourism activities achieve higher growth rates than areas that do not have this concentration of activity. Similarly, areas that are more vulnerable to external sector-specific shocks are characterised by a low level of unrelated variety (Frenken, Van Oort and Verburg 2007).

This recalls an evolving paradigm related to the concept of related variety (Frenken and Boschma 2003; Frenken, Van Oort and Verburg 2007). A related-variety industry is defined in terms of industrial sectors that are related because of shared or complementary competences in a cognitive-based definition. In other words, a certain degree of cognitive proximity gives rise to effective communication and interactive learning among different industries. This contributes to an increased capacity to absorb innovations from neighbouring sectors though cross fertilisation. In other words, related variety implies a relationship between industrial sectors and economic activities in terms of effective and potential competences, innovation and transfers of knowledge. In this context, related variety should promote creativity and innovation in local systems due to transversality and the spillover of innovation processes to other sectors.

The concept of related variety has recently been applied to the creative industries (Lazzeretti, Innocenti and Capone 2015) with particular emphasis on the process of cross fertilisation and cognitive relationships between different industries.

However, to date, no studies have applied this concept to the clustering and development of tourist destinations, although interest is increasing (Debbage and Ioannides 2004). Brouder and Eriksson (2013) identify synergies between tourism studies and evolutionary economic geography (EEG). They argue that this approach is appropriate to the concept of tourism development as the tourism sector is widely regarded as a conglomeration of related industries. As tourism is a composite product offer, the more businesses that offer various products and services, the greater the related variety present in a destination (Brouder and Eriksson 2013). Sanz-Ibáñez and Clavé (2014) attempt to relate clustering theories to the recent development of EEG and relational economic geography, but only from a theoretical perspective. This approach is particularly useful for the analysis of tourism as tourist clusters are usually based on activities with high cognitive proximity.

The next section aims to define what is meant by tourism. It does so by looking at a series of related activities, using a definition provided by the European Commission as a starting point. This is followed by the identification of tourist clusters in Italy using the methodology of location quotients (LQ).

3 Definition of the tourism industry and identification of tourist destinations

Before identifying clusters of tourist firms in particular destinations, this section attempts to define the tourism industry. In general, the tourism industry is regarded as comprising of accommodation, recreation, touring and transportation, etc.

The European Commission helps clarify this definition (EC 2003). It presents a model of competitiveness for the European sector of tourist enterprises that includes transport, accommodation, restaurants and other food facilities, and recreational activities. The model, shown in Figure 3.1, illustrates a process for 'supplying tourist services'. In the vertical column, the model illustrates an 'integrated *filière*' of tourism consisting of transportation (recreational) attractions, accommodations and restaurants (Capone and Boix 2008). The intermediaries related to the tourism *filière* or industry (travel agents, tour guides and tour operators) are represented in the central square, whereas the horizontal row shows horizontally integrated activities comprising producers, distributors and intermediaries whose occupation is not strictly associated with tourism.

This chapter offers an in-depth analysis of the tourism industry based on the European Commission's model (Figure 3.1). The model is integrated with a

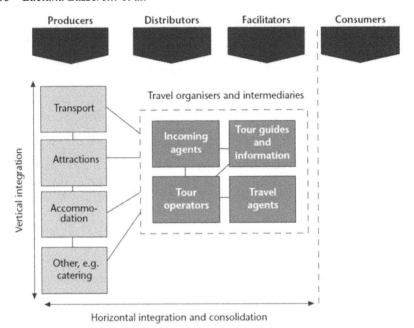

Figure 3.1 A tourism sector model

Source: EC (2003).

vertical value chain (accommodation, transport, recreation and catering) and categories of intermediaries, such as travel agents and tour operators.

We decided to include a wide set of industries in our definition of tourism as there is a trend in the literature to connect tourism with creativity, the experience economy and the cultural and creative industries (Richards 2011; Lazzeretti and Capone 2015). This approach includes not only tourism, but all creative activities centred on the experience of consumers and visitors. The activities of the proposed value chain are presented in Table 3.1 according to the three-digit nomenclature of economic activities (NACE) definitions (Rev. 2).

This definition of the tourism *filière* (Table 3.1) starts with activities that exclusively involve tourists, such as accommodation, travel agents and tour operators. It also includes activities that are relevant to both residents and tourists, such as restaurants and cafés, and cultural activities, such as the creative arts and entertainment, recently referred to as creative tourism and the creative industries (Richards 2011). Finally, factors that add to the attractiveness of a destination are considered, such as libraries and museums, together with activities related to the experience economy, such as sports and recreational activities.

To identify specific tourist destinations, we selected those places that have high concentrations of tourist firms. To identify clusters, we followed an approach that has been recognised at an international level and has been applied in various

European countries (De Propris 2005) to map tourism (Capone and Boix 2008) and creative industry clusters (De Propris *et al.* 2009; Boix *et al.* 2014).

Data on tourist firms were taken from the 2011 Census of Industry and Services (ISTAT 2011). Tourist clusters were expected to present a stronger specialisation in the activities presented in Table 3.1. We used the local labour market (LLM) as a geographical unit of analysis (Sforzi 1997), as this is a particularly appropriate way to study the clustering of firms. LLM units not only embody an agglomeration of firms but also a labour market. In order to identify them, we applied a concentration index for each NACE macro-definition:

$$LQ_{is} = \frac{E_{is} \, / \, E_s}{E_i \, / \, E}$$

where E_{is} is the number of tourist firms in the LLMs specialised in the sector i, E_s is the number of firms in the LLMs, E_i is the number of tourist firms specialised in the industry i and E is the total number of firms in Italy. An LQ score above 1 indicates that the destination has a tourism concentration above the national average. The index can be calculated for firms or employees. We decided to calculate the index using employees in order to include a measure of firm size. Accordingly, the index equates better destinations with larger firms.

Table 3.1 Tourism *filière* per NACE economic activities

Accommodation	*Libraries, archives, museums and*
55.1 Hotels and similar accommodation	*cultural activities*
55.2 Holiday and other short-stay	91.01 Library and archives activities
accommodation	91.02 Museums activities
55.3 Camping grounds, recreational	91.03 Operation of historical sites and
vehicle parks and trailer parks	buildings and similar visitor
55.9 Other accommodation	attractions
	91.04 Botanical and zoological gardens
	and nature reserves activities
Restaurant and food/beverage service	*Sports activities and amusement*
activities	*and recreation activities*
56.1 Restaurants and mobile food	93.1 Sports activities
service activities	93.2 Amusement and recreation
56.2 Event catering and other food	activities
service activities	
56.3 Beverage serving activities	
Creative, arts and entertainment activities	*Travel agencies and tour operators*
90.01 Performing arts	79.1 Travel agency and tour operator
90.02 Support activities to performing arts	activities
90.03 Artistic creation	79.9 Other reservation service and
90.04 Operation of arts facilities	related activities

Source: Our elaboration from EC (2003).

3.1 Mapping tourist destinations in Italy

There are 214 tourist destinations in Italy with an LQ above 1. Data are represented in four classes: no concentration, low, medium and high concentration (see Figure 3.2).

The highest values are concentrated in the North (Trentino and Alto Adige) and Centre (Liguria, Toscana and Lazio). The figure also shows art cities, such as Florence, Rome and Venice, places specialised in sun, sand and sea, skiing destinations (the Alps, in particular Trentino-Alto Adige), and lake localities (such as around Lake Garda). In addition, localities from the South are well represented by Capri, Amalfi and island tourist destinations.

Employment in the identified tourist destinations accounts for around 7.6 million employees, of which 1.4 million are in the selected tourism activities (18.6% of total employment). Average firm size in the tourist destinations is around eight employees. The industrial structure is based mainly on small and medium-sized enterprises (SMEs) with 90% of the firms having less than 20 employees.

Since the clustering of tourism activities has already been linked to the growth of tourist destinations in the literature, we investigated the factors underlying the clustering of tourist firms and then applied different weights to these factors.

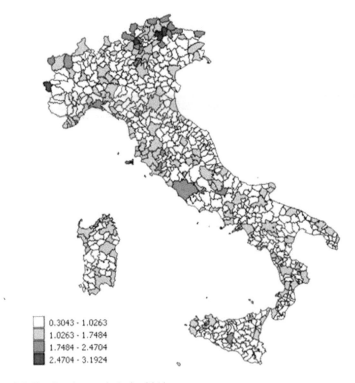

□ 0.3043 - 1.0263
▨ 1.0263 - 1.7484
▦ 1.7484 - 2.4704
■ 2.4704 - 3.1924

Figure 3.2 Tourist clusters in Italy, 2011

Source: Our elaboration.

4 Analysing the reasons for the clustering of tourist firms in tourist destinations

This section is divided as described below. First, we present the spatial analysis model. We then look at the variables used in the model. We then present the results using ordinary least square regression (OLS) and with the application of spatial models.

4.1 Spatial models

Spatial effects can also be measured in a regression model (Anselin 1988; 1992). Spatial models are typically required where the model variables are spatially related to each other, or where there is a pattern of spatial dependence in the errors. In both cases, the matrix W of weights or contacts should be used to ensure that the influence of spatial observations is included. For example, where the variable under study is spatially correlated, the linear regression model, referred to as a spatial lag model, is as follows:

$$Y = \rho W_1 y + X\beta_1 + u$$
$$u \sim N(0, \sigma^2 I)$$

where y is a vector ($N \times 1$), Wy is the spatial lag of the variable y, X is a matrix of k exogenous variable, u is the error, N is the number of observations and ρ is the parameter that indicates the disturbance. It should also be noted that if the spatial lag is omitted, the spatial dependence would move to the error, and would seem spatially correlated.

The second model is called the spatial error model (or spatial measurement error model), which is presented in the following form:

$$Y = X\beta_1 + u$$
$$u = \lambda Wu + \varepsilon$$
$$\varepsilon \sim N(0, \sigma^2 I)$$

In this model, referred to as a model of the first order, the matrix of contacts is inserted only in the error. The meaning of the terms is similar to the previous model: y is a vector ($N \times 1$), Wu is the spatial lag of the error, X is a matrix of k the exogenous variable, N is the number of observations, and, finally, λ is the parameter that indicates the disturbance of the error.

The third spatial model captures patterns of spatial dependence in the error and in the explanatory variables. The interpretation of symbols is similar to the previous example except that there are two groups of variables and two matrices that indicate the respective dependencies. Further to previous models, the matrix R ($N \times K'$) is a vector of exogenous variables that are spatially delayed thanks to the matrix W_2.

$$Y = \rho W_1 Y + X\beta_1 + W_2 R\beta_2 + u$$
$$u = \lambda W_3 u + \varepsilon$$
$$\varepsilon \sim N(0, \sigma^2 I)$$

We note that a mistake in the specification of the contact matrix is highly significant both for error checking the model and for the overall estimation. The recommended approach is to first estimate a classical linear function using OLS or robust OLS. Next, diagnostics should be carried out for the spatial effects. The next task is to verify which of the spatial models described above gives a better estimate of the phenomenon through models of maximum likelihood (ML).

The final stage is to construct a matrix of spatial contacts (W), assuming that the adjacent LLMs share a degree of contact, information flows, goods and services.

4.2 Variables

To analyse the factors that underlie the clustering of firms, we refer to the model of Porter's (1998a) Diamond, the diamond of localisation advantages, originally developed for the competitive advantages of nations (Porter 1990) and then extended to the cluster. To investigate the forces that most influence the process of clustering and the major factors behind competitive advantage for locations, Porter (1998a) proposes four conditions: factor conditions, rivalry and structure of the local industry, demand conditions, and related and supporting industry. This model has been applied to the tourism industry several times and to the competitiveness of destinations (Nordin 2003; Jackson and Murphy 2006; and others).

The factor conditions identify the local resources of the cluster, such as raw materials, human capital and infrastructure. In this study, we analyse the resources of tourist destinations, such as the presence of artistic, cultural and environmental heritage through a number of variables. To make clear any positive connections, the rivalry and structure of the local industry emphasises structure and competition in the destination and is analysed by the level of concentration of firms (LQ), the industrial structure of the various sectors (industry, services, etc.), and the level of local related variety. Finally, to investigate any connections outside the main industry,[1] related and supporting industries are analysed indirectly through the construction of an enlarged tourism *filière* (see Table 3.1) and through the indices of variety and unrelated variety. The specific variables of the model are described below.

All explanatory variables are expressed and calculated for 2001 (ISTAT 2001), in order to analyse the causal relationship between those variables and the concentration of tourism activities in the area until 2011. The dependent variable is the LQ of tourism activities for the year 2011, and was drawn up using data from the of the 2011 Census (ISTAT 2011). All the variables are described in Table 3.2.

With regard to variety, we used the entropy measures following the rules adopted in Frenken, Van Oort and Verburg (2007), and Hartog, Boschma and Sotarauta (2012). Variety is measured as the sum of the entropy at the chosen digit level and designates the variety in the industrial composition of the area. The value of this variable will be higher in areas characterised by a highly diversified industrial composition (Hartog, Boschma and Sotarauta 2012).

This measure was then broken down into two different indicators. The first, unrelated variety, was measured as the total amount of entropy at the two-digit

Table 3.2 Variables of the model

Clustering of tourist firms (LQ) 2011	$LQ_{is} = \dfrac{E_{is} / E_s}{E_i / E}$	Agriculture	$E^{2001}_{i;AGR} / E^{2001}$
Population/square metres	Population$_i^{2001}$/square metres$_i$	Manufacturing	$E^{2001}_{i;MAN} / E^{2001}$
Variety	$\displaystyle\sum_{g=1}^{G} Pi \, log_2 \left(\dfrac{1}{Pi}\right)$	Construction	$E^{2001}_{i;CON} / E^{2001}$
Related variety[a]	$\displaystyle\sum_{g=1}^{G} Pg \, Hg$	Commerce	$E^{2001}_{i;COMM} / E^{2001}$
Unrelated variety[b]1	$\displaystyle\sum_{g=1}^{G} Pg \, log_2 \left(\dfrac{1}{Pg}\right)$	Services	$E^{2001}_{i;SERV} / E^{2001}$
LQ CCIs	$LQ_{is} = \dfrac{E_{is} / E_s}{E_i / E}$	Cultural, artistic and environmental heritage (CAEH) (UNESCO, blue flags, ski destinations, parks, etc.)	1–0

Source: Our elaboration.

Notes: E = employment; (a) where *Hg* measures the degree of variety within the two-digit class of every Italian LLM: $H_g = \displaystyle\sum_{i \in S_g} \dfrac{P_i}{P_g} \, log_2 \left(\dfrac{1}{P_i / P_g}\right)$ (b) where *Pg* is the two-digit shares, calculated summing the three-digit shares P_i already used for the variety index: $P_g = \displaystyle\sum_{i \in S_g} P_i$.

[1]Where *Pg* is the two-digit shares, calculate summing the three-digit shares *Pi* already used for the variety index:. $P_g = \displaystyle\sum_{i \in S_g} P_i$

level, assuming that the sectors that do not share the same two digits are unrelated to each other. The higher this value, the more the area will be composed of dissimilar industrial sectors. High levels of this variable are associated with low knowledge spillovers (Frenken, Van Oort and Verburg 2007).

Related variety, the second indicator, is the weighted sum of the entropy within each two-digit sector.

In order to measure the local structure of the destinations, we also tested the existence of input–output effects outside the *filière*, using the initial share of the main sectors on total employment (agriculture, manufacturing, construction and services).

As tourism studies have paid increasing attention to the CCIs (Richards 2011; Lazzeretti and Capone 2015), we decided to include the clustering of CCIs, calculated as traditional LQ, in order to measure cultural tourism and the experience and event economy.

The creative industries were analysed for the first time in the *Creative Industries Mapping Document* (DCMS 2001). These industries need individual creativity to grow and develop. The UK's Department for Culture, Media and Sport (DCMS) taxonomy has arguably stood the test of time and has become a *de facto* world standard notwithstanding some criticism (Bakhshi, Freeman and Higgs 2013). CCIs are classed according to the DCMS (2001) categories of Architecture, Publishing, Movie and video, Software, Film and TV, Design activities, Photography, and Sound recording and music.

In addition to the variables discussed above, dummy variables for Cultural, Artistic and Environmental heritage (CAEH) were also included as these seem to be relevant for tourist destinations and the clustering of firms. These variables were built according to the integration of multiple data sources. In the first instance, we tried to assess the presence of different levels of artistic, cultural and environmental heritage in the territory, knowing that our approach was primarily a first attempt. We used the list of UNESCO world heritage sites as a proxy for artistic and cultural heritage. For natural heritage, we used three integrated indicators: (1) the presence in the territory of national parks (parks), (2) blue flags to guarantee the quality of beaches, and (3) the presence of ski destinations as registered by the Touring Club of Italy.

4.3. Results

We used multiple linear regression with robust standard errors. Table 3.3 presents the results. We started by analysing the non-spatial models. In the first model, the variable of interest is variety. In this case, we added only one control variable, population density, used as a control for urbanisation. In the second model, related and unrelated variety were included as variables of interest, whereas the control variable remained unchanged. The purpose of the second model was to identify whether there was a relationship between the concentration of tourism activities in the area and the two different types of industrial variety in the tourism *filière*. The third and fourth model were both full models, which linked the related and unrelated variety of the tourism industry in the area with the concentration and clustering of tourism activities. In these cases, we added numerous control variables. The difference between them relates to the dummy variables in specific tourist attractions. The presentation of the results follows the methodology of stepwise regression.

The first model shows that variety is significant and positively correlated with the concentration of tourism activities. The population density is significant, but negatively related to the tourism LQ of the area. This indicates that there is a lower concentration of tourism activities in highly urbanised areas. As expected, therefore, a high level of variety in an area promotes concentration and clustering of tourism activities.

Table 3.3 Robust OLS estimations

Dependent variable: Location quotient 2011

	Model 1	Model 2	Model 3	Model 4	5. Spatial lag	6. Spatial error
Constant	2.3814***	2.6247***	2.4375***	2.1981***	0.9704***	2.1492***
	(0.2184)	(0.2354)	(0.2931)	(0.2906)	(0.2547)	(0.2703)
Variety	0.2433**					
	(0.0884)					
Unrelated variety		-0.7299**	-0.5863*	-0.6620**	-0.4399	-0.5130
		(0.2548)	(0.2359)	(0.2285)	(0.2648)	(0.2856)
Related variety		0.4617***	0.3811***	0.3235***	0.2357*	0.1892*
		(0.0896)	(0.0895)	(0.0866)	(0.1034)	(0.1092)
Ln Density	-0.3358***	-0.2915***	-0.2382***	-0.1711***	-0.1453***	-0.1529***
	(0.0459)	(0.0464)	(0.0505)	(0.0460)	(0.0362)	(0.039)
Lq CCIs			-0.1334	-0.0145	0.1334	0.2185
			(0.1966)	(0.1795)	(0.1409)	(0.1489)
Agr			-1.2117***	-1.3002***	-1.8458***	-2.2448***
			(0.2988)	(0.3568)	(0.4901)	(0.5154)
Manu			-0.0058*	-0.0056	-0.0062	-0.0070
			(0.0029)	(0.0030)	(0.0048)	(0.0049)
Const			-0.0219	-0.0561*	-0.0700*	-0.0663*
			(0.0229)	(0.0265)	(0.0345)	(0.0346)
Serv			0.0069**	0.0100***	0.0114**	0.0117**
			(0.0022)	(0.0026)	(0.0035)	(0.0036)
CAEH			0.3640***			
			(0.0777)			
Sky				1.5080***	1.2231***	1.1766***
				(0.2437)	(0.1229)	(0.1348)

(Continued)

Table 3.3 Continued

Dependent variable: Location quotient 2011

	Model 1	Model 2	Model 3	Model 4	5. Spatial lag	6. Spatial error
Parks				-0.0759	-0.0061	0.0521
				(0.0791)	(0.0749)	(0.0791)
Blueflags				0.3401***	0.3572***	0.3588***
				(0.0830)	(0.1017)	(0.1011)
Unesco				0.3172***	0.3454**	0.3322*
				(0.0889)	(0.1303)	(0.1301)
R2	0.12808	0.1425	0.1912	0.3069	0.3655	0.3631
Akaike	1652.38	1642.88		1514.89	1465.34	1468.11
Schwarz	1665.97	1661		1573.79	1528.77	1527.01
CN	15.16	18.41		25.65		
Jarque-Bera	2749.04***	2723.75***		3334.98***		
Koenker-Bassett	17.91***	23.45***		42.50***		
Log likelihood	-823.191	-817.44		-744.446	-718.66	-721.05
Breusch-Pagan					228.17***	234.38***
LM error	258.22***	209.77***		79.68***		
LM lag	180.31***	172.47**		111.96***		
W_LQ_2011					0.7573***	
					(0.0678)	
Lambda (λ)						0.8090***
						(0.0641)
OBS	686	686	686	686	686	686

Notes: * p < 0.05; ** p < 0.01; *** p < 0.001; standard errors in parentheses.

Source: Our elaboration.

The second model, which tests for related and unrelated variety, shows significance in both variables of interest. Related variety is able to foster concentration of tourism activities, whereas the relationship between unrelated variety and LQ is negative, indicating that a large number of tourism activities that are not technologically connected can become an obstacle to the clustering of tourist firms in the area.

In the third model, additional control variables were included. Here, the variables of interest maintain the significance and the same sign as in the second model. Unrelated variety is significant and negative, whereas related variety is significant and positively correlated with the clustering of tourism activities. The variable measuring the clustering of creative businesses is not significant. This means that we cannot determine a connection between the concentration of firms in the tourism sector and the clustering of creative industries in the same area.

Other variables that are connected to the industrial structure of the area show a negative relationship between agriculture and tourist clustering. The same result occurs with the manufacturing sector, whereas there is no significance with respect to the construction industry. Instead, the variable linked to the service variable is positively significant, which indicates that there is a tendency towards a greater concentration in the tourism sector in areas with a high degree of services specialisation. The last control variable is a dummy called CAEH (cultural, artistic and environmental heritage), which indicates the presence of attractions in the area (UNESCO heritage sites, ski resorts, blue flag beaches or natural parks). The results indicate that tourism activities tend to cluster more in these areas.

In the fourth and last model, we divided the CAEH variable, splitting the tourist sites by type and inserting a dummy for each category. In this model, the R2 level was significantly higher than in the previous models.

In this case, the variables of interest are significant and retain the same signs observed in the two previous models and with population density. The control variables related to the local structure all retain the same sign as in the previous models. However, in this case, the manufacturing variable is not significant, whereas the construction field is significant with a negative sign. As in the previous case, a positive relationship is found exclusively in the case of a local service-oriented structure.

In this model, the control variable indicating the presence in the area of tourist attractions has been broken down by type, showing positive significance for ski resorts, for locations where there is a UNESCO heritage site and for blue flag beaches. However, we found no significance with regard to the presence of a national park in the area.

We now look at the results of the spatial models. First, we present the Moran's I global test for the presence of clustering effects that spread between neighbouring local systems. Figure 3.3 shows a value of 0.11 for the I of Moran and highlights the existence of spatial effects between adjacent local systems. This highlights how the clustering of tourist firms has a pattern of spatial diffusion through spillover processes.

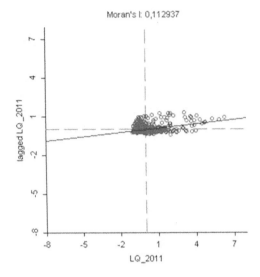

Figure 3.3 Scatterplot of Moran's I on LQ

Source: Our elaboration.

Tourist clusters (with high concentrations of tourist firms) tend to be located adjacent to other tourist clusters. This is explained by tourist behaviour. Tourists realise that trips in one area can lead to neighbouring destinations from a local starting point. The tourist is not locked into one destination, even if the one destination is particularly large.[1]

A process of spatial spillovers is assumed. In the development phase, when a destination is growing, this leads to a concentration of tourism activities in the area. Gradually this leads to the development and concentration of tourism activities in neighbouring destinations.[3] We investigate this aspect further in spatial models.

The fifth model stresses the spatial lag, which analyses the lag of clustering ($W \times$ LQ) even in neighbouring systems. The sixth model uses the spatial error in assessing whether the error (λ) has a spatial correlation with neighbouring systems (Cliff and Ord 1981).

The spatial lag and spatial error models were estimated using ML. The spatial parameters were statistically significant (0.75, lag and 0.80, error). Akaike and Schwarz tests confirmed that the spatial lag model was more appropriate than either the spatial error or the non-spatial model.

The fifth model shows that the lag of the clustering process parameter was positive. Neighbouring systems were affected by a kind of joint clustering. In other words, a phenomenon of widespread clustering at the local level goes beyond local boundaries and spreads to many destinations that can be quite far apart. The signs of the other parameters were in line with previous models. The index of related variety was significant and positive, whereas unrelated variety was negative, but not significant.

The sixth model showed a positive parameter for spatial error, emphasising that the error was related to neighbouring local systems. Spatially correlated variables should be included in future models to arrive at a better understanding of the clustering phenomenon. However, in our tests, the spatial lag model achieved the most accurate results.

5 Conclusions

This chapter aimed to investigate the factors underlying tourist clusters. We looked at the reasons for the formation of clusters in tourist destinations. This is particularly relevant given that the presence of tourist clusters in destinations is considered a key element for their competitiveness and growth.

We developed a model to analyse the reasons for the clustering of tourist firms in Italy by analysing the evolution of tourist destinations over a decade from 2001–11. We applied spatial analysis models and the related-variety approach to the clustering phenomenon.

Our research is mainly quantitative and offers a robust measurement of the factors underlying the clustering of firms in tourist destinations. The chapter adds to the international debate about the drivers for the competitiveness of destinations, tourist cities and regions.

The estimated models have provided results with high levels of statistical significance. The results show that related variety is an important determinant of the clustering of tourist firms. This emphasises that the existence of a *filière* of related activities is essential for the development of tourist destinations because the tourist benefits from the presence of a coordinated system of tourist enterprises in a particular destination.

The chapter also shows that another important factor is constituted by the elements connected to natural resources such as UNESCO sites and to environmental resources, such as the presence of blue flag beaches, natural parks or ski resorts.

We then used spatial models to identify clustering processes that spread into neighbouring areas. This enabled us to examine destination networks and spillover effects. The spatial tests were significant, suggesting the diffusion of processes to neighbouring destinations. The positive results of spatial correlation and a positive coefficient of the error show that the competitiveness of a destination is related to the competitiveness of other neighbouring destinations.

The relevance of the identified spatial correlation indicates that it is necessary to focus on destination networks and to enlarge the participation of local actors. This work, which requires further study and database refinements, is a solid basis from which to estimate the advantages of Italian tourist destinations. It highlights governance suggestions for destinations.

The application of related variety gave the most interesting results. Variety results provide an important factor for the clustering of tourist firms. However, this effect is even more evident with regard to related variety, which is robustly significant and one of the main drivers (along with the artistic and cultural resources). This aspect is confirmed by the fact that destinations specialised in the tertiary sector show higher levels of clustering.

In conclusion, the clustering of firms is not the only factor underlying the competitiveness of destinations and firms, although relevant in this sector. The results need to be evaluated according to the period of analysis, a period that takes into account development from 2001–11 and that includes a serious economic and financial crisis for all tourist firms in Italy.

Despite the limitations of this study, this chapter is part of an interesting line of research into the competitiveness of tourist destinations and the processes which underlie the clustering of firms in tourist destinations. The chapter adds a new perspective: the use of the related-variety approach and spatial models allow the existence of spillovers between neighbouring destinations to be considered.

Notes

1   In this study we do not analyse the factor of the demand condition as a variable linked to the demand (attendance, nights spent, etc.). It would have shown a high correlation between the resources and the clustering of firms.
2   As before, we used the local labour market as a territorial unit.
3   Consider, for example, rental and land purchase costs. If these prices increase significantly in a destination, there is a natural process, which involves looking for land and properties with lower prices in neighbouring destinations. See Capone and Boix (2008) to examine the role of spillovers in the growth of tourist destinations.

References

Acs, Z. J., Braunerhjelm, P., Audretsch, D. B. and Carlsson, B. (2009) 'The knowledge spillover theory of entrepreneurship', *Small Business Economics*, 32(1): 15–30.

Anselin, L. (1988) *Spatial Econometrics: Methods and Models*, Dordrecht, The Neederlands: Kluwer Academic Publishers.

Anselin, L. (1992) *SpaceStat Tutorial: A Workbook for Using SpaceStat in the Analysis of Spatial Data*, Urban-Champaign, IL: University of Illinois.

Bakhshi, H., Freeman, A. and Higgs, P. (2013) *A Dynamic Mapping of the UK's Creative Industries*, London: NESTA.

Baptista, R. (1998) 'Clusters, innovation and growth: A survey of the literature', in G. Swann, M. Prevezer and D. Stout (eds), *The Dynamics of Industrial Clustering: International Comparisons in Computing and Biotechnology*, Oxford: Oxford University Press, pp. 13–51.

Beatty, C. and Fothergill, S. (2004) 'Economic change and the labour market in Britain's seaside towns', *Regional Studies*, 38(5): 461–80.

Boix, R., Capone, F., De Propris, L., Lazzeretti, L. and Sanchez, D. (2014) 'Comparing creative industries in Europe', *European Urban and Regional Studies*, published online 21 August 2014.

Branzanti, C. (2014) 'Creative clusters and district economies: Towards a taxonomy to interpret the phenomenon', *European Planning Studies*, published online 16 July 2014.

Brouder, P. and Eriksson, R. H. (2013) 'Tourism evolution: On the synergies of tourism studies and evolutionary economic geography', *Annals of Tourism Research*, 43(October): 370–89.

Bull, P. J. and Church, A. (1994) 'The geography of employment change in the hotel and catering industry of Great Britain in the 1980s. A subregional perspective', *Regional Studies*, 28(1): 13–25.

Capone, F. and Boix, R. (2008) 'Sources of growth and competitiveness of local tourist production systems: An application to Italy (1991–2001)', *The Annals of Regional Science*, 42(1): 209–24.

Cliff, A. D. and Ord, J. K. (1981) *Spatial Processes: Models and Applications*, London: Pion.

DCMS – Department for Culture, Media and Sport (2001) *Creative Industries Mapping Document*, London: DCMS.

Delgado, M., Porter, M. E. and Stern, S. (2015) 'Defining clusters of related industries', *Journal of Economic Geography*, doi:10.1093/jeg/lbv017.

De Propris, L. (2005) 'Mapping local production systems in the UK: Methodology and application', *Regional Studies*, 39(2): 197–211.

De Propris, L., Chapain, C., Cooke, P., MacNeill, S. and Mateos-Garcia, J. (2009) *The Geography of Creativity*, London: NESTA.

EC – European Commission (2003) *Structure, Performance and Competitiveness of European Tourism and its Enterprises*, Luxembourg: Office for Official Publications of the European Communities.

Enz, C., Canina, L. and Liu, Z. (2008) 'Competitive dynamics and pricing behavior in US hotels: The role of co-location', *Scandinavian Journal of Hospitality and Tourism*, 8(3): 230–50.

Frenken, K. and Boschma, R. (2003) 'Evolutionary economics and industry location', *Review of Regional Research*, 23(1): 183–200.

Frenken, K., Van Oort, F. and Verburg, T. (2007) 'Related variety, unrelated variety and regional economic growth', *Regional Studies*, 41(5): 685–97.

Hartog, M., Boschma, R. and Sotarauta, M. (2012) 'The impact of related variety on regional employment growth in Finland 1993–2006: High-tech versus medium/low-tech', *Industry and Innovation*, 19(6): 459–76.

Debbage, K. and Ioannides, D. (2004) 'The cultural turn? Toward a more critical economic geography of tourism', in A. Lew, M. Hall and A. Williams (eds), *A Companion to Tourism*, Oxford: Blackwell, pp. 99–109.

ISTAT – Istituto Nazionale di Statistica (2001) *VIII Censimento generale dell'industria e dei servizi 2001*, Rome: ISTAT.

ISTAT – Istituto Nazionale di Statistica (2011) *IX Censimento generale dell'industria e dei servizi*, Rome: ISTAT.

Jackson, J. and Murphy, P. (2006) 'Clusters in regional tourism: An Australian case', *Annals of Tourism Research*, 33(4): 1018–35.

Lazzeretti, L. and Capone, F. (2009) 'Spatial spillovers and employment dynamics in local tourist systems in Italy (1991–2001)', *European Planning Studies*, 17(11): 1665–83.

Lazzeretti, L. and Capone, F. (2015) 'Narrow or broad definition of cultural and creative industries: Some evidence from Tuscany, Italy', *International Journal of Cultural and Creative Industries*, 2(2): 4–18.

Lazzeretti, L. and Petrillo, C. S. (eds) (2006) *Tourism Local Systems and Networking*, Amsterdam: Elsevier.

Lazzeretti, L., Boix, R. and Capone, F. (2012) 'Reasons for clustering of creative industries in Italy and Spain', *European Planning Studies*, 20(8): 1–20.

Lazzeretti, L., Innocenti, I. and Capone, F. (2015) 'Does related variety matter for creative industries?' *Papers in Evolution Economic Geography*, #15.10. Utrecth University.

Lorenzen, M. and Frederiksen, L. (2008) 'Why do cultural industries cluster? Localisation, urbanization, products and projects', in P. Cooke and L. Lazzeretti (eds), *Creative Cities, Cultural Clusters and Local Economic Development*, Cheltenham, UK: Edward Elgar, pp. 155–79.

Lue, C. C., Crompton, J. L. and Fesenmaier, D. R. (1993) 'Conceptualization of multi-destination pleasure trips', *Annals of Tourism Research*, 20(2): 289–301.

Michael, E. J. (2003) 'Tourism micro-cluster', *Tourism Economics*, 9(2): 133–46.

Nordin, S. (2003) *Tourism Clustering and Innovation*, Östersund, Sweden: Etour.

Novelli, M., Schmitz, B. and Spencer, T. (2006) 'Networks, clusters and innovation in tourism: A UK experience', *Tourism Management*, 27(6): 1141–52.

Porter, M. E. (1990) *The Competitive Advantage of Nations*, New York: Free Press.

Porter, M. E. (1998a) *On Competition*, Boston, MA: Harvard Business School Press.

Porter, M. E. (1998b) 'Cluster and the new economics of competition', *Harvard Business Review*, 76(6): 77–90.

Richards, G. (2011) 'Creativity and tourism. The state of the art', *Annals of Tourism Research*, 38(4): 1225–53.

Sanz-Ibáñez, C. and Anton Clavé, S. (2014) 'The evolution of destinations: Towards an evolutionary and relational economic geography approach', *Tourism Geographies*, 16(4): 563–79.

Sforzi, F. (ed.) (1997) *I sistemi locali in Italia*, Rome: ISTAT.

Shaw, G. and Williams, A. (2009) 'Knowledge transfer and management in tourism organisations: An emerging research agenda', *Tourism Management*, 30(3): 325–35.

Steinle, C. and Schiele, H. (2002) 'When do industries cluster? A proposal on how to assess an industry's propensity to concentrate at a single region or nation', *Research Policy*, 31(6): 849–58.

Stewart, S. I. and Vogt, C. A. (1997) 'Multi-destination trip patterns', *Annals of Tourism Research*, 24(2): 458–61.

Tallman, S., Jenkins, M., Henry, N. and Pinch, S. (2004) 'Knowledge, clusters and competitive advantage', *Academy of Management Review*, 29(2): 258–71.

Townsend, A. (1992) 'New directions in the growth of tourism employment. Propositions of the 1980s', *Environment and Planning A*, 24(6): 821–32.

Yang, Y. and Fik, T. (2014) 'Spatial effects in regional tourism growth', *Annals of Tourism Research*, published online 16 April 2014.

Yang, Y. and Wong, K.K.F. (2012) 'A spatial econometric approach to model spillover effects in tourism flows', *Journal of Travel Research*, 51(6): 768–78.

Yang, Y. and Wong, K.K.F. (2013) 'Spatial distribution of tourist flows to China's cities', *Tourism Geographies*, 15(2): 338–63.

4 Defining tourist clusters in Europe

A micro-level data approach

Francesco Capone and Rafael Boix

1 Introduction

From the time of its introduction, the issue of the cluster concept (Porter 1998a; 1998b) has received growing attention, particularly in terms of the role that concentration may play for firms' competitiveness, innovation and performance (Ketels 2003; 2011; Asheim, Cooke and Martin 2006). Although it was born from a vision of the manufacturing world, the concept of cluster has then been applied to the service industry (Keeble and Nachum 2002), to culture (Cooke and Lazzeretti 2008), to creative industries (Lazzeretti, Boix and Capone 2008; De Propris *et al.* 2009), and others.

Even in tourism studies, many authors have employed this concept in the analysis of the advantages of firm concentration and have started investigating the tourist destinations that are traditionally clustered. Several contributions prove that the cluster concept has been suitably adapted to the peculiarities of the tourism sector and provides a spatial and organisational model promoting competitiveness, innovation and local development (Michael 2003; Nordin 2003; Lazzeretti and Petrillo 2006; Novelli, Schmitz and Spencer 2006).

However, notwithstanding the relevant use of the concept in tourism studies, most of the researches in specialised literature have been based on case studies (Jackson and Murphy, 2008; Novelli, Schmitz and Spencer, 2006; Nordin, 2003), so that there is a lack of quantitative analyses that attempt to characterise the territorial co-localisation of firms, apart from very few exceptions (Capone and Boix 2008; Lazzeretti and Capone 2009; Segarra-Oña *et al.* 2012). From this also derives the lack of benchmarking analyses either cluster-to-cluster or among different countries, except for some studies at the European level (e.g. Kaae *et al.* 2007).

The present work attempts to fill this gap by means of a survey on the methodologies used to recognise clusters and concentrations of firms in the territory, from which to select a suitable method to map tourist clusters throughout Europe. Its final aim is to produce a map of tourist clusters in Europe, which should also provide an input for the subsequent parts of a broader research programme designed to develop international comparisons among the main European clusters and propose policy and managerial implications. This chapter contributes to this strand of research given that, from our point of view, behind the lack of effort on mapping tourist clusters there is still a lack a quantitative methodology able to solve the difficulties in identifying concentrations of tourist firms at a local level.

Avoiding the limitations of previous research, we propose a novel methodology that uses micro-data at the firm level and an ecological algorithm (nearest neighbour clustering) to identify tourist clusters. We apply this methodology to 15 European countries on a *filière* of tourism activities for 2014, based on the Amadeus database at the European level.

This chapter should therefore provide the key preliminary elements on which to build the identification of tourist clusters in Europe. It is therefore necessary to underline how some authors have rightly pointed out that the advantages of clustering are not only gained with spatial concentration, but definitely with the presence of a variety of characteristics, like – among many others – the development of networks, of trust, of a competition-cooperation process among firms (Santos, Almeida and Teixeira 2008). Judd (1995), for example highlighted that agglomeration economies apply to tourist clusters not principally because concentration lowers the costs or increases the efficiency of business transactions, but because a full panoply of services and businesses is necessary to make the space maximally attractive to consumers of the tourist space. Even Porter (1998a; 1998b) drew attention to the fact that in a tourist cluster, the quality of visitors' experiences depends on the quality and efficiency of complementary businesses (hotels, restaurants, transports, etc.), since the cluster members are mutually dependent, and the good performance of one can boost the success of the others.

Hence, this work represents a first investigation for the recognition of potential tourist clusters at the European level, which will then require further *ad hoc* in-depth analyses at the local level to verify the existence of positive externalities from the cluster, such as relationship dynamics among firms, trust, a common image, shared strategies and so on.

Our results underline that tourist firms are highly clustered, and that clusters are concentrated in the most important European art cities and famous rural and natural destinations stretching from the southern to the northern European countries. The work provides a first analysis of tourist clusters in Europe that it is original.

This chapter is divided into five parts. After this introduction, section 2 presents a literature review on cluster identification methodologies, with a particular focus on the studies of tourist clusters. Section 3 illustrates the research approach and the methodology applied. Section 4 explains the main findings, while section 5 is devoted to the discussion of the results and their implications.

2 Identification and mapping of tourist clusters

Porter (1998a; 1998b; 2003) has provided empirical evidence that the benefits generated by clusters emerge only when the cluster reaches a certain threshold of concentration of firms in the territory. This research strand has then been developed in a wide research project called 'US Cluster Mapping Project' (www.clustermapping.us), a national economic initiative that provides wide information to identify and investigate regional clusters in the United States. It is based at the Institute for Strategy and Competitiveness of the Harvard Business School. Delgado, Porter and Stern (2010; 2014; 2015) in their latest work develop a novel clustering algorithm that systematically assesses and generates sets of cluster definitions (i.e. groups of closely related industries). They use 2009 data for USA industries (six-digit NAICS [the North American Industry Classification System]), and propose a new set of benchmark cluster definitions that incorporates measures of inter-industry linkages based on co-location patterns, input–output links, and similarities in labour occupations. Ketels and Protsiv (2014) analyse the evolution of methodology in clusters mapping in the USA; in particular, they focus on how the detection of related industry is a crucial element for cluster identification.

From the industrial point of view, in fact, there are many contributions that have tried to analyse the concentration of firms in the territory and the related so-called *externalities* (Sforzi 1997; Ellison and Glaeser 1999; Rosenthal and Strange 2004; De Propris 2005; Boix and Galletto 2006). This literature includes a wide range of methods for identifying industrial clusters, depending on the type of cluster and data availability (Bergman and Feser 1999; Vom Hofe and Chen 2006; Jacquez 2008; Titze, Brachert and Kubis 2011). These include the identification of path dependency; the use of expert opinion (i.e. Delphi, MSQA); the identification in a region of a critical mass of firms in the same or complementary sectors; the use of concentration indices (such as location quotients, Gini indices, or Ellison-Glaeser measures), the use of input-output methods (such as triangularisation, and factor and principal components analysis), the use of network analysis, and the employment of spatial econometrics.

From the point of view instead of service sectors, tourism and culture, this rigorous method was not followed, although there are some interesting studies. A significant interest has been devoted to the identification, for instance, of cultural and creative industries' clusters (Cunningham and Higgs 2008; Lazzeretti 2013). Many of these studies converge on a methodology of identification of employment concentrations through location quotients (LQs). This was first developed for Italy and Spain (Lazzeretti, Boix and Capone 2008), England (De Propris *et al.* 2009), Austria (Trippl, Tödtling and Schuldner 2013), the whole of Europe (Lazzeretti 2013; De Miguel *et al.* 2014) and Russia (Vladimirovna 2014).

In tourism, there are few contributions that adopt a quantitative methodology for the identification of tourist clusters. Some authors point out that it is essential to first use a quantitative methodology and then a qualitative methodology to investigate the aspects of social capital, trust and relations among firms (Santos, Almeida and Teixeira 2008). Even in tourism, the main methodology to map the clusters of tourist firms uses indices of concentration (LQ) (Della Lucia 2006; Capone and Boix 2008; Lazzeretti and Capone 2008; Peiró-Signes *et al.* 2015; and others).

In this strand of research, the earlier works that map tourist clusters are from Lazzeretti and Petrillo (2006) and Capone and Boix (2008), who analyse destinations in Italy through LQs on a tourism *filière* defined at the European level (EC 2003). The authors then proceed to develop a cluster analysis in order to propose a taxonomy of destinations based on the characteristics of the local value chain.

Lazzeretti and Capone (2009) use local labour markets to analyse the growth of tourist destinations in Italy, applying models of spatial analysis and investigating the spatial spillovers in the territory. Segarra-Oña *et al.* (2012) identify tourist clusters in Spain through a similar methodology in order to investigate the performance of tourist firms.

However, this methodology does not really identify the clusters in the area; rather, it is primarily an index of local/regional specialisation and consequently it allows to map mainly those places that have a specialisation on certain industries. This methodology has also been criticised as it uses arbitrarily cut-off values (Crawley, Beynon and Munday 2013) and because it puts too much emphasis on large metropolitan centres, underestimating the importance of rural areas (Collis, Freebody and Flew 2011). This phenomenon has been particularly emphasised in the concentrations of the cultural and creative industries. Collis, Freebody and Flew (2011) present the advantages and limits of the use of LQs in mapping cultural and creative industries, proposing the use of a 'density sensitive index', using land area as a measure of size or urbanisation to adjust the index. They explain that the main problems of the LQ approach is that it inhibits 'seeing' the outer suburban geographies of industries, thus favouring those locations with larger workforces.

Among the most interesting alternative methods, Baggio (2008), and Scott, Cooper and Baggio (2008a; 2008b) propose a method to analyse tourist destinations and clusters using social network analysis. They investigate an Italian island in Tuscany, Elba, surveying local tourist firms and analysing the relationship dynamics among firms. Biggiero and Samarra (2010) develop an interesting study to identify cluster actors. They survey the main industry-leading firms in a cluster in order to reconstruct the 'core' cluster and then apply the snowball methodology in order to identify other actors cited as collaborating partners. Alberti and Giusti (2012) use the same methodology to identify the Motor Valley cluster in Italy and evaluate its tourism attractiveness and regional competitiveness. Estevão and Ferreira (2012) identify tourist clusters in Portugal using a cluster analysis in order to group places with similar characteristics and performances, using as a basis the 2008 turnover of the companies of continental Portugal and islands based on data of the National Institute of Statistics (INE).

In this general overview, we can summarise that the identification of tourist clusters has been mainly based on firm concentration, primarily from a supply side perspective. Nonetheless many authors have tried to map tourist destinations or clusters using demand data. D'Agata, Gozzo and Tomaselli (2013) apply social network analysis to map the spatial distribution of tourism mobility in Sicily, using survey data collected on a sample of tourists (who visited at least two destinations) leaving from airports and ports of the main Sicilian cities. Yang and Wong (2013) identified Chinese tourist cities using exploratory techniques to map tourist clusters using tourist flows and spatial statistics. They investigated the spatial distribution and determinants of inbound tourism flows to 341 cities in China from 1999–2006 and those of domestic tourism flows from 2002–06. Nielsen and Kaae (2008) present an interesting analysis of tourist beds at the Nomenclature of

Territorial Units for Statistics (NUTS) second level in order to depict a geographical disaggregation of tourism loads within Europe. These authors investigate the determinants of the geographical distribution of tourism loads, considering sustainability of land use. In this strand of research, Capone (2005) analyses national and foreigner tourist expenditures and nights spent in order to map tourist destinations in Italy from a demand perspective.

Boix, Hervás and De Miguel (2014) seek to overcome the problems involved in the definition of administrative boundaries by identifying clusters of creative industries at the European level with micro-firm level data. This chapter contributes to this strand of research as, notwithstanding all the supported endeavours on mapping (tourist) clusters, there is still a lack of a quantitative methodology to identify clusters of tourist firms at broad level.

In our opinion, it is necessary to overcome the limits of administrative boundaries (whether they be municipal, provincial or local labour markets), in order to identify real clusters and not the specialisation of territorial units. In the next section, we describe the methodology chosen for this process of identification based on micro-firm level data, analysed through geographic information system software.

3 Research design and methodology approach

The methodology we propose to map tourist clusters was proposed by Boix, Hervás and De Miguel (2014) for the study of creative industries. The methodology uses a mix of an extended geographical analysis machine (Openshaw, Charlton and Craft 1988; Sforzi 2009), and the logic put forward by Capone and Boix (2008) and Lazzeretti, Boix and Capone (2008) for identifying tourist and creative local systems. First, we define an operative notion of a tourist cluster. Second, a list of tourism industries is proposed. Third, firms' data are extracted, treated and geocodified. Fourth, a geostatistical algorithm is selected – in this case the spatial Nearest Neighbour Clustering (NNC) – and the procedure runs on the selected sample of firms.

3.1 Operative approaches to the notion of cluster

The first stage is to operationalise the notion of a tourist cluster. There is an intense discussion in the literature about the notion of *cluster* – see for example the connections between the core literatures on clustering in Feser and Sweeney (2002), and the taxonomical discussions in Gordon and McCann (2000) and Vom Hofe and Chen (2006). Gordon and McCann (2000) distinguish three stylised forms of spatial clustering, depending on the dominant or characteristic process occurring in the cluster: *pure agglomeration*, based on geographical proximity and agglomeration economies; *industrial complex*, based on input-output linkages and co-location in order to minimise transactions costs; and *social-network*, based on high levels of embeddedness and social integration. We could even distinguish other additional stylised forms of clusters such as artificial clusters (e.g. the 22@ in Barcelona) (González 2011). This multi-perspective approach results in an eclectic and polycentric notion of clusters, with the consequence that there can be no single method for identifying and mapping clusters (Benneworth *et al.* 2003).

Among the various problems that usually arise when trying to empirically delineate clusters, we can mention the difficulty in identifying a cluster's core industries, the lack of inter-industry trade data for subnational geographical areas the problems of collecting data on the basis of pre-given administrative and political units, the difficulties of identifying a cluster's geographical boundaries, the issue of which data to select (such as data relating to employment, number of firms, added value or level of productivity), and the arbitrariness of the rules for distinguishing clusters (Boix, Hervás and De Miguel 2014).

In fact, the literature includes a wide range of methods for identifying industrial clusters, depending on the type of cluster and data availability (Bergman and Feser 1999; Vom Hofe and Chen 2006; Jacquez 2008; Titze, Brachert and Kubis 2011). These include the identification of path dependency, the use of expert opinion (i.e. Delphi, MSQA), the identification of a critical mass of firms in a region in the same or complementary sectors, the use of concentration indices (such as LQs, Gini indices, or Ellison-Glaeser measures), the employment of input–output methods (such as triangularisation, and factor and principal components analysis), the use of network analysis, and the employment of spatial econometrics.

Hitherto, the ideal models for clusters described by Gordon and McCann (2000) have been used for guiding empirical research on tourist clusters, but none of them have stood out as more effective than the others. Moreover, the only characteristic of tourist clusters that so far has been identified has proved to be spatial agglomeration. Given the existing limited knowledge, we propose to proceed incrementally, starting initially with a modest approach (focusing on agglomeration clusters), but with the aim of enhancing our research later by extending our interest to other types of clusters (i.e. industrial complex and social network clusters).[1]

3.2 A list of tourism industries

At a second stage, it is necessary to select a list of tourism industries. The current value chain used in the study of tourism is broad and complex (OECD 2014). The tourism value chain as viewed in the *Tourism Satellite Accounts in Europe* (Eurostat 2013), and mainly in UNWTO (2015) and OECD (2014) include Accommodation for visitors; Food and beverages; Railway passenger transport; Road and passenger transport; Water passenger transport; Air passenger transport; Transport equipment rental; Travel agencies and other reservation services activities; Cultural activities; and Sports and recreation activities. The tourism value chain includes activities that take place in the outbound country and in the inbound country, activities that are a direct part of the tourism industry and activities that are only indirectly linked to it.

This list is too wide for the purpose of this article. Even restricting the measurement to local companies (inbound-local), in order to define geographic clusters with significant data constraints we are forced to focus only on those activities

that are to be used predominantly by tourists (Table 4.1): Short-term accommodation activities (including Hotels and similar accommodation and Holiday and
other short-stay accommodation); Camping grounds, recreational vehicle parks
and trailer parks; Travel agency, tour operator, reservation service and related
activities. The class ISIC 55.9[2] Other accommodation was excluded as it is not
predominantly addressed to tourists and would introduce a certain distortion
in the statistics. The use of such a restricted list of activities is a clear cost of
working at a detailed geographical level and with such a wide coverage. The use
of an extended chain adds richness, but dissolves the geographical specificity,
being unable to separate which part serves residents and which tourists. At the
same time, the use of a restricted chain can bias downward the importance of
tourist places.

3.3 From macro- to micro-geographic data

The third and fourth stages involve the selection of observations and appropriate
data, and the selection of an algorithm. Until now, research on tourist clusters in
Europe has been affected by two constraints. First, the level of the region is too
big to provide an appropriate detailed geography of tourist clusters (e.g. Segarra-
Oña *et al.* 2012), because of a number of effects. These include the average effects
of regional units (i.e. the ecological fallacy), the possibility that several clusters of
the same industry exist in the same region, the heterogeneity in the size definition
of NUTS2 (Hautdidier 2011), and an incapacity to identify actual locations and
boundaries of clusters. In addition, it is impossible to detect cross-regional and
cross-national clusters (Crawley and Pickernell 2012).

A second constraint has arisen when a strategy involved the collection of data at
infra-regional administrative levels such as municipalities and local labour markets (e.g. Capone and Boix 2008). Eurostat does not centralise this information
and the only option is to collect it from national statistical offices, which is difficult, slow and costly.

For the above reasons, and following recent studies on patterns of industrial
location (Feser and Sweeney 2002; Combes and Overman 2004; Duranton and
Overman 2005), we use micro-geographic data for cluster identification. This type

Table 4.1 Tourism activities predominantly focused on non-residents, Nomenclature of
Economic Activities (NACE) Rev. 2 codes

Code	Description
55.1	Short-term accommodation activities
55.2	Camping grounds, recreational vehicle parks and trailer parks
55.3	Camping grounds, recreational vehicle parks and trailer parks
79.1	Travel agency, tour operator, reservation service and related activities
79.9	Other reservation service and related activities

Source: Our elaboration.

of data permits the use of geostatistics in continuous space, which in turn permits the definition of concentration (agglomeration) on the basis of the locational density of firms in space.

3.4 Spatial nearest neighbour clustering algorithm

There are many techniques for identifying hot spots, including point location methods (total number of cases, i.e. fuzzy mode), hierarchical grouping (i.e. nearest neighbour methods), partitioning the sample in groups (i.e. spatial k-means), clumping (using partitioning techniques, but with overlapping), calculating the density of cases (i.e. kernel methods), and risk-based approaches (weighting using a risk variable, such as population, i.e. Kulldorff scan).

The Nearest Neighbour Clustering (NNC) approach was selected by us because of the occurrence of some advantageous properties. First, it works well with a very large number of observations in a continuous space. Second, it does not require a reduction of the space to grids, such as for example required using kernel techniques, which means we can avoid having to select the size of grids (Sweeney and Feser 2003). Third, it is possible to select a threshold random distance for the firms in the cluster, or to provide this distance on the basis of economic or relational criteria. Fourth, it is not necessary to assume any shape for the search radius, such as happens in scan methods. The NNC approach can detect large and small clusters, even inside cities. Fifth, it is possible to see the enveloping shape of the cluster (geographical boundaries).

In addition, the NNC approach also offers the possibility, if necessary, of taking into account the localisation of firms belonging to other industries (through a method similar to that typically used by specialisation indices). However, as we are looking for evidence of pure agglomeration, it would be more consistent to consider only the pure density of firms in the targeted industry since the continuous space is already acting as a corrective base for the index.

The output meets most of the desirable qualities for the measurement of spatial concentrations proposed by Combes and Overman (2004). It is comparable across activities and spatial scales; it proves to be reasonably robust to the existence of a deterministic component; the significance of results can be controlled; it is not sensitive to changes in administrative boundaries; it is reasonably unbiased in respect to changes in the industrial classification (the firm-level data report old and new NACE classifications); and it can have theoretical considerations applied to it. The relevance of some of these aspects depends on the choices we make during the application of the methodology.

The spatial NNC approach (NIJ 2004) starts from the matrix of distances d_{AB} between all the pairs of points. The second step is the selection of a threshold distance t_{AB} below which a pair of points could be considered as clustered. Those pairs of points, where $d_{AB} < t_{AB}$, form the random distance matrix d'_{AB}. Next, for each point the pairs of distances d'_{AB} are sorted in a descending order. The point with the largest number of threshold distances (the most connected point) is selected for the initial seed of the first cluster, and those points within the threshold distance of the initial seed are included in the first cluster. We can fix the condition of a minimum number of points in the cluster (size criterion) ranging from 2 to N; in our case, and following Boix, Hervás and De Miguel (2014), we consider that a minimum of 50 firms is necessary for the cluster to be counted as significant.[3] If the cluster satisfies the criterion of size, then it is retained and we proceed with the next most connected point not included in a previous cluster until all the selectable points have been assigned to a cluster, or discarded (Figure 4.1).

At the end of the procedure, a convex hull (an irregular polygon) can be calculated for each cluster as the enveloping line to the points of the cluster, which allows us to identify basic features such as the area of the cluster.

3.5 Selection of the distance

It is possible to manually select the distance threshold, although there is not yet general agreement about what constitutes an appropriate distance radius for clusters. For example, Funderburg and Boarnet (2008) found an average of 5–7.5 miles in their study of manufacturing clusters in Southern California. Feser and Sweeney (2002) described a distance of 26 kilometres for manufacturing industries in the San Francisco Bay area. May, Mason and Pinch (2001) indicated a range of up to 50 miles for the British high-fidelity industry. Boix, Hervás and De Miguel (2014) found an average of 16.5 kilometres in their study of creative service industries in 16 European countries. Rosenthal and Strange (2004) argue that the spatial range of agglomeration economies is short for localisation economies

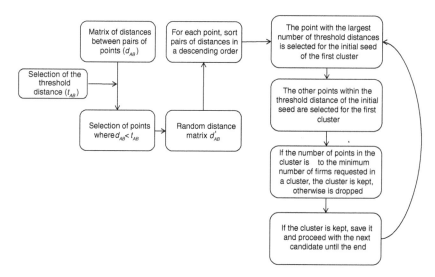

Figure 4.1 Spatial nearest neighbour hierarchical clustering algorithm

Source: Our elaboration.

in agglomerated industries, falling to as little as 15 miles, whereas for urbanisation economies it could extend to hundreds of miles.

One way of avoiding the problem is by selecting as a threshold a random distance to the nearest neighbours based on the probability of selecting any pair of points on the basis of a random distribution. Most software packages (e.g. ArcGis, Crimestat) compute the mean random distance to the first neighbour () because it is easy to relate on a confidence interval defined for a specific one-tailed probability, and to compare it with Student t tables. However, the hypothesis that firms are related only to the nearest single firm in the cluster is unreal, and we should select a number of n nearest neighbours with which a firm could be linked. As the high-order pairs are correlated, it is not possible *a priori* to fix a level of statistical significance, and to calculate the radius departing from this level, for more than the fourth neighbour (Aplin 1983). Several solutions have been suggested in the literature (see Dixon 2002a for a synthesis), none of them definitive: Kolmogorov-Smirnov-type statistics using Monte Carlo tests, squared distances, graphical methods, the use of auxiliary functions, and the use of a point of inflexion.

We propose in this case the use of an auxiliary function such as the Ripley's K statistic in order to obtain the average distance of clustering of tourist firms. Ripley's K draws circles around each observation, increasing the size of this circle successively and providing the degree of clustering for each radio, so that it can be evaluated to what distance occurs the biggest degree of clustering (Dixon 2002b; NIJ 2004). The spatial NNC can be calculated using Ripley's K distance where the clustering maximises, and the statistical significance of the results of the NNH can be assessed retrospectively by Monte Carlo simulation (Dixon 2002a; 2002b; NIJ 2004).

4 Identification of tourist clusters in Europe

4.1 Data

The micro-geographic data used in the research comes from the Amadeus database (Bureau van Dijk). Amadeus provides data for all the EU countries, detailed by firms' postal addresses, and at the four-digit NACE Rev 2 level. The area of our analysis covers the EU-15 countries (Austria, Belgium, Denmark, Finland, France, Germany, Greece, Ireland, Italy, Luxembourg, The Netherlands, Portugal, Spain, Sweden and the UK). French overseas regions were not included.

The data covers 230,000 active enterprises belonging to narrow list of tourism industries as principal activity (Table 4.1) in the EU-15 in 2014. Secondary activity codes are not considered. The postal addresses of the firms were translated to geographic coordinates which are used by the geostatistical algorithm. The NNC can deal with jobs or establishments, although the latter is more usual in geostatistics (Sweeney and Feser 2003). Furthermore, information about the number of employees by firm is poor and irregular in Amadeus, and the average firm size in the tourism industry is small (less than 8.5 persons employed per enterprise and 85% of micro-enterprises). For this reason we use the firm as the basic observation for the procedure.[4]

Eurostat Structural Business Statistics (SBS) are used as a proxy to provide a basic control on the quality of the sample. The coverage of our sample for 2013 (230,000 enterprises) is 76% of Eurostat SBS for 2013 (300,000 enterprises). This is an excellent coverage: the sampling error considering $P(-Z < z < Z) = 0.99$ stays below 0.1%, and the coverage is twice that in Feser and Sweeney (2002), and Boix, Hervás and De Miguel (2014). Country controls are difficult to establish accurately, due to a certain heterogeneity in the elaboration of national SBS statistics and to the fact that the other source available, Tourism Statistics (also for the year 2013), covers not enterprises but establishments and only in the accommodation sector. Amadeus sample covers more than 50% of the firms in Eurostat SBS for all the countries, except Ireland, Germany and Greece, being more than 100% for Sweden, The Netherlands, Denmark and Belgium, and more than 200% for Finland and the UK. Although these differences could open a debate on the coverage of the sample, the truth is that the comparison between Eurostat databases (SBS and Tourism Statistics) shows even more mixed results. The general impression is that different statistical sources are not directly comparable, and that the coverage of our sample is good, even if Amadeus has some limitations, in particular that the coverage of firms below 20 employees is irregular.

To reduce the 'national bias', we apply the algorithm to each country (or groups of countries) separately. This not only has the advantage of reducing the problems that arise from potential sample heterogeneity, but also allows taking into account the different characteristics of each country in terms of geography, infrastructure or structure of settlements. Thus, Ripley's K and NNC will be calculated separately for each country, with the only exceptions being Belgium, The Netherlands and Luxembourg, which will be grouped together (Benelux), and Ireland, which will be grouped with Northern Ireland to cover the whole island.

4.2 Tourist clusters in Europe

Tourist enterprises are located throughout the whole geography of the EU-15 (Figure 4.2). However, their geographical distribution is unequal. A kernel density map (Figure 4.3) reveals that the density of enterprises is particularly high in England and Wales, Benelux and West Germany, the centre and north of Italy, Austria, the Mediterranean Coast of Spain, and around some other large metropolitan areas such as Paris, Berlin, Munich, Stockholm or Athens.

The algorithm identifies 863 tourist clusters in the EU-15 (Figure 4.4). Monte Carlo simulations (1,000 replications) show that all clusters are statistically significant at 5%. About 67% of the tourist enterprises in the sample are located in a tourist cluster. In Sweden, France, Austria and Germany, more than 60% of tourist enterprises are located in tourist clusters, whereas in Spain this increases to 78.5% and in the UK to about 92% (Table 4.2). In the rest of the countries, the percentage of tourist firms in tourist clusters is less than 60%, being particularly low in Denmark (30.5%) and Luxembourg (0%). As can be seen in Figure 4.4, tourist clusters spreads not only across the most urbanised areas but also across rural areas, although in the latter case their size tends to be smaller.

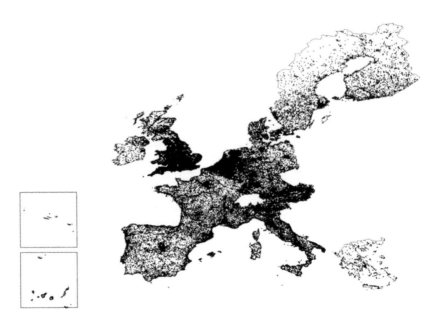

Figure 4.2 Tourist enterprises in the EU-15 by address (sample of 230,000 enterprises), 2014

Source: Our elaboration from Amadeus database (Bureau van Dijk).

Figure 4.3 Quadratic kernel density map of tourist enterprises in the EU-15 by address[*] (sample of 230,000 enterprises), 2014

Note: *Kernel function based on the quadratic kernel function (Silverman 1986: 76).

Source: Our elaboration from Amadeus database (Bureau van Dijk).

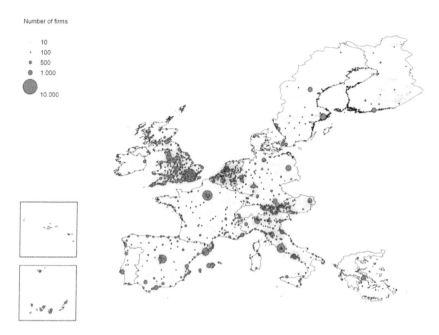

Number of firms

- 10
- 100
- 500
- 1.000
- 10.000

Figure 4.4 Tourist clusters in the EU-15 (hot spots with 50 or more enterprises), 2014

Source: Our elaboration from Amadeus database (Bureau van Dijk).

Table 4.2 Degree of clustering by country

Country	Tourist enterprises	Number of tourist clusters	Tourist enterprises in clusters	% of tourist enterprises in clusters
United Kingdom	46,147	177	42,428	91.9
Spain	28,814	107	22,607	78.5
Germany	20,663	86	13,125	63.5
Austria	13,894	63	8,771	63.1
Italy	39,272	152	24,069	61.3
France	27,884	111	16,967	60.8
Sweden	9,975	36	6,015	60.3
Greece	4,162	15	2,441	58.6
Netherlands	15,308	67*	8,625*	56.3*
Belgium	8,278	30*	4,143*	50.0*
Portugal	5,326	14	2,631	49.4
Finland	4,937	18	2,290	46.4
Ireland	1,220	2	542	44.4
Denmark	3,172	5	969	30.5
Luxembourg	335	0	0	0.0
EU-15	229,387	883*	155,623*	67.8*

Source: Our elaboration from Amadeus database (Bureau van Dijk).

Note: * Some clusters are shared between countries and counted twice. The net number of clusters is 863.

There are 392 clusters (45.5%) that have more than 100 tourist enterprises (Figure 4.5). These clusters have about 53% of the tourist enterprises of the sample and about 79% of the tourist enterprises located in tourist clusters. Most of these clusters are located in the tourist high-density areas (Figure 4.5).

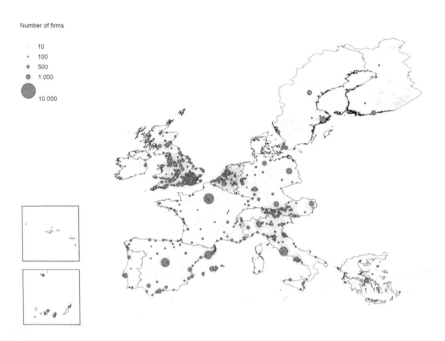

Figure 4.5 Tourist clusters in the EU-15 (hot spots with 100 or more enterprises), 2014

Source: Our elaboration from Amadeus database (Bureau van Dijk).

Table 4.3 Main identified clusters, hot spots with 1,000 enterprises

Tourist cluster/ destination	Nation	Number of firms	Number of firms in the nation	% of firms on total in the nation
London	England	7,699	46,147	16.7
Paris	France	4,369	27,884	15.7
Rome	Italy	3,327	39,272	8.5
Madrid	Spain	2,896	28,814	10.1
Barcelona	Spain	2,370	28,814	8.2
Stockholm	Sweden	1,747	9,975	17.5
Amsterdam	The Netherlands	1,592	15,308	10.4
Lancashire	England	1,428	46,147	3.1
Berlin	Germany	1,376	20,663	6.7
Milan	Italy	1,267	39.272	3.2
Munich	Germany	1,093	20,663	5.3
Wien	Austria	1,032	13,894	7.4
Palma de Mallorca	Spain	1,026	28,814	3.6

Source: Our elaboration from Amadeus database (Bureau van Dijk).

Only 13 clusters have more than 1,000 tourist enterprises (large tourist clusters) (Table 4.3). These clusters are located in London (7,699 enterprises), Paris (4,369), Rome (3,327), Madrid (2,896), Barcelona (2,370), Stockholm (1,747), Amsterdam (1,592), Lancashire (1,428), Berlin (1,376), Milan (1,267), Munich (1,093), Wien (1,032), and Palma de Mallorca (1,026). These 13 large tourist clusters have about 14% of the tourist enterprises of the sample and concentrate about 20% of the firms located in tourist clusters.

5 Conclusions

The aim of the present work was to propose a methodology for the identification of clusters in the territory and produce a map of the main tourist clusters at European level. We have analysed and georeferenced more than 230,000 EU-15 firms selected from the Amadeus database, and built a map of tourist clusters that is utterly new in specialised literature.

The suggested methodology proved to be satisfactory, although it required several *ad hoc* adjustments for the case under study and a continuous process of revision. Notwithstanding the limitations already mentioned, the maps presented in this chapter constitute an important outcome, as they evidence which are the main tourist destinations of Europe and allow to develop further policy and governance implications for the tourism competitiveness of the old continent.

The analysis confirms that tourist firms are highly concentrated and form clusters of tourist destinations. Their cartographic representation brings to light a heterogeneous kaleidoscope of competitiveness in the European destinations. The results show that there are 863 tourist clusters in the EU-15, only considering the selected activities (hotels, other accommodation, tour operators and travel agencies). These tourist clusters account for about 67% of tourist firms: 471 clusters have between 50 and 100 enterprises and 14% of the total tourist firms, while other 392 have more than 100 tourist enterprises and 53% of the total tourist firms.

We have found 13 macro-clusters with more than 1,000 firms, which are localised in the main European capitals – London, Paris, Rome, Madrid and Barcelona – as well as in the seaside destinations – such a Palma de Mallorca. There are also other clusters corresponding to equally relevant destinations, but not renowned at worldwide level. Finally, the remaining clusters distinguish minor, peripheral destinations that emphasise the existence of a multitude of 'tourisms' in the European nations.

The resulting scenario underlines, at a national level, the stronger competitiveness of the more tourism-based countries, like Italy, Spain, France and England. Also, two macro-national localisations emerge with forceful clarity: one is the whole Mediterranean Coast, which crosses Italy, France and Spain, where the level of international tourism supply is very high; another is in Northern Europe and comprises some parts of The Netherlands and South England.[5] In addition to these two macro-areas, many minor destinations, like the clusters localised in the north of Italy, Austria, and south of Germany, complete the geography of European tourism.

Further research developments in this field have been highlighted in this chapter, most importantly, the methodology, although we were only able to analyse a section of European tourist firms, those belonging to the tourism sector in a strict sense (accommodation, tour operators and travel agencies). What we want for the future is to enlarge this sample, even if it is clear that such an attempt must face many problems, namely the introduction of activities that are shared by resident people, which increases the difficulty of reading the results.

As already mentioned, this work is aimed at identifying tourist clusters in the territory with a georeferencing methodology applied to the firms in the tourism sector. Such a process does not investigate other key elements in the existence of clusters, like inter-firm relations, possible role of trust, sharing at territorial level of a value system or a local image, processes of cooperation, shared public goods, and so on. This is why we consider this study as a first phase, useful for a territorial benchmarking procedure at European level, but needing to be followed by a second phase of *ad hoc* studies that analyse the local specificities of clusters and verify the possible presence of positive externalities deriving from the concentration of firms. Obviously, for reasons of space and time, these aspects are not the object of this work, but we want to stress their importance in terms of the stringency of application of the cluster concept.

In conclusion, this work constitutes an important contribution to the analysis and mapping of tourist clusters in Europe. It is of great consequence and novelty from the point of view of both the methodology applied and the results obtained, and offers an important knowledge base for further studies and researches.

Notes

1   In the taxonomy of Gordon and McCann (2000), the 'pure agglomeration cluster' is considered to be a result of a normative process based on agglomeration economies. However, in section 2 we have introduced a wider range of factors that could lead to the same outcome. Our identification methodology describes the *ex post* results of these processes, but it is not conditional nor does it explain the process of agglomeration itself, being neutral in this respect.
2   Following United Nations (2008) ISIC Rev. 4, this class includes the provision of temporary or longer-term accommodation in single or shared rooms or dormitories for students, migrant (seasonal) workers and other individuals.
3   This number introduces a certain arbitrariness since there is no rule about what is the minimum number of firms in a cluster.
4   Actually, the algorithm does not assign weights to events, and so the relevant data is the location of the firm, regardless of its size. In the pure agglomeration logic, this is an advantage since the result is not distorted by the effect of large companies. However, this feature could also be considered a limitation for some research. If so, the algorithm could be adapted to be allowed for the different sizes of firms.
5   As already specified, this finding may suffer from an overestimate of the phenomenon in the Eurostat data.

References

Alberti, F. and Giusti, J. (2012) 'Cultural heritage, tourism and regional competitiveness: the Motor Valley cluster', *City, Culture and Society*, 3(4): 261–73.

Aplin, G. (1983) *Order-neighbour Analysis*, Norwich: Geo Books.

Asheim, B., Cooke, P. and Martin, R. (2006) 'The rise of the cluster concept in regional analysis and policy', in B.T. Asheim, P. Cooke and R.L. Martin (eds), *Cluster and*

Regional Development. Critical Reflections and Explorations, London: Routledge, pp. 1–30.

Baggio, R. (2008) *Network Analysis of a Tourism Destination*, PhD Dissertation Thesis, University of Queensland, Australia.

Benneworth, P., Danson, M., Raines, P. and Whittam, G. (2003) 'Confusing clusters? Making sense of the cluster approach in theory and practice', *European Planning Studies*, 11(5): 511–20.

Bergman, E. M. and Feser, E. J. (1999) *Industrial and Regional Clusters: Concepts and Comparative Analysis*, Morgantown, WV: West Virginia University Press.

Biggiero, L. and Samarra, A. (2010) 'Does geographical proximity enhance knowledge exchange? The case of the aerospace industrial cluster of Centre Italy', *International Journal of Technology Transfer and Commercialisation*, 9(4): 283–300.

Boix, R. and Galletto, V. (2006) 'Sistemas locales de trabajo y distritos industriales marshallianos en España', *Economía Industrial*, 359: 165–84.

Boix, R., Hervás, J. L. and De Miguel, B. (2014) 'Micro-geographies of creative industries clusters in Europe: From hot spots to assemblages', *Papers in Regional Science*, published online 20 January 2014.

Capone, F. (2005) *I sistemi locali turistici in Italia. Identificazione, analisi e misurazione delle fonti di competitività*, Firenze: Firenze University Press.

Capone, F. and Boix, R. (2008) 'Sources of growth and competitiveness of local tourist production systems: An application to Italy (1991–2001)', *The Annals of Regional Science*, 42(1): 209–24.

Collis, C., Freebody, S. and Flew, T. (2011) 'Seeing the outer suburbs: Addressing the urban bias in creative place thinking', *Regional Studies*, 47(2): 148–60.

Combes, P. and Overman, H. (2004) 'The spatial distribution of economic activities in the European Union', in J.V. Henderson and J.F. Thisse (eds), *Handbook of Regional and Urban Economics*, vol. 4, Amsterdam: Elsevier, pp. 2911–77.

Cooke, P. and Lazzeretti, L. (eds) (2008) *Creative Cities, Cultural Clusters and Local Economic Development*, Cheltenham, UK: Edward Elgar.

Crawley, A. and Pickernell, D. (2012) 'European urban and regional studies: An appraisal of the European cluster observatory', *European Urban and Regional Studies*, 19(2); 207–11.

Crawley, A., Beynon, M. and Munday, M. (2013) 'Making location quotients more relevant as a policy aid in regional spatial analysis', *Urban Studies*, 50(9): 1854–69.

Cunningham, S. D. and Higgs, P. L. (2008) 'Creative industries mapping: Where have we come from and where are we going?' *Creative Industries Journal*, 1(1): 7–30.

D'Agata, R., Gozzo, S. and Tomaselli, V. (2013) 'Network analysis approach to map tourism mobility', *Quality & Quantity*, 47(6): 3167–84.

De Miguel, B., Hervás, J. L., Boix, R. and De Miguel, M. (2012) 'The importance of creative industry agglomerations in explaining the wealth of the European regions', *European Planning Studies*, 20(8): 1263–80.

De Propris, L. (2005) 'Mapping local production systems in the UK: Methodology and application', *Regional Studies*, 39(2): 197–211.

De Propris, L., Chapain, C., Cooke, P., MacNeill, S. and Mateos-Garcia, J. (2009) *The Geography of Creativity*, London: NESTA.

Delgado, M., Porter, M. E. and Stern, S. (2010) 'Cluster and entrepreneurship', *Journal of Economic Geography*, 10(4): 495–518.

Delgado, M., Porter, M. E. and Stern, S. (2014) 'Clusters, convergence and economic performance', *Research Policy*, 43(10): 1785–99.

Delgado, M., Porter, M. E. and Stern, S. (2015) 'Defining clusters of related industries', *Journal of Economic Geography*, doi:10.1093/jeg/lbv017.

Della Lucia, M. (2006) 'Local development in the tourist sector: The application of a model to analyse industrial development', paper presented at the Proceeding of the 4th International Doctoral Colloquium in Tourism and Leisure, Barcelona, 3 May.

Dixon, P. M. (2002a) 'Nearest neighbor methods for spatial point processes', in A. H. El-Shaarawi and W. W. Piegorsch (eds), *Encyclopedia of Environmetrics*, vol. 3, Chichester: John Wiley & Sons, pp. 1370–83.

Dixon, P. M. (2002b) 'Ripley's K function', in A. H. El-Shaarawi and W. W. Piegorsch (eds), *Encyclopedia of Environmetrics*, vol. 3, Chichester: John Wiley & Sons, pp. 1796–1803.

Duranton, G. and Overman, H. G. (2005) 'Testing for localization using micro-geographic data', *Review of Economic Studies*, 72(4): 1077–1106.

EC – European Commission (2003) *Structure, Performance and Competitiveness of European Tourism and its Enterprises*, Luxembourg: Office for Official Publications of the European Communities.

Ellison, G. and Glaeser, E. (1999) 'The geographic concentration of an industry: Does natural advantage explain agglomeration?' *American Economic Association Papers and Proceedings*, 89(2): 311–16.

Estevão, C. and Ferreira, J. J. (2012) 'Tourism cluster positioning and performance evaluation: The case of Portugal', *Tourism Economics*, 18(4): 711–30.

Eurostat (2013) *Tourism Satellite Accounts (TSAs) in Europe*, Luxembourg: Eurostat.

Feser, E. J. and Sweeney, S. H. (2002) 'Theory, methods and cross-metropolitan comparison of business clustering', in P. McCann (ed.), *Industrial Location Economics*, Cheltenham, UK: Edward Elgar, pp. 229–59.

Funderburg, R. G. and Boarnet, M. G. (2008) 'Agglomeration potential: The spatial scale of industry linkages in the Southern California economy', *Growth and Change*, 39(1): 24–57.

González, S. (2011) 'Bilbao and Barcelona "in motion". How urban regeneration "models" travel and mutate in the global flows of policy tourism', *Urban Studies*, 48(7): 1397–1418.

Gordon, I. R. and McCann, P. (2000) 'Industrial clusters: Complexes, agglomeration and/ or social networks?', *Urban Studies*, 37(3): 513–32.

Hautdidier, B. (2011) 'Featured graphic: What's in a NUTS? Visualizing hierarchies of Europe's administrative/statistical regions', *Environment and Planning A*, 43(8): 1754–55.

Jackson J. and Murphy P. (2008) 'Clusters in regional tourism, An Australian Case', *Annals of Tourism Research*, 33(4): 1018–1035.

Jacquez, G. M. (2008) 'Spatial cluster analysis', in J.P. Wilson and A.S. Fotheringham (eds), *The Handbook of Geographic Information Science*, Oxford: Blackwell Publishing, pp. 395–416.

Judd, D. R. (1995) 'Promoting tourism in US cities', *Tourism Management*, 16(3): 175–87.

Kaae, B. C., Nielsen, T.S., Hasler, B. and Neye, S. (2007) *Sustainability Impact Assessment: Tools for Environmental, Social And Economic Effects of Multifunctional Land Use in European Regions*, part of EU SENSOR project, draft, November, EU.

Keeble, D. and Nachum, L. (2002) 'Why do business service firms cluster? Small consultancies, clustering and decentralisation in London and Southern England', *Transactions of the Institute of British Geographers*, 27(1): 1–24.

Ketels, C.H.M. (2003) *The Development of the Cluster Concept. Present Experiences and Recent Developments*, Ministry of Economic Affairs and Energy, Dusseldorf, North Rhine-Westphalia, Germany.

Ketels, C.H.M. (2011) 'Clusters and competitiveness: Porter's contribution', in R. Huggins and H. Izushi (eds), *Competition, Competitive Advantage and Clusters: The Ideas of Michael Porter*, Oxford: Oxford University Press, pp. 173–92.

Ketels, C.H.M. and Protsiv, S. (2014) *Methodology and Findings Report for a Cluster Mapping of Related Sectors*, European Cluster Observatory Report.

Lazzeretti, L. (ed.) (2013) *Creative Industries and Innovation in Europe*, London: Routledge.

Lazzeretti, L. and Capone, F. (2008) 'Mapping and analysing local tourism systems in Italy, 1991–2001', *Tourism Geographies*, 10(2): 214–32.

Lazzeretti, L. and Capone, F. (2009) 'Spatial spillovers and employment dynamics in local tourist systems in Italy (1991–2001)', *European Planning Studies*, 17(11): 1665–83.

Lazzeretti, L. and Petrillo, C. (eds) (2006) *Tourism Local Systems and Networking*, Amsterdam: Elsevier.

Lazzeretti, L., Boix, R. and Capone, F. (2008) 'Do creative industries cluster? Mapping creative local production systems in Italy and Spain', *Industry and Innovation*, 15(5): 549–67.

May, W., Mason, C. and Pinch, S. (2001) 'Explaining industrial agglomeration: The case of the British high-fidelity industry', *Geoforum*, 32(3): 363–76.

Michael, E. J. (2003) 'Tourism micro-cluster', *Tourism Economics*, 9(2): 133–46.

Nielsen, T. S. and Kaae, B. C. (2008) 'Tourism geography in Europe', in K. Helming, M. Pérez-Soba and P. Tabbush (eds), *Sustainability Impact Assessment of Land Use Changes*, Berlin-Heidelberg: Springer, pp. 181–209.

NIJ – National Institute of Justice (2004) *Crimestat III: A Spatial Statistics Program for the Analysis of Crime Incident Locations*, Washington, DC: The National Institute of Justice.

Nordin, S. (2003) *Tourism Clustering and Innovation*, Östersund, Sweden: Etour.

Novelli, M., Schmitz, B. and Spencer, T. (2006) 'Networks, clusters and innovation in tourism: A UK experience', *Tourism Management*, 27(6): 1141–52.

OECD – Organisation for Economic Co-operation and Development (2014) *Aid for Trade and Value Chains in Tourism*, Paris: OECD Publishing.

Openshaw, S., Charlton, M. and Craft, A. (1988) 'Searching for leukaemia clusters using a geographical analysis machine', *Papers of the Regional Science Association*, 64(1): 95–106.

Peiró-Signes, A., Segarra-Oña, M., Miret-Pastor, L. and Verma, R. (2015) 'The effect of tourism clusters on US hotel performance', *Cornell Hospitality Quarterly*, 56(2): 155–67.

Porter, M. E. (1998a) *On Competition*, Boston, MA: Harvard Business School Press.

Porter, M. E. (1998b) 'Cluster and the new economics of competition', *Harvard Business Review*, 76(6): 77–90.

Porter, M. E. (2003) 'The economic performance of regions', *Regional Studies*, 37(6–7): 549–78.

Rosenthal, S. and Strange, W. (2004) 'Evidence on the nature and sources of agglomeration economies', in J. V. Henderson and J. F. Thisse (eds), *Handbook of Regional and Urban Economics*, vol. 4, Amsterdam: Elsevier, pp. 2119–71.

Santos, C., Almeida, A. and Teixeira, A. (2008) *Searching for Clusters in Tourism. A Quantitative Methodological Proposal*, FEP Working Papers no. 293, Oporto University, Spain.

Scott, N., Cooper, C. and Baggio, R. (2008a) 'Destination networks. Theory and practice in four Australian cases', *Annals of Tourism Research*, 35(1): 169–88.

Scott, N., Cooper, C. and Baggio, R. (2008b) *Network Analysis and Tourism: From Theory to Practice*, Clevedon, UK: Channel View.

Segarra-Oña, M., Miret-Pastor, L.G., Peiró-Signes, A. and Verma, R. (2012) 'The effects of localization on economic performance: Analysis of Spanish tourism clusters', *European Planning Studies*, 20(8): 1319–34.

Sforzi, F. (ed.) (1997) *I sistemi locali in Italia*, Rome: ISTAT.

Sforzi, F. (2009) 'The empirical evidence of industrial districts in Italy', in G. Becattini, M. Bellandi and L. De Propris (eds), *A Handbook of Industrial Districts*, Cheltenham, UK: Edward Elgar, pp. 327–42.

Silverman, B. W. (1986) *Density Estimation for Statistics and Data Analysis*, New York: Chapman and Hall.

Sweeney, S. H. and Feser, E. J. (2003) 'Business location and spatial externalities: Tying concepts to measures business location and spatial externalities', in M. Goodchild and D. G. Janelle (eds), *Spatially Integrated Social Science: Examples in Best Practice*, Oxford: Oxford University Press.

Titze, M., Brachert, M. and Kubis, A. (2011) 'The identification of regional industrial clusters using qualitative input–output analysis (QIOA)', *Regional Studies*, 4(45): 89–102.

Trippl, M., Tödtling, F. and Schuldner, R. (2013) 'Creative and cultural industries in Austria', in L. Lazzeretti (ed.), *Creative Industries and Innovation in Europe*, London: Routledge, pp. 86–102.

United Nations (2008) *International Standard Industrial Classification of All Economic Activities. Revision 4*, New York: United Nations.

UNWTO – United Nations World Tourism Organization (2015) *Yearbook of Tourism Statistics*, Madrid: UNWTO.

Vladimirovna, R. N. (2014) 'Identification of tourist clusters in the Pribaikal Region', *International Journal of Econometrics and Financial Management*, 2(4): 163–67.

Vom Hofe, R. and Chen, K. (2006) 'Whither or not industrial cluster: Conclusions or confusions?', *The Industrial Geographer*, 4(1): 2–28.

Yang, Y. and Wong, K.K.F. (2013) 'Spatial distribution of tourist flows to China's cities', *Tourism Geographies*, 15(2): 338–63.

Part II

Tourist clusters and performance, creative and experience economy

5 Do tourist clusters boost hotels' performance?

Resilience in a crisis period in Italy

Francesco Capone

1 Introduction

The application of the cluster concept to the tourism industry has aroused much interest for a long time, initially from the analysis of competitiveness and to promote innovation and development. (Nordin 2003). Research literature reveals that cluster theory has been suitably adapted to the peculiarities of the tourism sector and provides a spatial and organisational model that promotes competitiveness, innovation and local development (Cooper 2006; Lazzeretti and Petrillo 2006; Novelli, Schmitz and Spencer 2006; Shaw and Williams 2009).

The concentration of firms in a territory as a determinant of enterprise competitiveness extended some time ago to the tourism industry (Novelli, Schmitz and Spencer 2006), cultural and creative industries, leading to the coining of terms such as *tourist cluster* and *district* (Getz 1993; Pearce 1998; Hjalager 2000; Maulet 2006; Lazzeretti and Capone 2008), *cultural cluster* and *district* (Lazzeretti 2003; Cinti 2008; Santagata 2002) and *creative cluster* (De Propris *et al.* 2009).

Literature on clusters, despite intense criticism (Martin and Sunley 2003), has widely recognised that the concentration of businesses in a specific area promotes the competitiveness of local enterprises and their innovation capabilities (Baptista 2000; Porter 2003; and others).

Despite the importance of the cluster concept in the field of tourism studies, because much literature has focused on the agglomeration of manufacturing firms in a territory, the effect of concentrations of tourist firms on their performances is often taken for granted, and only recently some contributions started to investigate the relation between agglomeration of tourist firms and their performances (Tsang and Yip 2009; Kukalis 2010; Sainaghi 2010; Peiró-Signes *et al.* 2015).

The aim of this research is to test and measure the effects of clustering in the tourism industry and establish whether tourist firms, in particular in the hotel industry, have a better performance if they are located inside a cluster, particularly in a crisis period. This work departs from a recent strand of research investigating the contribution of clusters to tourist firms' performances (Canina, Enz and Harrison 2005; Enz, Canina and Liu 2008; Bernini 2009; Bresciani, Thrassou and Vrontis 2012; Peiró-Signes *et al.* 2015) and contextualises it in the recent concept of resilience (Holling 1973; Simmie and Martin 2010; Martin, 2012;

Lazzeretti L. and Cooke P. 2015). This work aims to contribute to this debate by focusing on the hotel industry in Italy, as a country based on concentrations of small and medium-sized enterprises (SMEs) and a nation highly specialised in the tourism industry.

To investigate this aspect, we first proceed to map tourist clusters in the Italian territory using 2011 the Italian National Institute of Statistics (ISTAT) Census of Industry and Services and the methodology of location quotients (LQs), as applied by other contributions on the tourism industry (Capone and Boix 2008). We then analyse the economic performances (ROA, ROS, RevPAR, etc.) of more than 11,000 hotels located in the Italian territory over the last five years taken from the Aida and Amadeus (Bureau van Dijk) databases to verify whether their performances are affected by their location in the identified tourist cluster, its structural characteristics or recent economic trends.

The results allow us to show that hotels within tourist clusters have a greater resilience than isolated firms and have registered significantly better performances in the last five years than those located outside the clusters. However, results significantly change depending on the type of tourist cluster and the characteristics of the hotel.

2 Tourist clusters, resilience and firm performances: focus on the hotel industry

The growing interest in industrial clusters began with the studies carried out by Porter (1998) and later widened to a world level. Porter (1998) pointed out that in a globalised economy, competitive advantages are increasingly associated with local, territorially embedded economies. He defined a cluster as a geographic concentration of interconnected companies and institutions in a particular field. The European Community (EC 2003) adopted this viewpoint, stressing that clusters can be important for policies supporting innovation and that attention should be given to the relationships and interdependencies among actors in the production value chain of goods and services.

The intuition that similar or complementary economic activities tend to concentrate in one area can be traced back to the seminal work of Marshall and his formulation of external economies of localisation (Becattini, Bellandi and De Propris 2009). It is widely recognised that geographical clustering results in enhanced returns and growth for local firms (Tallman *et al.* 2004). In this literature, it is possible to recognise three different forms of external economies (Tallman *et al.* 2004): qualified labour pools, specialised suppliers and knowledge spillovers.[1]

Also Porter pointed out that:

> a host of linkages among cluster members result in a whole greater than the sum of its part. In a typical tourism cluster, for example, the quality of a visitor's experience depends not only on the appeal of the primary attraction but also on the quality and efficiency of complementary businesses such as hotels, restaurants, shopping outlets and transportation facilities. Because

members of the cluster are mutually dependent, good performance by one can boost the success of the others.

(Porter 1998: 77)

Most researchers hypothesizes that tourist clusters improve firms' competitiveness (Lazzeretti and Petrillo 2006; Cristina, Ferreira and Vitor 2010). Despite the relevance of the cluster concept in tourism studies, the impact of the agglomeration on the performance of tourist firms is often taken for granted.

Other researchers interpreted the cluster concept as a means of developing the tourism industry, with a particular emphasis on developing countries (Nordin 2003; Cunha and Cunha 2005; Feng and Chang 2009); Kim and Wicks (2010) propose a competitiveness cluster model in a global value chain perspective. Others (Novelli, Schmitz and Spencer 2006) focused more on specific case studies, such as the healthy lifestyle tourist cluster in the UK, on which they investigated the concepts of cluster, network and tourism business innovation, or the South Carolina tourist cluster (Flowers and Easterling 2006).

Despite the wide use of the cluster concept in the tourism industry (Cristina, Ferreira and Vitor 2010), few quantitative studies exist on the effects of the cluster on tourist firms (Brouder and Eriksson 2013).

A series of seminal contributions on the localisation effect on hotels is one of Baum and collaborators, which analyses the Manhattan hotel industry in the USA. Baum and Mezias (1992) found that a hotel's competitors and customers are partly determined by the hotel's location, while Baum and Haveman (1997) found some results in other enlarged contexts. Ingram and Baum (1997) analysed the failures of Manhattan hotels between 1898 and 1980, underlining that chain affiliation aids survival in longitudinal hotel failures and that the size of the hotel matters. Ingram and Inman (1996) analysed hotels at Niagara Falls, focusing on the evolution of hotel populations, failures and foundings of the new hotels. The authors underlined that when institutions promote collaborations with other hotels, failures decline. Ingram (1996) analysed USA hotel chains' strategies and failures between 1896 and 1980, increasingly underlining the role of chain and affiliation strategies. More recently, Ingram and Roberts (2000) surveyed the Sydney hotel industry focusing on friendship networks and performances.

Chung and Kalnins (2001) analysed the population of hotels and motels operating in Texas in 1992 and found that independent and smaller hotels gain the most from a central localisation, while smaller establishments are harmed. Kuah (2002) reviewed the advantages of locating small businesses in a tourist cluster, while Michael (2003) pointed out that in Australia, the rural towns' micro-market clustering theory offers one alternative for enhancing local economic growth.

Enz, Canina and Liu (2008) analysed the competitive dynamics and pricing behaviour of the USA hotel industry, identifying strategies of co-location in geographical clusters and finding that the benefits of co-location are higher for low-quality hotels than for luxury ones. Canina, Enz and Harrison (2005) focused on the agglomeration effects in the USA lodging industry, and later (Enz and Canina 2010; Enz, Canina and van der Rest 2015) investigated the European hotel industry and its performances (RevPAR) at the country level, while Capone and Boix (2008) found that a higher concentration of hotels in a territory leads to increased growth in the tourism industry.

Sainaghi (2011) analysed the hotel industry in Milan, identifying the most important performance determinant in the centrality within the destination. Focusing on performance determinants, Tsang and Yip (2009) analysed Beijing, and Urtasun and Gutierrez (2006) analysed Madrid from 1936–98. The studies underlined that results change according to the hotel location, but they also depend on the size and quality of the firm.

Many studies focus on innovation as an effect of localisation in tourist clusters (Hjalager 2000); Jackson (2006) confirmed this aspect in China's tourist clusters. Other studies verify that tourist clusters are important for local economic development (Iordache, Ciochina and Asandei 2010). Shaw and Williams (2009) reviewed the importance of the role of cluster in knowledge transfer. Weidenfeld, Williams and Butler (2010), examining the tourist attractions in Cornwall, underlined that knowledge transfer and innovation diffusion are more common among firms that offer a similar product and are located far apart geographically.

Another group of studies dealt with cluster mapping and identification, using qualitative and quantitative methodologies (Santos, Almeida and Teixeira 2008). Even though some studies applied the concepts of industrial district systems to tourism (Hjalager 2000) or local tourism systems (Lazzeretti and Capone 2008), quantitative methodologies identified tourism agglomerations with LQs. Scott, Cooper and Baggio (2008) proposed a method for mapping tourist destinations and clusters using social network analysis, while Yang and Wong (2013) identified Chinese tourist cities using exploratory techniques to map clusters, employing tourist flows and spatial analysis.

Few studies have analysed the contribution of clusters in a period of crisis considering the emerging strand of the *resilience* concept (Lazzeretti and Capone, 2015). In his seminal contribution, Holling (1973) explains the concepts of 'engineering resilience', defined as the resistance to disturbance and the speed to return to the pre-existing equilibrium, and of 'ecological resilience', defined as a system's capacity to face disturbances and shocks, and to move into another regime of behaviour. Cioccio and Michael (2007) discuss the ability of local communities and tourist businesses to manage and recover from natural disasters, while Luthe and Wyss (2014) deal with tourism governance and resilience with regard to interrelated impacts of global environmental change. Anyhow, to our knowledge there are no quantitative studies in tourism on the concept of resilience. Resilience as a concept has much explanatory power that requires more attention in tourism research, both from a quantitative network governance and a more qualitatively informed research perspective (Luthe and Wyss 2014).

Several studies have identified the important role of the cluster concept for the overall competitiveness of tourism businesses, but few studies have focused on a crisis period. This work tries to test also the ability of hotels to respond to the overall crisis. In the presented literature, it is possible to identify some main research strands.

A line of research at the intra-regional level analysed central vs peripheral locations in a metropolis, for example with Baum and Mezias (1992), Chung and Kalnins (2001), Sainaghi (2010; 2011), leading to a stream of research on hotels' location strategies.

Other researchers analysed the effect of the cluster on specific cases to identify the contribution of concentration to innovation (Hjalager 2010; Nordin 2003), dissemination of knowledge (Shaw and Williams 2009) and competitiveness (Weidenfeld, Williams and Butler 2010).

The quantitative research focused more on analysing how the performances of tourist firms change, particularly that of hotels, such as in Enz and collaborators (Canina, Enz and Harrison 2005; Enz, Canina and Liu 2008) and Segarra-Oña *et al.* (2012), which investigated different performances of hotels based on their location in geographical clusters.

We identified some common determinants that provoke different performances at the firm level, which will be useful in the empirical part of this work:

1   The size of the hotel, its quality (in stars) and its possible affiliations to well-known, international chains sometimes change the consequences of location because large firms may in some cases be equally competitive in a poor cluster, whereas small firms fail to compensate for the deficiencies of the system alone (Canina, Enz and Harrison 2005; Enz, Canina and Liu 2008).
2   Depending on the analysed segments of tourism and the type of tourist clusters in which firms are located, the results differ depending on their location. For example, the role of the local system is crucial in urban tourism, while in rural tourism other variables come into play (Segarra-Oña *et al.* 2012).
3   The structure of the local system where the firm is located and whether the local system can reconstruct autonomously affect the ability of a whole tourism value chain to satisfy visitors (Capone and Boix 2008).
4   The life cycle of the cluster (Butler 1980; Getz 1992; and others) in which the hotel is located can affect firm performance; for example, a firm may be located in a highly concentrated cluster, but if the destination is in a cycle of decline, the firm's performance will not improve.

3 Research methodology

To verify the hypotheses proposed earlier in this chapter, we need to first identify tourist clusters in the Italian territory, then propose a methodology to map a tourist cluster using a tourism *filière* and finally analyse the different economic performances of hotels on the basis of their locations along a time period. Subsection 3.1 will deal with the first issue, and 3.2 with the second one.

3.1 Identification of geographical clusters

The concentrations of the tourism industry at national level can be examined using simple industry-specialisation statistics (such as the concentration index and the

Gini index) or more sophisticated measures (Ellison and Glaeser 1997). However, these statistics are non-spatial and only rely on the industrial dimension, so that they do not provide information about the place where an industry is concentrated. The territorial dimension is taken into account by territorial indices of specialisation or clustering, where a wide range of methodologies are available (Vom Hofe and Chen 2006).

Our choice is to identify tourist clusters using the LQ mapping methodology as it has been widely applied in several different contexts and countries (Porter 2003; De Propris *et al.* 2009) and also to the tourism industry (Capone and Boix 2008). The 'clustering' is usually calculated through LQs. The LQ measures whether a territory (city, region, etc.) presents a higher concentration of a particular industry in comparison to the national average. In other words, it reveals whether a place is specialised in the selected industry.[2]

We must then define which economic activities to include in the 'tourism industry'. The tourism industry is generally considered as comprising a number of various activities such as recreation, accommodation, tour operators and transport activities. In other studies (Lazzeretti and Capone 2008), the tourism industry was analysed as being mainly composed of the activities in the hotel, restaurant and café (HoReCa) sector – and represented by HoReCa employees. A wider set of economic activities has been included in other contributions (Segarra-Oña *et al.* 2012) as there is no formal consensus in defining tourism statistically.

We refer here to the contribution by the European Commission (EC 2003) introducing a model of competitiveness for the tourism sector which includes transport, accommodation, restaurant and other food facilities and recreational activities. Therefore we collected data on Hotels and other accommodation; Restaurants, bars and catering; Travel agencies and tour operators; and Art, entertainment and recreation activities. The NACE Rev. 2 economic activities selected are presented in Table 5.1.

Therefore, in order to identify tourist clusters, we apply to the Italian local labour systems (LLSs) the concentration index, constructed in its classical form:

$$LQ_{fs} = \frac{E_{fs} / E_s}{E_f / E}$$

where E_{fs} is the number of employees in local units in the local system s specialising in the *tourism filière*; E_s is the number of employees in local units in the local system s; E_f is the number of employees in the country specialising in the *tourism filière*; and E is the total employment in the country. An LQ above 1 indicates that the place has a specialisation (concentration) in tourism activities that is above the national average. Data were collected from the 2011 Italian Census of Industry and Services at a three-digit level.

Regarding the territorial dimension, we use LLSs which interpret the daily work commuting flows of a locality. The use of LLSs for territorial analysis has two main advantages, as they allow to go beyond the administrative definitions and refer to the actual industrial organisation of each territory; also, LLSs are

Table 5.1 Tourism *filière* per NACE economic activities

Accommodation	Libraries, archives, museums and cultural activities
55.1 Hotels and similar accommodation 55.2 Holiday and other short-stay accommodation 55.3 Camping grounds, recreational vehicle parks and trailer parks 55.9 Other accommodation	91.01 Library and archives activities 91.02 Museums activities 91.03 Operation of historical sites and buildings and similar visitor attractions 91.04 Botanical and zoological gardens and nature reserves activities
Restaurant and food/beverage service activities	*Sports activities and amusement and recreation activities*
56.1 Restaurants and mobile food service activities 56.2 Event catering and other food service activities 56.3 Beverage serving activities	93.1 Sports activities 93.2 Amusement and recreation activities
Creative, arts and entertainment activities	*Travel agencies and tour operators*
90.01 Performing arts 90.02 Support activities to performing arts 90.03 Artistic creation 90.04 Operation of arts facilities	79.1 Travel agency and tour operator activities 79.9 Other reservation service and related activities

Source: Our elaboration from EC (2003).

territorial units more suitable for socio-economic analysis, and refer to the intensity of links between the residents and the labour force in a given place.

4 Tourist clusters in Italy

There are 214 tourist clusters with an LQ larger than 1. For a better representation of LQs, data in Figure 5.1 are represented in four classes: no specialisation, low, medium and high specialisation.

The highest values are concentrated in the north (Trentino and Alto Adige) and centre of Italy (Liguria, Toscana and Lazio). The figure also shows art cities like Florence, Rome and Venice, places specialising in the three Ss (Sun, Sand and Sea), skiing destinations (the Alps, in particular Trentino-Alto Adige), and lake localities (such as the Lake Garda area). Also south localities as Capri and Amalfi are well represented, as well as island tourist destinations.

The total employees of the *filière* add up to 2.4 million (14.7% of the employment in Italy), in line with other estimations of the industry in 2001. Employment in the tourist clusters accounts for around 7.6 million employees, where 1.4 million are in the selected tourism activities (18.6% of their total employment). In the tourist clusters, the average firm size is around eight employees per firm, and 90% of the firms have less than 20 employees, confirming an industrial structure mainly based on SMEs.

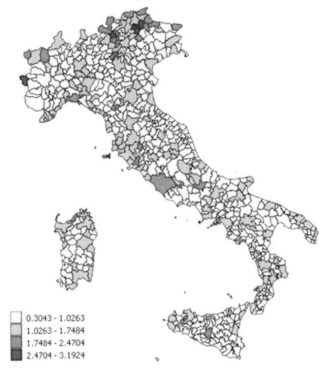

Figure 5.1 Tourist clusters in Italy, 2011

Source: Our elaboration.

5 Analysis of hotels' performance

5.1 Research design and methodology

To validate the previous hypothesis, a sample is analysed comprising a total of 11,759 hotels in Italy, taken from the 2013 Aida database (Bureau van Dijk) for the period of 2008–12. The analysed sample represents around 48% of the total hotel population in Italy, which in the 2011 ISTAT Census of Industry and Services amounts to 24,381.

Of the hotels under analysis, 7,197 are located outside the identified tourist clusters, while 1,451 are located in highly specialised clusters, 1,330 in medium-specialised clusters, and 1,785 in low-concentrated clusters, as defined in the previous sections according to the LQ concentrations.

Moreover, as different hotel characteristics could lead to different results, a variable *size* is also considered in order to take into account the dimension of the hotel and therefore the overall quality of the analysed sample.[3] The 'micro' hotels are those with less than 10 employees and they represents 66% of the sample (7,000), 'small' hotels are those with less than 50 employees and they are 33% of the sample (over 3,000), 'medium hotels' are those with less than 100 employees and they are 3% (over 200), while large hotels employ more than 100 employees and represent 2% of the sample (115).

Finally, in order to take into account different typologies of tourist clusters and eventually diverse tourism segments, we adopt the ISTAT taxonomy that divides the Italian territory on the basis of its main specialisation, i.e. urban systems, tourism systems, agricultural systems, port and shipbuilding systems, industrial districts and large enterprises systems (ISTAT 2006). This helps to differentiate the analysis and consider the impact of different characteristics of clusters on hotel performances, i.e. that clusters localised in urban systems could boost more hotel performances than in other systems.

In the second part of the study, an Analysis of Variance (ANOVA) was performed. The analysis compares whether the performances of hotels located inside clusters significantly differ from the values achieved by hotels located outside clusters, as already done in other contributions (Peiró-Signes *et al.* 2015).

The ANOVA analysis specifies whether the null hypothesis indicating the equality of the means for a given level of significance should be accepted or rejected. In other words, it is an attempt to verify whether the means of the variables analysed are significantly different between the groups analysed.

Usually revenue per room (RevPAR) is the most used proxy to investigate hotel profitability (Chung and Kalnins 2001; Canina, Enz and Harrison 2005), but as the RevPAr is not available in the database, we decided to use traditional profitability variables as also accepted in other contributions (Kukalis 2010).[4]

Return on sales (ROS) together with earnings before interest, taxes, depreciation and amortisation (EBITDA) per employee was chosen as the variable to be used to measure 'profitability', since it is considered to be one of the most reliable and popular indicators for measuring and comparing financial profit (Segarra-Oña *et al.* 2012). All the variables regard a period of five years (2008–12). Also EBITDA/sales and a variable *size* have been considered in order to eliminate any correlation existing among size and economic results.

5.2 Results and discussion

First of all, we investigate the results of the analysis, presenting the evolution of about 11,000 hotel performances subdivided on the basis of localisation, whether inside or outside clusters. Figure 5.2 presents the average ROS from 2008–12 for the 11,000 analysed hotels. The hotels localised in the most specialised clusters (high and medium concentrations) demonstrate a relevant higher profitability during the whole period. In fact, the ROS goes from an average of 2% in 2008 to a 1.5% in 2012, remaining positive despite the crisis. Instead, the hotels located outside the cluster have recorded a negative ROS since 2009 and the trend worsens more and more. The hotels in clusters with low specialisation defend themselves better, but they also register a negative ROS in 2012. Similar results are also found using other indices of performances, such as earnings before interest, taxes and amortisation (EBITA), EBITDA/sales and return on investment (ROI), etc.

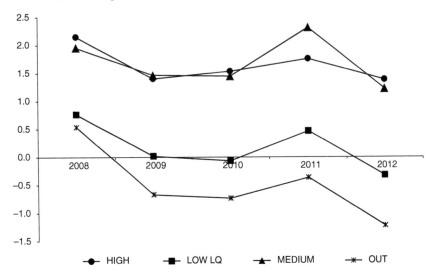

Figure 5.2 Hotel performances per cluster concentration, ROS mean, 2008–12

Source: Our elaboration.

We now analyse the hotel performances based on location as from the taxonomy of local systems as proposed by ISTAT (2006) (Figure 5.3). As expected, the hotels located in the tourism systems registered better performances than others. The other local systems have similar performances and it is difficult to identify some particular trends. The hotels located in urban systems have better performances than the others, while from 2010 onwards hotels located in low-specialised systems record better results. This could be due to the fact that systems with low specialisation in manufacturing have a better relationship with the environment and the territory, like the ones diffused in the south of Italy.

It is then also possible to analyse the hotels' performances depending on their dimension. Figure 5.4 presents the hotels' performances per firm size. The overall trend is declining, however the medium and small hotels, on average, have better performances, while large ones record the worst performances with a sharp decline from 2008–12. Micro-hotels, which are the vast majority, stand in the middle.

Tables 5.2–5.5 present the results of the ANOVA. The analysis of ROS, subdivided per different types of clusters, is significant for all the considered years (Table 5.2). The ROS of hotels localised in clusters with high and medium concentration is similar (in 2012, the latter had a little lower performance). The ROS of the hotels in clusters with low concentration has been around zero in recent years (between -0.3 and +0.4 in the period of 2009–12), while it is negative for the hotels outside the identified tourist clusters (from -0.3 in 2011 up to -1.2 in 2012). The same results emerge from the comparison of performances between the ROS of hotels localised in clusters with high concentration and those outside, but here

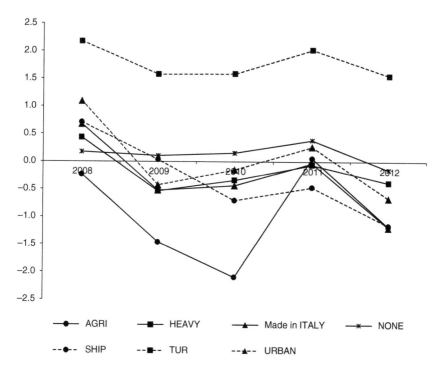

Figure 5.3 Hotel performances per typology of destinations, ROS mean, 2008–12
Source: Our elaboration.

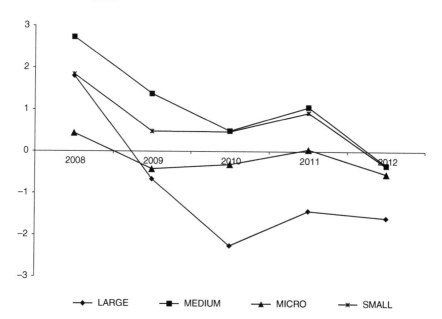

Figure 5.4 Hotel performances per firm size, ROS mean, 2008–12
Source: Our elaboration.

Table 5.2 ANOVA on ROS per cluster concentration (LQ)

Concentration	ROS					Observations
	2012	2011	2010	2009	2008	
High	1.3826	1.7567	1.4020	1.5342	2.1501	1,451
Medium	1.2212	2.3138	1.4633	1.4447	1.9554	1,330
Low	−0.3239	0.4648	0.0176	−0.0665	0.7641	1,785
Outside	−1.2256	−0.3668	−0.6690	−0.7323	0.5388	7,197
Test F	*29.272****	*27.154****	*22.147****	*25.363****	*14.944****	–
High	1.3826	1.7567	1.4020	1.5342	2.1501	1,451
Outside	−1.2256	−0.3668	−0.6690	−0.7323	0.5388	7,197
Test F	*2.268*	*3.439**	*3.864**	*0.928*	*21.734****	–

Source: Our elaboration.

Notes: * $p < 0.1$; *** $p < 0.001$.

Table 5.3 ANOVA on EBITDA on sales per cluster concentration (LQ)

Concentration	EBITDA on sales					Observations
	2012	2011	2010	2009	2008	
High LQ	8.9697	9.9194	10.6554	10.0734	10.1256	1,451
Outside	−3.0498	1.0136	2.3431	1.8288	4.0131	7,197
Test F	*14.487****	*3.108**	*2.009*	*0.659*	*0.076*	–

Source: Our elaboration.

Notes: * $p < 0.1$; *** $p < 0.001$.

Table 5.4 ANOVA on ROS per size of hotel

Size	ROS					Observations
	2012	2011	2010	2009	2008	
Large	−1.5944	−1.4280	−2.2552	−0.6622	1.8002	116
Medium	−0.3377	1.0584	0.4892	1.3775	2.7298	246
Small	−0.3608	0.9238	0.4731	0.4771	1.8389	3,658
Micro	−0.5400	0.0442	−0.3090	−0.4196	0.4334	7,743
Total	−0.4904	0.3244	−0.0683	−0.1055	0.9319	11,763
Test F	*0.512*	*5.559***	*5.352***	*6.565***	*18.476****	–

Source: Our elaboration.

Notes: ** $p < 0.01$; *** $p < 0.001$.

the significance is not valid for all years (see for instance 2008, 2010 and 2011). The analysis of EBITDA and EBITD/sales has similar trends (Table 5.3).

The analysis of performances based on the *size* variable confirms previous evidences (Table 5.4). Hotels localised in small and medium-sized firms have the best results, particularly in recent years, although the analysis for 2012 is not

Table 5.5 ANOVA on ROS per typology of destination

Typology	ROS					Observations
	2012	2011	2010	2009	2008	
Agriculture	−1.1830	0.0565	−2.0963	−1.4649	0.2333	186
Touristic	1.5528	2.0213	1.5871	1.5784	2.1735	1,521
Industrial district	−1.1942	−0.0339	−0.4361	−0.5216	0.6744	2,619
Heavy industry	0.3864	−0.0608	−0.3398	−0.5365	0.4328	873
Urban systems	−0.6676	0.265	−0.1488	−0.4268	1.0946	3,997
Shipbuilding industry	−1.1594	−0.4697	−0.7060	0.355	0.7093	1,374
Test F	*9.736****	*6.6632****	*7.487****	*7.348****	*6.103****	–

Source: Our elaboration.

Note: *** $p < 0.001$.

significant. Regarding the typology of local systems by ISTAT, we found that tourist local systems record the best performances followed by urban systems all along the period (Table 5.5).

Finally, we carried out an ordinary least-squares (OLS) regression analysis with dummy variables in order to isolate the effects of localisation in clusters with different levels of concentration (high, medium, low, outside), dimensions of hotels (micro, small, medium and large) and types of local systems.

ROS and EBITDA/sales are the dependent variables of the models. The results of the analysis are presented in Table 5.6. As variables are dummies, the coefficient estimates can be interpreted as direct predictors of performances.[5]

The performances of the hotels are substantially better in the higher concentrated clusters, confirming previous analyses. These are twice as high in the tourist clusters with medium and high concentration of Model 1, as compared to the hotels outside the cluster. The hotels localised in low-concentrated clusters record a differential of 0.9 greater than those localised outside. The difference of performance in being in the most concentrated clusters rather than outside amounts to about 2%. The ROS of hotels localised in clusters with high concentration is twice that of hotels localised in low-concentrated clusters.

The estimations on *size* are not significant, only the size 'small' is statistically significant and indicates a better performance of small hotels than others, in particular of micro-hotels. We remind that this is also the most numerous group and therefore more statistically significant.

The result of the analysis of various typologies of local systems is partly significant. Only the tourism systems confirm the results of the previous section. Urban systems record a positive contribution to performances. Even port and shipbuilding systems record a positive value, probably identifying sun and sea destinations.

Finally, the performance of the hotels identified are different depending on their size. There are in fact hotels of small and medium-sized dimension that benefit from being located in clusters, which underlines the importance of the cluster to external economies of small SMEs.

Table 5.6 OLS estimations

Dependent variable		Model 1 (ROS 2012)			Model 2 (EBITDA on sales)			Model 3 (ROS 2012)			
Constant		-1.226*** (0.000)	-1.199*** (0.000)	-1.372*** (0.000)	-3.050*** (0.000)	-4.882*** (0.000)	-5.878*** (0.000)	0.668*** (0.000)	0.336 (0.123)	0.308 (0.698)	0.080 (0.922)
Outside								-1.894*** (0.000)	-1.561*** (0.000)	-1.558*** (0.000)	-1.492*** (0.000)
Concentration	High	2.608*** (0.000)	2.617*** (0.000)	1.735** (0.000)	12.020*** (0.000)	11.267*** (0.000)	9.172* (0.037)		1.047** (0.007)	1.055** (0.006)	-0.191 (0.787)
	Medium	2.446*** (0.000)	2.313*** (0.000)		10.344*** (0.000)	9.766*** (0.000)	9.538*** (0.000)				
	Low	0.902** (0.005)	0.900** (0.005)	0.934** (0.000)	4.553*** (0.017)	4.322* (0.023)	4.167* (0.032)				
Hotel size	Micro									0.043 (0.956)	0.042 (0.957)
	Small			-0.054 (0.826)		5.909*** (0.000)	5.772*** (0.000)			0.021 (0.979)	0.014 (0.986)
	Medium			-0.002 (0.998)		4.562 (0.328)	4.252 (0.362)				
	Large			-1.085 (0.341)		9.334 (0.165)	8.592 (0.203)			-1.027 (0.453)	-1.054 (0.441)
Typology of destinations	Urban			0.210 (0.443)			2.230 (0.169)				0.187 (0.495)
	Tourist			1.159 (0.107)			3.472 (0.415)				1.623* (0.021)

	(1)	(2)	(3)	(4)	(5)	(6)	(7)	(8)	(9)	(10)
Shipbuilding			0.183 (0.637)							0.146 (0.707)
Industrial district						2.351 (0.306)				
Heavy industry			0.664 (0.146)			-1.628 (0.547)				0.728 (0.111)
R^2	0.086	0.087	0.089	0.065	0.076	0.078	0.076	0.080	0.080	0.084
R^2 adj.	0.007	007	0.008	0.004	0.005	0.005	0.006	0.006	0.006	0.006
Test F	29.272***	14.781***	9.315***	16.584***	11.328***	7.198***	67.984***	37.691***	15.252***	9.307***
Obs.	11,763	11,763	11,763	11,763	11,763	11,763	11,763	11,763	11,763	11,763

Source: Our elaboration.

Notes: * p < 0.1; ** p < 0.01; *** p < 0.001.

The large hotels record a positive, but smaller effect on performance. They are the only ones who show less negative performances even in low-concentrated clusters, confirming that, from a certain point of view, big facilities can avoid being in a cluster, but their performances still benefit if they are localised inside clusters. Hotels outside clusters record the worst performances, but large hotels suffer the most, confirming the notion that the experience of tourists is a complex product and therefore customer satisfaction also depends on the quality of the tourism industry at local level.

Finally, we have also tested whether the life-cycle phase of the cluster[6] explains why some hotels perform better than others, but the results for the different phases of the cluster life cycle are not statistically significant.

6 Conclusions and implications

The purpose of this research was to assess and measure the contribution of the cluster to the tourism industry performances, with a specific case study on the hotel sector in Italy, in the crisis period.

The hotels located in the identified tourist clusters show better performances and a better ability to face the crisis than the hotels outside the cluster. The performances also depend on other variables. The main drivers are the quality and size of the hotels and the typology of the tourist cluster in which the firms are located.

These are some of the main implications arising from the study. Large firms demonstrate a better ability to face the crisis in low-concentrated clusters, but they also benefit from a location in high-concentrated clusters and, at the same time, they record bad performances out of the cluster. This shows that even large companies are dependent on others and on the local tourism system, in fact they can only partially overcome the shortage of the local tourist supply.

Small and medium-sized businesses, which are the majority of the sample, show the most location-dependent performance. This highlights even more that being in a competitive cluster is fundamental for SMEs. This result is true even for small facilities located in urban clusters that gain the greatest benefits from their location in a cluster.

The clustering process emerges as an important determinant of the hotel performance and the localisation is confirmed as an important strategy for the hotel, not only in terms of proximity to natural resources and artistic heritage, but also because of the externalities achievable in the destination or cluster. It is confirmed that visitors' satisfaction is closely linked to the local industries and businesses – composing the overall visitors' experience – and the competitiveness of destinations necessarily goes through the management and configuration of the local tourist supply. In this context, local governance receives an increasing importance as it has the task of matching the configuration of the local tourist offer (the various multi-sectoral local businesses) with the demand (the visitors). Local governance should then be planned at cluster level in a multi-industry perspective in order to consider the several different businesses that compose the local system.

Referring then to the limitations of the study, one of main constraint is not to consider local resources. In this context, the artistic, cultural and environmental heritage is considered in literature as a crucial driver to generate and increase the competitiveness of a tourist destination or cluster, but this is more than empirically demonstrated.[7] It would be interesting to analyse and measure whether and how hotel performances depend also on the presence of an important endowment of artistic and cultural resources (e.g. using the ranking of Italian sites developed by UNESCO).

Another future development would be to analyse other tourist firms (for instance transport and travel agencies), given that clusters are composed of an integrated *filière* of different industries and most of the existing studies have focused only on the hotel industry. One last consideration regards the cluster life-cycle model and the effect of the economic recession on the data under study. In this work, the cluster life-cycle model is not particularly significant, and this should also influence the capacity of resilience of tourist firms. As to the period of analysis, this research investigates only five years, while in the resilience approach a longer period of time is usually analysed in order to grasp the capacity to face the crisis.

Despite its limitations, this study adds new knowledge to the application of the cluster concept to the tourism industry in a crisis period. However, further quantitative researches are needed to investigate the complex phenomenon.

Notes

The author expresses his gratitude to Rafael Boix for his advice and comments on this chapter.

1   The concentration of a certain industry in a particular territory allows the formation of a specialised labour pool, also thanks to knowledge diffusion in the territory. Second, being part of a cluster allows to turn to specialised suppliers who are geographically near, so that transportation as well as supervision and transaction costs are reduced, and face-to-face contacts intensified. Finally, clustering produces knowledge spillovers, i.e. a faster and cheaper spread of knowledge due to geographical proximity, more frequent contacts and the building of trust among operators, who develop a symbolic capital in reputation.
2   A faultless index for analysing concentrations in the territory does not exist, however the LQ is one of the most used and supported.
3   In this context, it could be useful to consider the hotel's stars, but unfortunately this variable was not available.
4   See Chen, Koh and Lee (2011) for a comparison of RevPAR, ROA and EPS.
5   The coefficient estimates can be interpreted as direct contributions of the performances in comparison to the omitted dummy variable. In order to interpret the results regarding the overall mean, it is better to use a fixed-effects model.
6   We have considered here the trend of occupation from 2008–11 in the cluster considering several phases, including: development, when employment increases at a high rate, maturity, with no or low employment growth, and decline.
7   See Chapter 3 for a preliminary analysis of this topic.

References

Baptista, R. (2000) 'Do innovations diffuse faster within geographical clusters?' *International Journal of Industrial Organization*, 18(3): 515–35.

Baum, J. and Haveman, H. (1997) 'Love thy neighbor? Differentiation and agglomeration in the Manhattan hotel industry, 1898–1990', *Administrative Science Quarterly*, 42(2): 304–39.

Baum, J. and Mezias, S. (1992) 'Localized competition and organizational failure in the Manhattan hotel industry, 1898–1990', *Administrative Science Quarterly* 37(4): 580–604.

Becattini, G., Bellandi, M. and De Propris, L. (eds) (2009) *Handbook of Industrial Districts*, Cheltenham, UK: Edward Elgar.

Bernini, C. (2009) 'Convention industry and destination clusters: Evidence from Italy', *Tourism Management*, 30(6): 878–89.

Bresciani, S., Thrassou, A. and Vrontis, D. (2012) 'The determinants of performance in the Italian hotel industry. An empirical analysis', in *Proceeding of the 5th Annual EuroMed Conference of the EuroMed Academy of Business*, EuroMed Press, pp. 191–202.

Brouder, P. and Eriksson, R. (2013) 'Tourism evolution: On the synergies of tourism studies and evolutionary economic geography', *Annals of Tourism Research*, 43(October): 370–89.

Butler, R.W. (1980) 'The concept of a tourist area cycle of evolution: Implications for management of resources', *Canadian Geographer*, 24(1): 5–12.

Canina, L., Enz, C.A. and Harrison, J. (2005) 'Agglomeration effects and strategic orientations: Evidence from the US lodging industry', *Academy of Management Journal*, 48(4): 565–81.

Capone, F. and Boix, R. (2008) 'Sources of growth and competitiveness of local tourist production systems: An application to Italy (1991–2001)', *The Annals of Regional Science*, 42(1): 209–24.

Chen, J., Koh, Y. and Lee, S. (2011) 'Does the market care about RevPAR? A case study of five large US lodging chains', *Journal of Hospitality & Tourism Research*, 35(2): 258–73.

Chung, W. and Kalnins, A. (2001) 'Agglomeration effects and performance: A test of the Texas lodging industry', *Strategic Management Journal*, 22(10): 969–88.

Cinti T., (2008) 'Cultural clusters and districts: the state of art', in P. Cooke and L. Lazzeretti, (2008) (eds), *Creative cities, cultural clusters and local economic development*, Cheltenham: Edward Elgar.

Cioccio, I. and Michael, E. J. (2007) 'Hazard or disaster: Tourism management for the inevitable in Northeast Victoria', *Tourism Management*, 28(1): 1–11.

Cooper, C. (2006) 'Knowledge management and tourism', *Annals of Tourism Research*, 33(1): 47–64.

Cristina, E., Ferreira, J. and Vitor, B. (2010) 'Entrepreneurial strategies within the tourism cluster of Serra da Estrela: Implications for regional competitiveness', *Advances in Management*, 3(6): 55–65.

Cunha, S. K. and Cunha, J. C. (2005) 'Tourism cluster competitiveness and sustainability: Proposal for a systemic model to measure the impact of tourism on local development', *Brazilian Administration Review*, 2(2): 47–62.

De Propris, L., Chapain, C., Cooke, P., MacNeill, S. and Mateos-Garcia, J. (2009) *The Geography of Creativity*, London: NESTA.

EC – European Commission (2003) *Structure, Performance and Competitiveness of European Tourism and its Enterprises*, Luxembourg: Office for Official Publications of the European Communities.

Ellison, G. and Glaeser, E. (1997) 'Geographic concentration in US manufacturing industries: A dartboard approach', *Journal of Political Economy*, 105(5): 889–926.

Enz, C. A. and Canina, L. (2010) 'Competitive pricing in European hotels', in J. S. Chen (ed.), *Advances in Hospitality and Leisure*, vol. 6, Oxford, UK: Elsevier, pp. 3–25.

Enz, C., Canina, L. and Liu, Z. (2008) 'Competitive dynamics and pricing behavior in US hotels: The role of co-location', *Scandinavian Journal of Hospitality and Tourism*, 8(3): 230–50.

Enz, C. A., Canina, L. and Van der Rest, J.-P. (2015) 'Competitive hotel pricing in Europe: An exploration of strategic positioning', *Cornell Hospitality Reports*, 15(2): 6–16.

Feng, W. and Chang, M. H. (2009) 'A review of researches on tourism cluster at home and abroad', *Human Geography*, 2(1): 16–21.

Flowers, J. and Easterling, K. (2006): 'Growing South Carolina's tourism cluster', *Business and Economic Review*, 52(3): 15–20.

Getz, D. (1992) 'Tourism planning and destination life cycle', *Annals of Tourism Research*, 19(4): 752–70.

Getz, D. (1993) 'Planning for tourism business districts', *Annals of Tourism Research*, 20(3): 583–600.

Hjalager, A. (2000) 'Tourism destinations and the concept of industrial districts', *Tourism and Hospitality Research*, 2(3): 199–213.

Hjalager, A. (2010) 'A review of innovation research on tourism', *Tourism Management*, 31(1): 1–12.

Holling, C. S. (1973) 'Resilience and stability of ecological systems', *Annual Review of Ecological Systems*, 4: 1–23.

Ingram, P. (1996) 'Organization form as a solution to the problem of credible commitment: the evolution of naming strategies among US hotel chains', *Strategic Management Journal*, 17(S1): 85–98.

Ingram, P. and Baum, J. (1997) 'Chain affiliation and the failure of Manhattan hotels, 1898–1980', *Administrative Science Quarterly*, 42(1): 68–102.

Ingram, P. and Inman, C. (1996) 'Institutions, intergroup competition, and the evolution of hotel populations around Niagara Falls', *Administrative Science Quarterly*, 41(4): 629–58.

Ingram, P. and Roberts, P. W. (2000) 'Friendships among competitors in the Sydney hotel industry', *American Journal of Sociology*, 106(2): 387–423.

Iordache, C., Ciochina, I. and Asandei, M. (2010) 'Clusters. Tourism activity increase competitiveness support', *Theoretical and Applied Economics*, 17(5): 99–112.

ISTAT – Istituto Nazionale di Statistica (2006) *Specializzazioni produttive e sviluppo locale*, Rapporto annuale, Rome: ISTAT.

ISTAT – Istituto Nazionale di Statistica (2011) *IX Censimento generale dell'industria e dei servizi*, Rome: ISTAT.

Jackson, J. (2006) 'Developing regional tourism in China: The potential for activating business clusters in a socialist market economy', *Tourism Management*, 27(4): 695–706.

Kim, N. and Wicks, B. E. (2010) 'Rethinking tourism cluster development models for global competitiveness', in *International CHRIE Conference*, 30 July, University of Massachusetts, Amherst, MA: ScholarWorks@UMass.

Kuah, A.T.H. (2002) 'Cluster theory and practice: Advantages for the small business locating in a vibrant cluster', *Journal of Research in Marketing and Entrepreneurship*, 4(3): 206–28.

Kukalis, S. (2010) 'Agglomeration economies and firm performance: The case of industry clusters', *Journal of Management*, 36(2): 453–81.

Lazzeretti, L. (2003) 'City of art as a high culture local system and cultural districtualization processes: The cluster of art restoration in Florence', *International Journal of Urban and Regional Research*, 27(3): 635–48.

Lazzeretti, L. and Capone, F. (2008) 'Mapping and analysing local tourism systems in Italy, 1991–2001', *Tourism Geographies*, 10(2): 214–32.

Lazzeretti, L. and Petrillo, C. (eds) (2006) *Tourism Local Systems and Networking*, Amsterdam: Elsevier.

Lazzeretti L. and Capone (2015), 'Innovations and innovators in a resilient city. The case of chemical innovations after the 1966 flood in Florence', *City, Culture and Society*, 6(3), doi: 10.1016/j.ccs.2015.02.004.

Lazzeretti L. and Cooke P. (2015), 'Introduction to the special issue "the resilient city"', *forthcoming* in *City Culture and Society*, 6(3).

Luthe, T. and Wyss, R. (2014) 'Assessing and planning resilience in tourism', *Tourism Management*, 44: 161–63.

Martin, R. and Sunley, P. (2003) 'Deconstructing clusters: Chaotic concept or policy panacea?', *Journal of Economic Geography*, 3(1): 5–35.

Martin, R. (2012) Regional economic resilience, hysteresis and recessionary shocks, *Journal of Economic Geography* 12 (1): 1–32.

Maulet, G. (2006) 'A framework to identify a localised tourism system', in L. Lazzeretti and C.S. Petrillo (eds), *Tourism Local Systems and Networking*, Amsterdam: Elsevier, pp. 25–42.

Michael, E. J. (2003) 'Tourism micro-cluster', *Tourism Economics*, 9(2): 133–46.

Nordin, S. (2003) *Tourism Clustering and Innovation*, Östersund, Sweden: Etour.

Novelli, M., Schmitz, B. and Spencer, T. (2006) 'Networks, clusters and innovation in tourism: A UK experience', *Tourism Management*, 27(6): 1141–52.

Pearce, D. G. (1998) 'Tourist districts in Paris: Structure and functions', *Tourism Management*, 19(1): 49–65.

Peiró-Signes, Á., Segarra-Oña, M., Miret-Pastor, L. and Verma, R. (2015) 'The effect of tourism clusters on US Hotel Performance', *Cornell Hospitality Quarterly*, 56(2): 155–67.

Porter, M. E. (1998) *On Competition*, Boston, MA: Harvard Business School Press.

Porter, M. E. (2003) 'The economic performance of regions', *Regional Studies*, 37(6–7): 549–78.

Sainaghi, R. (2010) 'Hotel performance: State of the art', *International Journal of Contemporary Hospitality Management*, 22(7): 920–52.

Sainaghi, R. (2011) 'RevPAR determinants of individual hotels: Evidences from Milan', *International Journal of Contemporary Hospitality Management*, 23(3): 297–311.

Santagata, W. (2002) 'Cultural Districts, Property Rights and Sustainable Economic Growth', *International Journal of Urban and Regional Research*, 26(1): 9–23.

Santos, C., Almeida, A. and Teixeira, A. (2008) *Searching for Clusters in Tourism. A Quantitative Methodological Proposal*, FEP Working Papers no. 293, Oporto University, Spain.

Scott, N., Cooper, C. and Baggio, R. (2008) 'Destination networks. Theory and practice in four Australian cases', *Annals of Tourism Research*, 35(1): 169–88.

Segarra-Oña, M., Miret-Pastor, L., Peiró-Signes, A. and Verma, R. (2012) 'The effects of localization on economic performance: Analysis of Spanish tourism clusters', *European Planning Studies*, 20(8): 1319–34.

Shaw, G. and Williams, A. (2009) 'Knowledge transfer and management in tourism organisations: An emerging research agenda', *Tourism Management*, 30(3): 325–35.

Simmie, J. and Martin, R. (2010) 'The economic resilience of regions: Towards an evolutionary approach', *Cambridge Journal of Regions, Economy and Society*, 3(1): 27–43.

Tallman, S., Jenkins, M., Henry, N. and Pinch, S. (2004) 'Knowledge, clusters and competitive advantage', *Academy of Management Review*, 29(2): 258–71.

Tsang, E.W.K. and Yip, P.S.L. (2009) 'Competition, agglomeration, and performance of Beijing hotels', *Service Industries Journal*, 29(2): 155–71.

Urtasun, A. and Gutierrez, I. (2006) 'Hotel location in tourism cities: Madrid 1936–1998', *Annals of Tourism Research*, 33(2): 382–402.

Vom Hofe, R. and Chen, K. (2006) 'Whither or not industrial cluster: Conclusions or confusions?' *The Industrial Geographer*, 4(1): 2–28.

Weidenfeld, A., Williams, A.M. and Butler, R.W. (2010) 'Knowledge transfer and innovation among attractions', *Annals of Tourism Research*, 37(3): 604–26.

Yang, Y. and Wong, K.K.F. (2013) 'Spatial distribution of tourist flows to China's cities', *Tourism Geographies*, 15(2): 338–63.

6   How does concentration affect hotels' performance?

An empirical study of USA panel data

Marival Segarra-Oña, Angel
Peiró-Signes and Rohit Verma

1 Introduction

Geographical agglomerations have been widely studied, especially for manufacturing industries (Isaksen 1997; Porter 1998; Enright 1999; Feser and Bergman 2000; Roberts and Enright 2004; Vale and Caldeira 2007; Maine, Shapiro and Vining 2010). These agglomerations, studied in the literature as the 'Emilian model' (Brusco 1982), 'clusters' (Porter 1998), 'geographical spillovers' (Bronzini and Piselli 2009), the 'district effect' (Signorini 1994), the 'Marshallian effect' (Cainelli and De Liso 2005) or 'synergic concentrations' (Segarra-Oña and De Miguel 2009), reinforce competitiveness, while research on service industries is still scarce.

While there may be some differences between the above-mentioned concepts, there is a common idea of referring to geographical concentrations of firms in the same industry. This rich concept explains regional development and wealth creation when the relations between the participants are based on links that can be established between competing and cooperating companies (e.g. Delgado, Porter and Stern 2014). This model has recently been applied to the tourism industry (e.g. Segarra-Oña et al. 2012) but, because of the specific characteristics of this sector, a great deal of research still needs to be conducted before we can fully understand the factors influencing the success of the different types of firms involved.

The tourism industry is gaining in economic importance; it is a growing industry and is leading the economic global recovery. This is why an urgent need has arisen to develop specific studies to disentangle the effects of location and the geographic effects of being close together and concentrated near competitors, suppliers and related services.

Taking into account the above, the objective of this work will be to assess whether the cluster effect can be extrapolated to the tourism industry in one of the world's leading destinations, the USA. To do this, we will study hotels, as a key part of the tourist cluster, with the object being to see, by analysing five-year economic data, if over time performance of hotels belonging to tourist clusters in the USA differs from the performance of those located outside clusters.

2 Previous findings and definitions

The academic literature has been intermittently interested in the geographic agglomeration of firms in a particular industry, using terms with similar meanings to 'cluster' (Porter 1998), which is defined as a geographical agglomeration of firms, with relations established among them and with related institutions and connected industries, all of which operate in a specific field, or 'regional cluster' (Enright 1999; 2000), which is understood to be an industrial cluster in which firms are geographically closely located, and in the same or related industries. Along the same lines, the term 'industrial districts' was previously defined (Brusco 1982; Becattini 1990) to mean agglomerations of firms involved in independent productive processes, very often in the same sector or related sectors, completely integrated into the local environment and within the area delimited by the every-day distance to work. In sum, all these terms imply the importance that territory and, therefore, business location holds for companies' competitiveness.

The importance of geographical concentration and the evidence of the existence of industrial clusters have been widely studied over time, especially since Porter (1998) revitalized this subject. It is considered a key question regarding regional development (Koo 2005; Asheim, Cooke and Martin 2008) and competitiveness (Isaksen 1997; Dayasindhu 2002; Karaev, Lenny Koh and Szamosi 2007), since it facilitates cooperation and competition (Rabellotti 1995; Rabellotti and Schmitz 1997; Brenner 2006) and, something that is gaining in importance in the era of globalization, the attraction of specialized knowledge due to the concentration of related activities in a specific area (Asheim 1996; Baptista and Swann 1998; Pinch *et al*. 2003; Asheim, Cooke and Martin 2008).

In addition, proximity and informal social networks facilitate the transfer of specific technological knowledge (Audretsch and Feldman 1996; Baptista and Swann 1998), knowledge about clients' preferences (Urban and von Hippel 1988), and knowledge about processes (Saxenian 1996).

Brusco (1982) studied several sectors in the north of Italy – from consumer goods to automatic machinery and packaging machinery in Bologna – and extended his comments to concentrations of firms in the service sector and particularly in the tourism industry (pointing out that 4 million foreign tourists went every year to the Adriatic Riviera), but he did not analyse the idea of geographical agglomerations related to the service industry.

Several authors have applied the cluster theory to explain the competitiveness of specific activities, such as the convention segment (Bernini 2009); Bernini stated that a close relationship with tourist attractions and related services enhances success in the convention industry. The more that this subsector is integrated into the tourism industry, the better the results that are obtained, in terms of destination attraction and performance. The study was performed in Italy but its conclusions can be extrapolated.

Novelli, Schmitz and Spencer (2006) and later Lai *et al*. (2014), highlighted the importance of small and medium-sized enterprises (SMEs) in the innovation process and the networking formation within a tourist cluster, enhancing the local activities and therefore, the development of the region.

A growing body of research has examined location-based competitive dynamics within the hotel industry (Segarra-Oña *et al*. 2012). Early work reported that hotels concentrate in city centres as shown for hotels in Toronto by Wall, Dudy-cha and Hutchinson (1985), and London hotels (Page and Sinclair 1989). Other authors highlighted the convenience of suburban areas due to their proximity to clusters of offices and shopping malls, amusement parks or other recreational activities (Relph 1991; Karakas 2012).

These types of analyses have mainly been performed in Europe, where tourism tends to be more concentrated and tourist destinations more clearly identified (Spain, Italy, France and Greece), as well as in specific locations (such as the Balearic Islands or the Adriatic Coast). Several studies have determined that location is a key aspect in a hotel's success (Arbel and Pizam 1977; Newell and Seabrook 2006) but most studies of hotel industry location have focused on analysing only one area (Arbel and Pizam 1977; Urtasun and Gutiérrez 2006).

In a previous work (Peiró-Signes *et al.* 2015), we analysed hotels located inside and outside tourist clusters in the USA, segmenting the sample according to scale levels and property types. Hotels in clusters performed consistently better than properties outside clusters at the same scale level. The results also showed that chain-managed hotels inside clusters performed better than chain-managed properties outside clusters.

However, hotels can also be organized in terms of quality and price – from top brands such as 'The Leading Hotels of the World' to those classified using the typical stars. In this chapter, we add value to the previous study by segmenting the sample into upper-priced and lower-priced hotels, to open a new field of analysis that mixes the study of the cluster effect applied to the hospitality industry and consumers' price perceptions.

Based on our previous analysis (Peiró-Signes *et al.* 2015) and the theoretical background, we would expect that:

The cluster effect will create positive externalities for upper-priced hotels located in tourist clusters but not for lower-priced hotels

On the one hand, we would expect clients with a higher income level to take advantage of the other tourist cluster components (Cunha and Cunha 2005). On the other hand, as Bernini (2009) has recently proved, the more embedded that attractions are within the tourist cluster, the higher their competitiveness; better results can therefore be expected.

3 Methodology

We used location quotients (LQs) and standard location quotients (SLQs) to identify tourist clusters. The same methodology has previously been used to analyze the performances of clusters in the region of Valencia (Miret-Pastor and Segarra-Oña 2011; Segarra-Oña *et al.* 2012), for cluster mapping (Porter 2003), and for the location of 'local production systems' specialising in tourism (Lazzeretti and Capone 2006). This method has some advantages, as it is easy and simple to apply and to understand, but it also has its critics. In recent years, other methods have appeared, such as Brenner's (2006), which is based on a comparison of spatial distributions. However, since our objective is to compare territories whose boundaries have already been determined, the LQ method is considered to be appropriate for our analysis.

The rate used to measure the specialization levels was the LQ.

$$LQ = \frac{E_{is} / E_s}{E_i / E},$$

where E_{is} is the number of employees in county s in sector i; E_s is the number of employees in county s; E_i is the number of employees in the USA in sector i; and E is the total number of employees in the USA.

Regarding the geographical division, we thought about using the local labour markets as the location variable measure, as was done in previous works to locate regional tourist clusters in Spain (Boix and Galletto 2008; Miret-Pastor and Segarra-Oña 2011) or at a national level in Italy (Lazzeretti and Capone 2006; Capone and Boix 2008). However, the resulting maps would be too fragmented. On the other hand, using state-level labour markets gives big areas within states that do not match up well with cluster findings or that do not show existing clusters because employment in other industries within the same state hides the evidence.

Therefore, we decided to use officially recognised geographic county areas, which makes the analysis simpler, more understandable and more useful, especially for agents responsible for tourism planning, since these entities have competencies in tourist promotion strategies. In addition, the metropolitan statistical areas (MSAs) defined by the United States Office of Management and Budget (OMB) were considered. MSAs are defined as one or more adjacent counties or county equivalents that have at least one urban core area with a population of at least 50,000, plus adjacent territory that has a high degree of social and economic integration with the core, as measured by commuting ties.

Since there is no formal definition of the tourism sector at a statistical level, we identified some of the sectors or subsectors represented in the North American Industry Classification System (NAICS) codes. The NAICS codes that identify the whole tourism industry are the Arts, entertainment, and recreation code (NAICS 71) and the Accommodation and food services code (NAICS 72). Data for the LQ calculation were extracted from the US Bureau of Labor Statistics database for the year 2010.

The LQ coefficient establishes an arbitrary cut-off for cluster consideration. We decided to set up a cluster greyscale scale so that we could show higher concentration and lower concentration clusters graphically. Counties with an LQ higher than 3 were considered to be highly concentrated tourist clusters and were tinted black. Then SLQ analysis determined an LQ cut-off of nearly 2 for counties which were considered to be tourist clusters with a medium concentration; these were tinted dark grey. Finally, counties with an LQ of over 1.25 were considered as tourist clusters with a low concentration and were tinted light grey. Figure 6.1 shows the tourist clusters within the USA.

To complete the necessary data collection for our analysis we used the Hotel Horizons database. Hotel Horizons is a PKF hospitality research tool with analysis for hotel segments across the 50 most important metropolitan areas in the USA. The data includes revenue per available room (RevPAR), average daily rate (ADR),

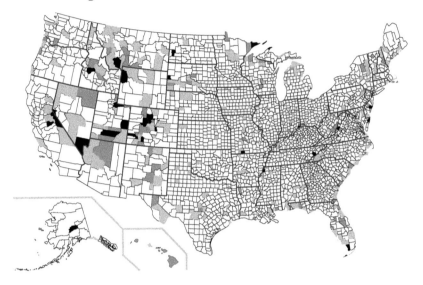

Figure 6.1 USA tourist clusters, 2010

Source: USA county map extracted from the US Census Bureau (Peiró-Signes *et al.* (2015).

Table 6.1 USA hospitality markets* from PKF Hotel Horizons database

Albuquerque	Houston	Phoenix
Anaheim	Indianapolis	Pittsburgh
Atlanta	Jacksonville	Portland
Austin	Kansas City	Raleigh-Durham
Baltimore	Long Island	Richmond
Boston	Los Angeles	Sacramento
Charlotte	Memphis	Salt Lake City
Chicago	Miami	San Antonio
Cincinnati	Minneapolis	San Diego
Cleveland	Nashville	*San Francisco*
Columbus	*New Orleans*	Seattle
Dallas	New York	Saint Louis
Denver	Newark	Tampa
Detroit	*Oahu*	Tucson
Fort Lauderdale	Oakland	Washington DC
Fort Worth	*Orlando*	*West Palm Beach*
Hartford	Philadelphia	

Source: Our elaboration.

Notes: *PKF analyses the historical and expected performance of 59 major US lodging markets (https://store.pkfc.com/hotel-horizons-reports); in-cluster markets are shown in italics.

occupancy rates (Occ), revenue, and demand and supply data. We retrieved data for all these variables from 2003–11 to perform the analysis.

Before the data analysis, markets were identified according to their tourist cluster membership. Table 6.1 shows, in italics, the markets located in the tourist clusters that had previously been identified.

A dummy variable that identifies whether a market is or is not located in a tourist cluster was introduced; it takes the value 1 if the market is in a tourist cluster and 0 if it is not.

To determine whether there are significant differences in the results of the hotel performance indicators, we ran an Analysis of Variance (ANOVA) tests including all the markets and segments (all, lower-priced and upper-priced[1]).

Additionally, in order to see if hotels in a cluster show significant differences in the evolution of the main variables from 2006–10, we ran an ANOVA test on the percentage of variation shown from 2006–10 in supply, demand, revenues, occupancy, ADR, and RevPAR. Note that in this case we can compare the supply, demand, and revenue variables between groups, as we are comparing the percentage in the increase from the reference year (2006), which is not dependent on the number of hotels introduced for the calculation of each location.

4 Results

The map (Figure 6.1) shows strong clusters in some well-known tourist areas like Las Vegas, Atlantic City, Orlando and Hawaii, among other destinations.

We can also see how 'hot tourist spots' have influenced nearby areas (counties), and that areas of high concentration are in the centre of a cluster while the concentration decreases with increasing distance.

The results in Table 6.2 show that hotels in clusters have higher Occs, higher ADRs and higher RevPAR than those located outside clusters. These results are maintained within the upper-priced and the lower-priced segments, although the upper-priced segment shows bigger differences than the lower-priced segment. It is remarkable that the standard deviations for each of the three variables in both groups, in-cluster and out-cluster, and for each of the cases, show little difference, which indicates that the data distribution for in- and out-cluster are well differentiated, as the means show them to be fairly separated.

The Table 6.3 results show no significance in the percentage increase/decrease in supply, demand, revenue and RevPAR for the markets, whether or not the market is in a cluster. Note that the percentage decreases in occupancy rate are significantly lower in markets located in clusters than in those outside clusters, although this variation is mainly because of the differences for the upper-priced hotels in the studied markets. By contrast, ADR decreased significantly more in markets that are in a tourist cluster than in those that are not in a cluster, although this difference is due to the lower-priced hotels in the markets.

As occupancy represents demand over supply, the results indicate that upper-priced hotels in clusters have been more efficient in filling up the rooms than those outside clusters.

On the other hand, the ADR results, which reflect revenue over demand, indicate that lower-priced hotels in tourist clusters have been unable to increase their revenues and demand, which has led to a dramatic decrease of 11.27% in ADR over a four-year period, while outside clusters this category only decreases by 3.03%. In the upper-priced category, the results show the same tendency, although no significant differences are shown.

Table 6.2 ANOVA results for hospitality performance variables, in-cluster vs out-cluster

		All			Lower-priced			Upper-priced		
		Mean	Std dev	F	Mean	Std dev	F	Mean	Std dev	F
Occ	Out-cluster	62.2	8.7	35.394***	59.4	9.3	29.401***	66.2	7.9	19.119***
	In-cluster	67.7	9.3		64.8	10.3		69.9	9.0	
ADR	Out-cluster	103.10	30.47	81.781***	73.62	18.90	31.201***	135.88	33.98	60.568***
	In-cluster	131.93	28.14		84.66	17.41		164.08	37.73	
RevPar	Out-cluster	65.72	28.91	69.237***	44.73	18.59	33.632***	91.40	33.12	50.693***
	In-cluster	91.11	29.30		56.13	19.12		116.56	37.10	

Source: Our elaboration.

Note: *** p < 0.01.

Table 6.3 ANOVA results for the percentage of increase/decrease for hotel performance variables, in–cluster vs out–cluster

		All			Lower–priced			Upper–priced		
		Mean	Std dev	F	Mean	Std dev	F	Mean	Std dev	F
ΔSupply	Out–cluster	11.92	5.86	0.623	8.62	5.60	0.358	16.53	8.74	1.287
	In–cluster	9.68	7.55		6.90	10.26		11.93	7.00	
ΔDemand	Out–cluster	2.42	6.01	2.344	-3.26	6.33	0.206	9.82	7.60	1.387
	In–cluster	7.10	10.31		-1.89	7.29		14.60	15.86	
ΔRevenue	Out–cluster	0.19	9.10	0.053	-6.06	10.11	1.860	4.58	10.12	0.008
	In–cluster	-0.86	14.41		-12.73	12.91		5.05	19.50	
ΔOcc	Out–cluster	-8.36	5.45	5.375**	-10.79	6.41	0.901	-5.59	4.94	8.604**
	In–cluster	-2.37	5.83		-7.95	5.83		2.29	11.01	
ΔADR	Out–cluster	-2.25	5.49	4.271**	-3.03	6.18	7.339**	-4.84	5.24	2.340
	In–cluster	-7.68	6.32		-11.27	8.93		-8.67	5.96	
ΔRevPAR	Out–cluster	-10.38	7.98	0.042	-13.42	9.28	1.030	-10.08	794	0.895
	In–cluster	-9.58	11.32		-18.02	12.70		-6.13	15.63	

Source: Our elaboration.

Note: ** p < 0.05.

Finally, RevPAR, which is calculated as revenue over supply or ADR times occupancy, represents a better overall performance measure for hotels. This indicator shows that there is no significant difference in its increase/decrease for in-cluster as opposed to out-cluster hotels. Overall, even though hotels in clusters had a significantly lower decrease in occupancy rates over the period of the study than out-cluster hotels (-2.37 vs -8.36), the result was compensated for by a significantly lower decrease in the daily rates of out-cluster versus in-cluster hotels (-2.25 vs -7.68). These results lead to an insignificant difference in the RevPar variation overall.

We can take two important insights from this analysis. First, taking into account that the period of the study is during the financial crisis in the USA, in-cluster hotels were able to sustain occupancy better than out-cluster hotels, while out-cluster hotels were able to sustain daily rates better than in-cluster hotels. This suggests either that a tourist cluster reduces the exposure to market changes in demand, or that in-cluster hotels had to reduce daily rates in order to fill up their rooms to maintain a certain level of operational capacity, which can have an impact on hotels' profits. Second, in any case, a lower impact on occupancy is a better overall result for the tourist cluster. In other words, even if hotels do not significantly improve their revenues over a period, other in-cluster tourist businesses at the destination will be benefitting from the ability of in-cluster hotels to maintain demand.

5 Conclusions

In this chapter we compared the performances of hotels located inside and outside tourist clusters in the North American market. These results suggest that the upper-priced and lower-priced segments inside and outside clusters do not evolve in the same way. Clustered markets grow more slowly than other markets, but are significantly more efficient in growing their occupancy than the corresponding markets outside a cluster if they are in the upper-priced segment. Demand has increased in the upper-priced segment and has reduced in the lower-priced segment, which, in addition to an insufficient increase or negative increase in revenues shown by each segment, has led to a sharp fall in ADR for the given period.

The results show that our hypothesis, that the cluster effect will create positive externalities on upper-priced hotels located in tourist clusters but not in lower-priced hotels, is fulfilled. Generally speaking, and as our previous analysis indicated (Peiró-Signes *et al.* 2015), hotels located within a tourist cluster perform better than those located outside. However, with this study we have carried out a dual-focused analysis. Upper-priced hotels are getting more benefits from being located in a cluster – higher occupancy rates and higher revenues.

As location is the differentiating factor, and upper-priced hotels are better than lower-priced hotels at taking advantage of the proximity of related services such as restaurants or cultural offers, a future line of research is to analyse the extent to which hotel clients play a role in the process of adding value to the cluster-hotel relationship. What types of network do the clients build within the cluster, how do the hotels link the different members of the tourist clusters, and how does this differ from the point of view of the users of upper-priced and lower-priced hotels?

As we have taken data from 2006–11 in order to have a large quantity of data, we checked that the results do not vary significantly from one year to another. Occupancy, ADR and RevPAR showed significant differences between markets inside and markets outside clusters, for every year. For the other variables, a few differences are shown during the overall period, and these might be explained by other factors that are not the aim of this work. However, this should be considered as a limitation of our study.

Notes

The authors would like to thank the Center for Hospitality Research at Cornell University that hosted A. Peiró-Signes and M. Segarra-Oña as visiting scholars.
1   As classified by PKF (https://store.pkfc.com/hotel-horizons-reports)

References

Arbel, A. and Pizam, A. (1977) 'Some determinants of urban hotel location: The tourists' inclinations', *Journal of Travel Research*, 15(3): 18–22.

Asheim, B. T. (1996) 'Industrial districts as "learning regions": A condition for prosperity', *European Planning Studies*, 4(4): 379–400.

Asheim, B. T, Cooke, P. and Martin, R. (2008) 'Clusters and regional development: Critical reflections and explorations', *Economic Geography*, 84(1): 109–12.

Audretsch, D. B. and Feldman, M. P. (1996) 'Knowledge spillovers and the geography of innovation and production', *The American Economic Review*, 86(3): 630–40.

Baptista, R. and Swann, P. (1998) 'Do firms in clusters innovate more?' *Research Policy*, 27(5): 525–40.

Becattini, G. (1990) 'The Marshallian industrial district as a socio-economic notion', in F. Pyke and W. Sengenberger (eds), *Industrial Districts and Local Economic Regeneration*, Geneva: International Institute for Labour Studies, pp. 37–51.

Bernini, C. (2009) 'Convention industry and destination clusters: Evidence from Italy', *Tourism Management*, 30(6): 878–89.

Boix, R. and Galletto, V. (2008) 'Marshallian industrial districts in Spain', *Scienze Regionali*, 7(3): 29–52.

Brenner, T. (2006) 'Identification of local industrial clusters in Germany', *Regional Studies*, 40(9): 1–14.

Bronzini, R. and Piselli, P. (2009) 'Determinants of long-run regional productivity with geographical spillovers: The role of R&D, human capital and public infrastructure', *Regional Science and Urban Economics*, 39(2): 187–99.

Brusco, S. (1982) 'The Emilian model: Productive decentralisation and social integration', *Cambridge Journal of Economics*, 6(2): 167–84.

Cainelli, G. and De Liso, N. (2005) 'Innovation in industrial districts: Evidence from Italy', *Industry and Innovation*, 12(3): 383–98.

Capone, F. and Boix, R. (2008) 'Sources of growth and competitiveness of local tourist production systems: An application to Italy (1991–2001)', *The Annals of Regional Science*, 42(1): 209–24.

Cunha, S.K. and Cunha, J.C. (2005) 'Tourism cluster competitiveness and sustainability: Proposal for a systemic model to measure the impact of tourism on local development', *BAR-Brazilian Administration Review*, 2(2): 47–62.

Dayasindhu, N. (2002) 'Embeddedness, knowledge transfer, industry clusters and global competitiveness: A case study of the Indian software industry', *Technovation*, 22(9): 551–60.

Delgado, M., Porter, M. E. and Stern, S. (2014) 'Clusters, convergence, and economic performance', *Research Policy*, 43(10): 1785–99.

Enright, M. J. (1999) 'Regional clusters and firm strategy', in A. Chandler, O. Solvell and P. Hagstrom (eds), *The Dynamic Firm*, Oxford: Oxford University Press, 315–42.

Enright, M. J. (2000) 'Regional clusters and multinational enterprises: Independence, dependence, or interdependence?' *International Studies of Management and Organization*, 30(2): 114–38.

Feser, E. J. and Bergman, E. M. (2000) 'National industry cluster templates: A framework for applied regional cluster analysis', *Regional Studies*, 34(1): 1–19.

Isaksen, A. (1997) 'Regional clusters and competitiveness: The Norwegian case', *European Planning Studies*, 5(1): 65–76.

Karaev, A., Lenny Koh, S. C. and Szamosi, L. T. (2007) 'The cluster approach and SME competitiveness: A review', *Journal of Manufacturing Technology Management*, 18(7): 818–35.

Karakas, B. (2012) 'Marketing business tourism in suburban areas', *International Journal of Hospitality and Tourism*, 1(2): 6–18.

Koo, J. (2005) 'Technology spillovers, agglomeration, and regional economic development', *Journal of Planning Literature*, 20(2): 99–115.

Lai, Y. L., Hsu, M. S., Lin, F. J., Chen, Y. M. and Lin, Y. H. (2014) 'The effects of industry cluster knowledge management on innovation performance', *Journal of Business Research*, 67(5): 734–39.

Lazzeretti, L. and Capone, F. (2006) 'Identification and analysis of tourist local systems: An application to Italy (1996–2001)', in L. Lazzeretti and C. S. Petrillo (eds), *Tourism Local Systems and Networking*, Amsterdam: Elsevier, pp. 25–40.

Maine, E. M., Shapiro, D. M. and Vining, A. R. (2010) 'The role of clustering in the growth of new technology-based firms', *Small Business Economics*, 34(2): 127–46.

Miret-Pastor, L. and Segarra-Oña, M. (2011) 'Estudio del clúster turístico de Benidorm a través de indicadores de aglomeración y especialización', in D. López, *Renovación de destinos turísticos consolidados*, Valencia: Tirant lo Blanch, pp. 69–86.

Newell, G. and Seabrook, R. (2006) 'Factors influencing hotel investment decision making', *Journal of Property Investment & Finance*, 24(4): 279–94.

Novelli, M., Schmitz, B. and Spencer, T. (2006) 'Networks, clusters and innovation in tourism: A UK experience', *Tourism Management*, 27(6): 1141–52.

Page, S. J. and Sinclair, T. M. (1989) 'Tourism and accommodation in London: Alternative policies and the docklands experience', *Built Environment*, 15(2): 125–37.

Peiró-Signes, A., Segarra-Oña, M., Miret-Pastor, L. and Verma, R. (2015) 'The effect of tourism clusters on US hotel performance', *Cornell Hospitality Quarterly*, 56(2): 155–67.

Pinch, S., Henry, N., Jenkins, M. and Tallman, S. (2003) 'From "industrial districts" to "knowledge clusters": A model of knowledge dissemination and competitive advantage in industrial agglomerations', *Journal of Economic Geography*, 3(4): 373–88.

Porter, M. E. (1998) 'Location, clusters, and the "new" microeconomics of competition', *Business Economics*, 33(1): 7–13.

Porter, M. E. (2003) 'The economic performance of regions', *Regional Studies*, 37(6–7): 549–78.

Rabellotti, R. (1995) 'Is there an "industrial district model"? Footwear districts in Italy and Mexico compared', *World Development*, 23(1): 29–41.

Rabellotti, R. and Schmitz, H. (1997) *The Internal Heterogeneity of Industrial Districts in Italy, Brazil and Mexico*, IDS Working Paper no. 59, Brighton: IDS.

Relph, E. (1991) 'Suburban downtowns of the greater Toronto area', *The Canadian Geographer*, 35(4): 421–25.

Roberts, B. H. and Enright, M. J. (2004) 'Industry clusters in Australia: Recent trends and prospects', *European Planning Studies*, 12(1): 99–121.

Saxenian, A. (1996) 'Beyond boundaries: Open labor markets and learning in Silicon Valley', in M.B. Arthur and D.M. Rousseau (eds) *The Boundaryless Career: A New Employment Principle for a New Organizational Era*, New York: Oxford University Press, pp. 23–39.

Segarra-Oña, M. and De Miguel, B. (2009) 'Evaluación de la concentración industrial sinérgica: propuesta metodológica y aplicación a un sector industrial', *Tec Empresarial*, 3(1): 65–72.

Segarra-Oña, M., Miret-Pastor, L. G., Peiró-Signes, A. and Verma, R. (2012) 'The effects of localization on economic performance: Analysis of Spanish tourism clusters', *European Planning Studies*, 20(8): 1319–34.

Signorini, L. F. (1994) 'The price of Prato, or measuring the industrial district effect', *Papers in Regional Science*, 73(4): 369–92.

Urban, G. L. and von Hippel, E. (1988) 'Lead user analyses for the development of new industrial products', *Management Science*, 34(5): 569–82.

Urtasun, A. and Gutiérrez, I. (2006) 'Hotel location in tourism cities: Madrid 1936–1998', *Annals of Tourism Research*, 33(2): 382–402.

Vale, M. and Caldeira, J. (2007) 'Proximity and knowledge governance in localized production systems: The footwear industry in the north region of Portugal', *European Planning Studies*, 15(4): 531–48.

Wall, G., Dudycha, D. and Hutchinson, J. (1985) 'Point pattern analyses of accommodation in Toronto', *Annals of Tourism Research*, 12(4): 603–18.

7 Tourism, creativity and entrepreneurship

New firm formation in Tuscany

Luciana Lazzeretti and Francesco Capone

1 Introduction

The aim of this chapter is to examine the relationship between tourism and creativity, with a specific focus on cultural and creative industries (CCIs). The study investigates the patterns of clustering and co-locations of firms in tourism and CCIs and their contribution to new firm formation through a case study of Tuscany.

The relevance of the creative economy continues to grow in recent years and important synergies with tourism are emerging, offering considerable potential for growing demand and developing new products, experiences and markets (Richards and Wilson 2007; OECD 2014). This contemporary debate focuses on the shift from conventional models of cultural tourism to new models of creative tourism based on intangible culture and contemporary creativity.

Richards and Wilson (2006) first identified the growth of 'creative tourism' as an extension of or a reaction to cultural tourism. They argued that in contrast to most cultural tourists, creative tourists are increasingly looking for more engaging, interactive experiences which can help them in their personal development and identity creation. Richards (2013) points out that some practical implementations are workshops, open ateliers, tasting experiences, itineraries, shop windows, etc.

Creative tourism has been defined by Richards and Raymond (2000: 18) as 'tourism which offers visitors the opportunity to develop their creative potential through active participation in courses and learning experiences which are characteristic of the holiday destination where they are undertaken'.

Creative tourism is a new approach to focus on local skills, traditions and habits from many areas. This new focus in part coincides with the event and experience economy and the increasing relevance of the experience of visitors (Lorentzen and Hansen 2009; Lorentzen 2012). In creative tourism, in fact tourists may wish to learn about arts and crafts, language, gastronomy and wine-making, nature, landscapes, spirituality, design and so on. In many different destinations some of these activities have been made part of the tourism supply for many years, but only in recent years have they acquired a crucial importance for local attraction and competitiveness (Richards 2013; Hjalager and Antonioli Corigliano, 2000). This is particularly relevant as creative tourism is more and more seen as a significant driver in developing local economies, improving destinations' image and competitiveness and supporting growth of new industries and markets (OECD 2014; Richards 2014).

Besides, the creative economy approach focuses on creativity, skill and talent as a potential trigger for wealth and firms creation (UNCTAD 2010; Bakhshi, Freeman and Higgs 2013). Originally, this strand of research has developed mainly from the Florida's contribution on the creative class (Florida 2002) and from the study on the creative city (Landry and Bianchini 1995; Landry 2000), and later on focuses increasingly on CCIs as an independent line of research (Capone, 2008; Belussi and Sedita, 2010; Flew and Cunningham 2010; Lazzeretti 2013).

In this context, the European Commission (EC 2010) discussing the potential of CCIs has reintroduced the distinction between creative and cultural industries, including tourism, to attach more importance to the recent phenomenon of creative tourism, and to its connections with culture, creativity, considering also the increasing trend of the event and experience economy. There is in fact a growing interest in the literature that connects the creative economy approach with tourism and economic development (Richards 2011; 2013; Tafel-Viia *et al.* 2014).

This chapter investigates the relationships of clustering and co-locations of firms in tourism and CCIs and their contribution to new firm formation through a case study of Tuscany. The analysis is based on the construction of an *ad hoc* database, elaborated from the Statistic Database of Local Units of Active Firms (ASIA) (ISTAT 2009), that includes data on firms and employees in 2009, subdivided by NACE Rev. 2 codes at three-digit level. We investigate the relationships between CCIs and the tourism industry, using a spatial perspective in order to analyse whether firms in CCIs and tourism tend to locate close to one another, forming clusters (Porter 1998). We also analyse the different contributions of CCIs and tourist clusters to new firm formation, as it is underlined in the literature that CCIs and tourist hot spots support and contribute to local development, new firm formation and entrepreneurship (Lee, Florida and Acs 2004; Stolarick and Florida 2006; Fritsch 2008).

The chapter is organised as follows. After this introduction, section 2 illustrates the contribution of CCIs and tourism for local development and in particular for firm formation and entrepreneurship. Section 3 traces an operational definition of CCIs and tourism. Section 4 investigates CCIs and tourist clusters in Tuscany, representing results in geographical maps. Section 5 investigates the co-location patterns of CCIs and tourism, while section 6 investigates their contribution to firm formation and presents the regression model and estimates. The work ends with conclusive remarks.

2 Cultural and creative industries, tourism and new firm formation

Several contributors suggest that there is a strong relationship between the presence of CCIs and development. Power (2011) shows that those European regions with clusters of CCIs are generally characterised by a higher economic prosperity. Lazzeretti (2013) states that large urban areas and capital city regions dominate the creative and cultural industries in Europe. Bakhshi, McVittie and Simmie (2008) analyse the contribution of creative industries to the wider economy. De Miguel *et al.* (2012) analyse the impact and importance of creative industries' clusters on the wealth of Europe. Boix, De Miguel and Hervás (2013) investigate creative service businesses and their performances in European regions. Stam, De Jong and Marlet (2008) analyse creative industries in The Netherlands separating them in three domains (arts, media and publishing, and creative business services). Barrowclough and Kozul-Wright (2008) investigate the potential of creative industries for economic growth in developing countries while Yusuf and Nabeshima (2005) focus on East Asia.

Also regarding new firm formation, a positive correlation is demonstrated between the clustering of CCIs, and new business formation and entrepreneurship (Lee, Florida and Acs 2004; Fritsch 2008). An influential line of research suggests that clusters of creative industries are associated with entrepreneurship, new firm formation and development (Florida 2002; Cooke and Lazzeretti 2008). De Propris *et al.* (2009) point out the importance of creative clusters in local and regional development and new firm formation, while Cook and Pandit (2010) analyse the relevance of London-based media clusters in the UK film and television industry due to the city's international linkages and entrepreneurship. The UK's Department for Culture, Media and Sport (DCMS 2006) was one of the first to investigate the connection between entrepreneurship and CCIs, while Henry (2007) developed a wide study of entrepreneurship and CCIs with international comparisons in several sectors. The seminal contribution of Scott (2006) investigates the concept of 'creative destruction' as innovative entrepreneurship in culture-related industries, pointing out the role of entrepreneurial behaviour and new firm formation.

In the international literature it is recognised that the clustering of CCIs promotes a series of benefits in the local economy: economic growth in terms of an increase of employment and birth of new creative businesses (Stolarick and Florida 2006). These benefits do not only manifest within creative industries themselves, but also in other industries thanks to spillovers (Chapain *et al.* 2010). Creative clusters have received an increasing attention over the last years (De Propris *et al.* 2009). CCIs are affected by agglomeration economies, which basically act as centripetal forces, fostering the incubation and attraction of creative industries in places with specific characteristics (localisation economies) or in large cities and metropolises (urbanisation economies) (Lorenzen and Frederiksen 2008).

Despite their importance for economic development, which is also recognised by supranational organisations and institutions (e.g. EC 2010; UNCTAD 2010), at the moment the definition of CCIs remains a topic of international debate (De Beukelaer 2014; Lazzeretti and Capone 2015). Recently, the European Commission (EC 2010) in its *Green Paper* has reintroduced a distinction between creative and cultural industries, reverting to the sectorial definitions typical of cultural economics and blending them with those of the creative economy, including tourism, the experience economy, and other activities. In addition to traditional cultural and creative activities, it also considers a more peripheral level, in which several other sectors that rely on content production are interdependent with CCIs, specifically cultural tourism and new technologies (EC 2010). The European Commission's aim is to attach more importance to the recent phenomenon of creative tourism, and to its connections with culture, creativity, and the increasing trend of the event and experience economy.

This approach is not only limited to the *Green Paper*. There is a growing interest in the literature that connects CCIs with tourism and economic development (Richards 2011; 2013; Tafel-Viia *et al.* 2014; Pilotti 2011). This approach comprises not only tourism, but also all the creative activities centred on the experience of consumers and visitors (Salman 2010). The arts (museums, historical sites, gardens) and all creative activities that depend on customer involvement can also be added to these. This outlook has been identified as overlapping with other cultural and creative sectors, leading some to consider fashion, design and enogastronomy as just some examples of products that can be lived through consumption or visitor experiences (Santagata 2009).

There are then other approaches that seek to enlarge the DCMS taxonomy of the creative sector and broaden this perspective to other industries such as tourism or heritage-related activities (Yang 2009; Sepe and Di Trapani 2010). In this research stream, Boix and De Propris in this book analyse the experience economy and creative industries in the UK, including tourism and the event economy, while Hong *et al.* (2014) also investigate the event economy and natural and cultural heritage activity in China.

Recently, tourism studies have increasingly included creative economy themes, and explored case studies and the interconnections between the cultural and creative sectors and visitors; for example in the case of East London (Pappalepore, Maitland and Smith 2014), of distressed neighbourhoods with arts-based communities (Aquino, Phillips and Sung 2012), and of small to medium-sized cities (Den Dekker and Tabbers 2012). Russo and Quagliari (2012) speak of 'post-Bohemian' districts which have facilitated the penetration of tourists into artistic areas such as creative Barcelona.

In light of these contributions, interest in CCIs and other related fields traditionally linked with cultural industries and tourism is increasing. Several concerns arise from the consideration of the two different sectors which interrelationships are not enough studied. This problem also appears in cultural heritage-based territories, such as Tuscany, where it is difficult to identify a coherent set of activities and even risky, in our opinion, to consider industries with different characteristics and evolutionary trends under the same umbrella.

Given the foregoing discussion, what are the implications of enlarging the definition of CCIs to tourism? And what are the relationships of these two industries at the local level? This issue has recently received greater interest as creativity and tourism are more and more analysed in the same context (OECD 2014; Richards 2014). This work attempts to contribute in this direction. The work focuses on a specific region, Tuscany, which is recognised in several contributions as a tourist and creative region (Lazzeretti and Capone 2015), analysing the different configurations of these industries and their contribution to new firm formation.

3 The definitions of cultural and creative industries and tourism industry

In its original contribution, according to the Anglo-Saxon perspective (DCMS 2001), CCIs included cultural industries and emerging creative industries such as technology and multimedia. The activities taken into account were essentially those based on creativity, talent, personal abilities and that which may have a potential for the increase of employment and wealth.

For its institutional value and the pioneering contribution, a milestone in the definition of creative industries is the one provided by the DCMS (2001) which includes 13 sectors: Advertising, Architecture, Arts, Ancient art markets, Design, Film, Video, Software, Music, Performing arts, Publishing, TV and Radio. This taxonomy has been adopted in several researches and has been accepted as the principal one at the European level (UNESCO 2013), in particular in its revised version (DCMS 2013).[1]

Table 7.1 presents NACE Rev. 2 economic activities that have been selected for the analysis. Table 7.1 includes CCIs following the definition of the DCMS (2013), and Tourism defined as the hotel, restaurant and café (HoReCa) sector plus Tour operator and Travel agency, that is considered together with cultural heritage activities such as Museum, Libraries, etc. and the experience economy, such as Performing arts.

The data source for the Tuscan case is the ISTAT ASIA 2009 database. The ASIA database collects the information from all the Italian Chambers of Commerce and includes all the firms active in Italy in 2009. Data on CCIs in 2001 refers to the Census of Industry and Services (ISTAT 2001).

Table 7.1 Cultural and creative industries and tourism

		NACE three-digits	
Cultural and creative industries	Software	62.1	Computer programming activities
		62.2	Computer consultancy activities
		63.1	Computer facilities management activities
	Cinema and film	59.1	Motion picture, video and television programme activities
	Music	59.2	Sound recording and music publishing activities
	TV and radio	60.1	Radio broadcasting
		60.2	TV programming and broadcasting
	Publishing	58.1	Publishing of books, periodicals and other publishing activities
	Architecture and engineering	71.1	Architectural and engineering activities and related technical consultancy
	Advertising	73.1	Advertising
		73.2	Market research and public opinion polling
	Design	74.1	Specialized design activities
	Photography	74.2	Photographic activities

		NACE three-digits	
Tourism industry	Performing arts	90.01	Performing arts
		90.03	Artistic creation
	Tourism – Hotel, restaurants, travel agencies	55.1	Hotels and similar accommodation
		55.2	Holiday and other short-stay accommodation
		55.3	Camping grounds, recreational vehicle parks and trailer parks
		56.1	Restaurants and mobile food service activities
		79.1	Travel agency and tour operator activities
	Cultural heritage	91.01	Library and archives activities
		91.02	Museums activities
		91.03	Operation of historical sites and buildings and similar visitor attractions
		91.04	Botanical and zoological gardens and nature reserves activities

Source: Our elaboration.

The analysis, conducted at the NACE three-digit level, results in some constraints on the definitions, but municipal data are only available at the three-digit level. The most important problem raised concerns Architecture, which is considered together with Engineering.[2]

4 Cultural and creative industries and tourism in Tuscany

This section presents the results obtained through the analysis of CCIs and tourism in Tuscany considering the selected economic activities and using the ISTAT 2009 ASIA database (active firms).

We first consider only cultural and creative firms in Tuscany, which amount to 32,000 units. From 2001–09, firms grew with a pace of 21%. At an absolute level, an increment of more than 6,000 new firms is reported in the period.

In 2001, the average dimension was of 2.08 employees per firm, whereas in 2009 this value decreased to 1.89 employees per firm. As expected, CCIs in Tuscany are mainly composed by family businesses, micro-firms, professionals and freelances (for instance in cultural services and multimedia) based on individual creativity and entrepreneurship.

Considering the weight of CCIs in the regional economy, they account for 5% of employment in Tuscany, whilst the weight of creative firms in the regional economy raises up to a relevant 9%. These percentages are in line with other studies where creative industries cover a percentage of national employment between 4 and 6% (De Propris *et al.* 2009; Lazzeretti 2013).

We now evaluate CCIs considering also tourism. The firms almost double reaching more than 50,000 units. They have also a crucial weight on the regional economy, as they represent 14% of total firms and 11% of the total employment in the region.

4.1 Clustering of creative industries in Tuscany

This section analyses CCIs in Tuscany through a territorial and geographical approach. The investigation focuses on territorial concentration indices (location quotients), according to a widely used approach (Boix et al. 2014). For each municipality, we assess whether there is a clustering of firms in CCIs and tourism and we compare them with the regional average. This method is applied to the 286 municipalities and to the economic activities NACE Rev. 2 using the location quotient, created in its classical structure:

$$\text{Location quotient} = LQ_{is} = \frac{E_{is} / E_s}{E_i / E}$$

where E_{is} is the number of firms in the municipality s specialised in industry i; E_s is the number of firms in the municipality s; E_i is the number of firms in Tuscany specialised in industry i; and E is the total amount of firms in Tuscany. A location quotient (LQ) above 1 indicates that the municipality is specialised in industry i (CCIs or tourism), i.e. there is a clustering of firms compared to the regional average.

Figure 7.1 shows the results of data elaboration obtained through the ArcView software, which allows us to georeferentiate the results on a territorial map. The municipalities of Tuscany have been identified according to the index of concentration, from the lightest (lower concentration) to the darkest (higher concentration).

Figure 7.1a presents clusters of firms in CCIs. They result to be mainly localised in the north centre of the region, with several highly interesting agglomerations. The first macro-area is the one based in Florence, which includes the municipality of Prato with the textile-clothing industrial district and the areas of San Casciano and Empoli. Separated from this area are the municipalities in the Valdarno area, all characterised by the presence of relevant local productive systems, like the Arezzo jeweler district. The other creative clusters are the ones centred on Pisa and Lucca with the surrounding municipalities, where many research and development activities are concentrated together with university-related services. Another clustering is represented by Siena and the neighbouring municipalities, specialised mainly in pharmaceutical and life sciences industries. Florence shows an index of concentration of 1.63, Pisa has an index of 1.7, whereas Lucca and Siena both show a concentration index of 1.2.

Figure 7.1b illustrates clusters of tourist firms. It especially highlights clusters in municipalities in Southern Tuscany, in particular areas such as Maremma and Versilia on the coast, which result to be mainly specialised in tourism. In the centre of the region, the area of Volterra and San Gimignano, Siena and Chianti and further south the area of Montalcino and Pienza are specialised in tourism and culture-related services. Concentration indexes of tourist firms show the prevalence of tourist clusters with high values of LQ in the Tuscan archipelago (between 3.5 and 5), Maremma (3.5), Versilia (2.7), Siena country side (Chianti) (2.7), etc.[3]

In synthesis, Figure 7.1a highlights CCIs localised in large urban centres and manufacturing clusters characterised by relevant R&D activities (Florence, Pisa, etc.), whereas Figure 7.1b highlights mainly tourist destinations connected to tourism and rural creativity, as in the case of Southern Tuscany.

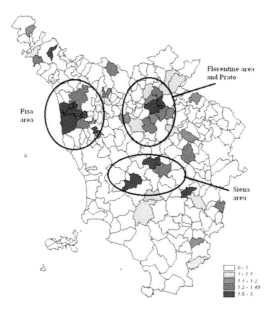

Figure 7.1a CCIs clusters in Tuscany, 2009

Source: Our elaboration on data from ISTAT (2009).

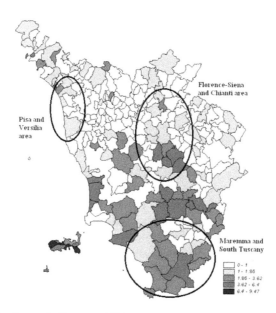

Figure 7.1b Tourist clusters in Tuscany, 2009

Source: Our elaboration on data from ISTAT (2009).

5 Correlation analysis of firms' co-location

We have found that CCIs and tourism have different spatial patterns of location, notwithstanding that the literature point out increasing synergies between these two industries, not only in cultural tourism. In this section, we investigate the relationships of CCIs and tourism, using a spatial perspective in order to analyse whether firms in CCIs and tourism tend to locate close to one another.

We use correlation analysis to investigate patterns of co-location. We calculate correlation coefficients between two LQs of each analysed activity of CCIs and tourism. Table 7.2 presents Spearman coefficients among different sectors at a 0.01% and 0.05% level of significance. A positive correlation indicates that firms in the two industries tend to co-locate together and therefore may have some kind of local interrelationships.

The analysis presents interesting results. First of all, CCIs and tourism show a significant and negative coefficient, therefore they do not tend to co-locate in the same destination or city. This confirms what emerged from the maps, i.e. that CCIs are more concentrated in few large urban areas and tourist firms are more concentrated in rural areas and tourist destinations. Nonetheless this aspect is not always in line with the literature as regards the idea of rural creativity (Bell and Jayne 2010; Collis, Freebody and Flew 2011).

Second, it is possible to analyse co-location patterns of firms in each CCIs and tourism activities. Of course, Hotel and restaurants show a positive and significant coefficient, in fact it is easy to imagine that they tend to cluster together, for instance in tourist destinations. Besides Tour operator and Travel agency show a negative coefficient, but not significant.

Regarding CCIs, as expected Hotel and restaurants are negatively correlated while higher and positive coefficients are registered with Architecture, Software and Design, three industries that tend to locate together in metropolitan areas and large urban centres (Lazzeretti, Boix and Capone 2012).

The coefficient of Cultural heritage activities is significant and positively correlated only with Travel agency, and negatively correlated with Hotel and restaurants. This could be possible as also Cultural heritage activities are more clustered in urban centres of art cities. Also Performing arts shows a similar pattern of co-location, pointing out that this part of the experience economy finds more synergies with CCIs than tourism activities.[4]

In conclusion, the results point out that firms in CCI and tourism have different patterns of location, therefore the relationships between these two groups of firms cannot be taken for granted. The main results confirm the hypothesis that CCIs and tourism generally tend to co-locate in different places, CCIs in large urban centres forming creative clusters, and tourism activities in travel destinations, among which are smaller localities. In the next section, we investigate the relationships between these two sectors and their contribution to the formation of new firms at local level.

Table 7.2 Correlation matrix

	Tourism	CCIs	Hotels	Restaurants	Travel agency	Performing arts	Cultural heritage	Publishing	Cinema and music	Tv and radio	Software	Architecture	Advertising	Design	Photo
Tourism	1.000	−0.328**	0.894**	0.892**	−0.076	−0.037	−0.108*	−0.156**	−0.176**	−0.220**	−0.282**	−0.207**	−0.370**	−0.411**	−0.274**
CCIs	−0.328**	1.000	−0.339**	−0.285**	0.118*	0.236**	0.138**	0.218**	0.322**	0.272**	0.497**	0.856**	0.363**	0.484**	0.264**
Hotels	0.894**	−0.339**	1.000	0.644**	−0.081	−0.044	−0.144**	−0.135*	−0.200**	−0.196**	−0.267**	−0.252**	−0.382**	−0.345**	−0.235**
Restaurants	0.892**	−0.285**	0.644**	1.000	−0.101*	−0.148**	−0.100*	−0.174**	−0.131*	−0.214**	−0.280**	−0.138**	−0.325**	−0.409**	−0.244**
Travel agency	−0.076	0.118*	−0.081	−0.101*	1.000	0.181**	0.216**	0.321**	0.342**	0.178**	0.273**	0.007	0.247**	0.172**	0.282**
Performing arts	−0.037	0.236**	−0.044	−0.148**	0.181**	1.000	0.080	0.172**	0.223**	0.059	0.284**	0.144**	0.244**	0.194**	0.141**
Cultural heritage	−0.108*	0.138**	−0.144**	−0.100*	0.216**	0.080	1.000	0.379**	0.167**	0.226**	0.144**	0.104*	0.200**	0.077	0.141**
Publishing	−0.156**	0.218**	−0.135*	−0.174**	0.321**	0.172**	0.379**	1.000	0.339**	0.297**	0.234**	0.087	0.285**	0.120*	0.329**
Cinema and music	−0.176**	0.322**	−0.200**	−0.131*	0.342**	0.223**	0.167**	0.339**	1.000	0.310**	0.344**	0.184**	0.319**	0.187**	0.243**
Tv and radar	−0.220**	0.272**	−0.196**	−0.214**	0.178**	0.059	0.226**	0.297**	0.310**	1.000	0.224**	0.163**	0.257**	0.147**	0.195**
Software	−0.282**	0.497**	−0.267**	−0.280**	0.273**	0.284**	0.144**	0.234**	0.344**	0.224**	1.000	0.188**	0.312**	0.270**	0.218**
Architecture	−0.207**	0.856**	−0.252**	−0.138**	0.007	0.144**	.200**	0.087	0.184**	0.163**	0.188**	1.000	0.156**	0.213**	0.140**
Advertising	−0.370**	0.363**	−0.382**	−0.325**	0.247**	0.244**	0.200**	0.285**	0.319**	0.257**	0.312**	0.156**	1.000	0.255**	0.214**
Design	−0.411**	0.484**	−0.345**	−0.409**	0.172**	0.194**	0.077	0.120*	0.187**	0.147**	0.270**	0.213**	0.255**	1.000	0.172**
Photo	−0.274**	0.264**	−0.235**	−0.244**	0.282**	0.141**	0.141**	0.329**	0.243**	0.195**	0.218**	0.140**	0.214**	0.172**	1.000

Source: Our elaboration.

Notes: * correlation is significant at the 0.05 level (1–tailed); ** correlation is significant at the 0.01 level (1–tailed).

6 Cultural and creative industries, tourism and new firm formation

The aim of this section is to investigate the different contribution of CCI and tourism to new firm formation. It is recognised in the literature that CCIs and tourist clusters support and contribute to local economic development and specifically to the formation of new businesses and entrepreneurship (Lee, Florida and Acs 2004; Stolarick and Florida 2006; Fritsch 2008), in particular through spillovers and cross-fertilisation processes (Lazzeretti 2009).

As longitudinal data on firms' births and deaths are not available, the growth of firms from 2001–09 is chosen as a proxy of new firm formation. Table 7.3 presents the variables used for the empirical analysis. The dependent variable in the model is the growth of firms in each Tuscan municipality in the period of 2001–09. All the independent variables are calculated at the year 2001 in order to avoid problems of causality. Independent variables are divided in two groups.

The first set of variables regards the industry structure of the municipality. First, we consider the industry share of CCIs and tourism in the municipalities in order to test the hypothesis of the creative economy approach. By this, we aim to assess which are the main determinants of new firm formation, hypothesising different factors according to the local industrial specialisation.

Second, we include a group of variables of the general industry structure. The existence of medium and large cities such as Florence suggests that CCIs are more related to large urban areas. A *size* variable is therefore introduced in order to evaluate whether the dimension of the municipality matters. We include the total population of the municipality in order to evaluate the effect of this urbanisation dimension. The proxy chosen for the size of the local system is the resident population, analysed in absolute (*population*) and relative terms (*population/km²*).

Moreover, we consider the share of firms in manufacturing and services activities in order to analyse the effects of cross-fertilisation and whether the growth in the period is more related to manufacturing or services in the municipality. The share of firms in services does not take into account the firms in the dependent variable.

The third group of variables regards the clustering of CCIs and tourism in the municipalities and is analysed with the help of LQs. Also the LQs are calculated for CCIs and tourism according to the different approaches adopted.

A stepwise regression model was applied to verify the statistical significance of the model. First, in order to separately test the contribution of the different factors to the growth of new firms, partial regressions have been estimated for the different groups of variables (industry structure and clustering). Second, a full model, including all the statistically significant variables in partial regressions, was estimated and reduced to a parsimonious specification. Table 7.4 presents the results of the partial and complete regressions. All the models are satisfactory with a good R^2, but with differences.

Model 1 deals with 'industry structure' and it has a R^2 of 0.68. All the variables have been used safe the share of firms in services that has been omitted due to collinearity problems. The variable *size* is negative, but it is not statistically significant. The share of firms in manufacturing activities is positive. The share of firms

Table 7.3 Variables of the model

Variables	Description
Dependent variable	Ln of percentage of growth of firms per municipality *i* in the period 2001–09
Independent variables	
% firms in tourism	Percentage of firms in tourism
% firms in CCIs	Percentage of firms in CCIs
Size (population)	Population
Size 2 (population density)	Population/km²
% firms in manufacturing	Percentage of firms in manufacturing activities
% firms in services	Percentage of firms in services
LQ CCIs	Location quotient in CCIs
LQ tourism	Location quotient in tourism

Source: Our elaboration.

Note: All the independent variables refer to the year 2001.

in CCI is negatively correlated with the growth of firms, but it is not significant. The share of firms in tourism are instead positively correlated to formation of new firms with the highest coefficients (0.819). This could be also related to the characteristics of Tuscany and its wide diffusion of tourist firms throughout the region.

Model 2 of clustering has an R^2 of 0.684, that is higher than in the previous model. LQs are all statistically significant, but with differences in sign and intensity. LQ in CCIs is negative and significantly correlated with firms' growth (-0.098), but very small. Besides, LQ in tourism is positively correlated with firm formation (0.810), and has the most relevant impact on firm formation. Under this light, the effects of the concentration of tourism seem to produce a greater total effect at regional level. However, this aspect is more widely investigated in the full model. In general, results confirm that the contribution of tourist clusters to firm formation prevails on that of CCIs.

Model 3 is the full model integrating all the previous variables and achieves an R^2 of 0.787, which is higher than in the other estimations. As expected, the share of CCIs is finally positively correlated (0.128). The coefficient of the share of tourism is omitted for collinearity. As for the clustering of CCIs and tourism, CCIs are still negatively correlated with growth, but close to zero (-0.096), while tourist clustering registers a positive and significant coefficient, the highest coefficient in the model (0.831). This confirm that clustering of tourist firms shows a larger contribution to firm formation than cluster of CCIs. This is specific for the case of Tuscany as a world known tourist region. This is also due to the different relationship between the two sectors. In fact, whilst the presence of tourist clusters results positive in rural areas, that of CCIs is positive in urban areas. Variable *size* is now positively correlated, but it is not significant. Here it seems confirmed an urban effect, where CCIs are more clustered in urban areas. The share of firms in manufacturing activities is negative, but not statistically significant.

Table 7.4 OLS estimations

Variables	Model 1 Industry structure	Model 2 Clustering	Model 3 Full model
Constant	0.182 (0.732)	1.751*** (0.000)	1.9891*** (0.000)
% firms in tourism	0.819*** (0.000)		
% firms in CCIs	−0.088 (0.022)		0.128*** (0.000)
Size (population)	−0.044 (0.276)		0.059 (0.093)
% firms in manufacturing	0.048 (0.243)		−0.17 (0.613)
LQ CCIs		−0.098* (0.009)	−0.096*** (0.000)
LQ tourism		0.810*** (0.000)	0.831*** (0.000)
R^2	0.688	0.684	0.787
Adjusted R^2	0.683	0.681	0.787
VIF mean	1.93	1.60	1.39
DF	4	2	5
Test F	125.28*** (0.000)	148.52*** (0.000)	167.44*** (0.000)
Durbin Watson	1.842	1.827	1.886
Obs	232	232	232

Source: Our elaboration on data from ISTAT (2001; 2009).

Notes: * $p < 0.01$; *** $p < 0.0001$; significance in brackets.

7 Conclusions

The aim of this chapter was to examine the relationship between tourism and creativity, with a specific focus on CCIs. The study has investigated the patterns of clustering and co-locations of firms in tourism and CCIs and their contribution to new firm formation through a case study of Tuscany.

The first results confirm the relevance of CCIs and tourism activities in the case of Tuscany, accounting for a relevance share of total firms in the region. Firms in CCIs grow more in the period and develop predominantly in large metropolitan areas as an urban phenomenon. These clusters are mainly localised in large urban areas such as Florence, Pisa and Siena, and are strongly linked to high-tech industries (R&D, software, design, etc.). Tourist clusters have instead a wider diffusion in the region and are strongly present in rural areas, smaller cities and tourist destinations.

Regarding the location analysis of firms in CCIs and tourism, they show different patterns of co-location, so that the interrelationships between these two groups of firms cannot be taken for granted. The main results confirm the hypothesis that CCIs and tourism in general tend to co-locate in different places, CCIs in large urban centres forming creative clusters, and tourist firms in travel destinations, smaller cities and localities.

Concerning the contribution of these two sectors to the formation of new firms and entrepreneurship at the local level, tourist clusters results are more important than that of CCIs, confirming the economic structure on which the regional economy is based. This is particularly true in regions like Tuscany, characterised by the presence of a widespread cultural and environmental heritage and only a few high-tech clusters, typical instead of Northern Europe, where the creative economy approach has taken hold.

In many countries, CCIs are more and more driving the interest and economic development, but according to our findings, tourism activities are at least as important for promoting new entrepreneurship and new firm formation. This suggests that a strong focus on CCIs in regions like Tuscany may be justified, but taking also into account other sectors, particularly tourism.

The last argument is related to the increasing attention on creative tourism and the interrelationships between tourism and creativity, analysed in our study in terms of CCIs' performance. The results underline that there are several differences between these two industries, from the different weight of employment and number of firms in the economy of Tuscany, to their different spatial configuration, and finally the different co-location strategies of firms. From this point of view, despite the interrelationships between tourism and CCIs are highly appealing, from the point of view of this analysis clear empirical evidences of synergies between these two sectors do not emerge. Therefore these relationships do not seem to have yet been sufficiently investigated.

Notwithstanding the limit of the analysis, the integration of the creative economy approach with tourism shows interesting results. Further research is needed in order to generalise results, nonetheless the case of Tuscany seems to point out again that CCIs and tourism are still important determinants in promoting new entrepreneurships and firm formation.

Notes

1 The revised classification of CCIs of DCMS (2013) focus on the creative intensity of industries, i.e. the percentage of creative employees on the total, in order to evaluate whether it is creative or not.
2 The analysis of 2001 data on employment in Florence shows that Architecture accounts for 1,671 employees while Engineering accounts for 671 employees. In a city of art like Florence, it is not surprising that the employees in Architecture constituted the majority for the macro-economic activity. This analysis is not possible for 2011 as data below the 3-digit level are not available at the municipal level.
3 This is also because LQs are higher in small places as they are relative indexes of specialisation.
4 On this topic see also Chapter 8 by Boix and De Propris in this book.

References

Aquino, J., Phillips, R. and Sung, H. (2012) 'Tourism, culture, and the creative industries: Reviving distressed neighbourhoods with arts-based community', *Tourism, Culture and Communication*, 12(1): 5–18.
Bakhshi, H., Freeman, A. and Higgs, P. (2013) *A Dynamic Mapping of the UK's Creative Industries*, London: NESTA.

Bakhshi, H., McVittie, E. and Simmie, J. (2008) *Creating Innovation: Do the Creative Industries Support Innovation in the Wider Economy?* London: NESTA.

Barrowclough, D. and Kozul-Wright, Z. (eds) (2008) *Creative Industries and Developing Countries: Voice, Choice and Economic Growth*, Abingdon: Routledge.

Bell, D. and Jayne, M. (2010) 'The creative countryside: Policy and practice in the UK rural cultural economy', *Journal of Rural Studies*, 26(3): 209–18.

Belussi F. and Sedita S. R. (eds.) (2010) *Managing situated creativity in cultural industries*, Abingdon: Routledge.

Boix, R., De Miguel, B. and Hervás, J. L. (2013) 'Creative service business and regional performance: Evidence for the European regions', *Service Business*, 7(3): 381–98.

Boix, R., Capone, F., De Propris, L., Lazzeretti, L. and. Sanchez, R. (2014) 'Comparing creative industries in Europe', *European Urban and Regional Studies*, published online August 2014.

Capone F. (2008) 'Mapping and analysing creative systems in Italy (1991–2001)', in P. Cooke and L. Lazzeretti (eds), *Creative cities, Cultural Cluster and Local Economic Development*, Cheltenham, Edward Elgar, pp. 338–364.

Chapain, C., Cooke, P., De Propris, L., MacNeill, S. and Mateos-Garcia, J. M. (2010) *Creative Clusters and Innovation*, London: NESTA.

Collis, C., Freebody, S. and Flew, T. (2011) 'Seeing the outer suburbs: Addressing the urban bias in creative place thinking', *Regional Studies*, 47(2): 148–60.

Cook, G.A.S. and Pandit, N. R. (2010) 'International linkages and entrepreneurship in media clusters: Evidence from the UK', in C. Karlsson, B. Johansson and R.R. Stough (eds), *Entrepreneurship and Regional Development. Local Processes and Global Patterns*, Cheltenham, UK: Elgar Edward, pp. 119–47.

Cooke, P. and Lazzeretti, L. (eds) (2008) *Creative Cities, Cultural Clusters and Local Economic Development*, Cheltenham, UK: Edward Elgar.

DCMS – Department for Culture, Media and Sport (2001) *Creative Industries Mapping Document*, London: DCMS

DCMS – Department for Culture, Media and Sport (2006) *Developing Entrepreneurship for the Creative Industries*, London: DCMS.

DCMS – Department for Culture, Media and Sport (2013) *Classifying and Measuring the Creative Industries*, London: DCMS.

De Beukelaer, C. (2014) 'Creative industries in "developing" countries: Questioning country classifications in the UNCTAD creative economy reports', *Cultural Trends*, 23(4): 232–51.

De Miguel, B., Hervás, J. L., Boix, R. and De Miguel, M. (2012) 'The importance of creative industry agglomerations in explaining the wealth of European regions', *European Planning Studies*, 20(8): 1263–80.

De Propris, L., Chapain, C., Cooke, P., MacNeill, S. and Mateos-Garcia, J. (2009) *The Geography of Creativity*, London: NESTA.

Den Dekker, T. and Tabbers, M. (2012) 'From creative crowds to creative tourism: A search for creative tourism in small and medium sized cities', *Journal of Tourism Consumption and Practice*, 4(2): 129–32.

EC – European Commission (2010) *Green Paper on Cultural and Creative Industries: Unlocking the Potential of Cultural and Creative Industries*, COM(2010) 183, Brussels: EU Commission.

Flew, T. and Cunningham, S.D. (2010) 'Creative industries after the first decade of debate', *The Information Society*, 26(2): 113–23.

Florida, R. (2002) *The Rise of the Creative Class*, New York: Basic Books.

Fritsch, M. (2008) 'How does new business formation affect regional development? Introduction to the special issue', *Small Business Economics*, 30(1): 1–14.

Hjalager, A.M. and Antonioli Corigliano, M., (2000), 'Food for tourists. Determinants of an image', International Journal of Tourism research, 2, 281–293.

Henry, C. (eds) (2007) *Entrepreneurship in the Creative Industries: An International Perspective*, Cheltenham, UK: Edward Elgar.

Hong, J., Yu, W., Guo, X. and Zhao, D. (2014) 'Creative industries agglomeration, regional innovation and productivity growth in China', *Chinese Geographical Science*, 24(2): 258–68.

ISTAT – Istituto Nazionale di Statistica (2001) *VIII Censimento generale dell'industria e dei servizi* 2001, Rome: ISTAT.

ISTAT – Istituto Nazionale di Statistica (2009) *Database ASIA 2009*, Rome: ISTAT.

Landry, C. (2000) *The Creative City: A Toolkit for Urban Innovators*, London: Earthscan.

Landry, C. and Bianchini, F. (1995) *The Creative City*, London: Demos.

Lazzeretti, L. (2009) 'The creative capacity of culture and the new creative milieu', in G. Becattini, M. Bellandi and L. De Propris (eds), *A Handbook of Industrial Districts*, Cheltenham, UK: Edward Elgar, pp. 281–94.

Lazzeretti, L. (ed.) (2013) *Creative Industries and Innovation in Europe*, London: Routledge.

Lazzeretti, L. and Capone, F. (2015) 'Narrow or broad definition of cultural and creative industries: Some evidence from Tuscany, Italy', *International Journal of Cultural and Creative Industries*, 2(2): 4–18.

Lazzeretti, L., Boix, R. and Capone, F. (2012) 'Reasons for clustering of creative industries in Italy and Spain', *European Planning Studies*, 20(8): 1–20.

Lee, S. Y., Florida, R. and Acs, Z. (2004) 'Creativity and entrepreneurship: A regional analysis of new firm formation', *Regional Studies*, 38(8): 879–91.

Lorentzen, A., Schrøder, L., Larsen K. T. (2012) (eds), Spatial Dynamics in the Experience Economy, Routledge: Abingdon.

Lorentzen, A. and Hansen, C. J. (2009) 'The role and transformation of the city in the experience economy: Identifying and exploring research challenges', *European Planning Studies*, 17(6): 817–27.

Lorenzen, M. and Frederiksen, L. (2008) 'Why do cultural industries cluster? Localisation, urbanization, products and projects', in P. Cooke and L. Lazzeretti (eds), *Creative Cities, Cultural Clusters and Local Economic Development*, Cheltenham, UK: Edward Elgar, pp. 155–79.

OECD – Organization for Economic Cooperation and Development (2014) *Tourism and the Creative Economy*, OECD Studies on Tourism, Paris: OECD Publishing.

Pappalepore, I., Maitland, R. and Smith, A. (2014) 'Prosuming creative urban areas. Evidence from East London', *Annals of Tourism Research*, 44(1): 227–40.

Pilotti, L. (2011) (eds) *Creatività, innovazione e territorio. Ecosistemi del valore per la competizione globale*, Il Mulino, Bologna.

Porter, M. E. (1998) 'Cluster and the new economics of competition', *Harvard Business Review*, 76(6): 77–90.

Power, D. (2011) *Priority Sector Report: Creative and Cultural Industries*, The European Cluster Observatory, Europe Innova Paper no. 16, Luxemburg: Publications Office of the European Union.

Richards, G. (2011) 'Creativity and tourism. The state of the art', *Annals of Tourism Research*, 38(4): 1225–53.

Richards, G. (2013) 'Tourism development trajectories: From culture to creativity?', in M. Smith and G. Richards, *Handbook of Cultural Tourism*, London: Routledge, pp. 9–16.

Richards, G. (2014) 'Tourism and the creative industries. Executive summary', in OECD, *Tourism and the Creative Economy*, OECD Studies on Tourism, Paris: OECD Publishing, pp. 7–9.

Richards, G. and Raymond, C. (2000) 'Creative tourism', *ATLAS news*, 23: 16–20.

Richards, G. and Wilson, J. (2006) 'Developing creativity in tourist experiences: A solution to the serial reproduction of culture?' *Tourism Management*, 27(6): 1408–13.

Richards, G. and Wilson, J. (2007) *Tourism, Creativity and Development*, Abingdon: Routledge.

Russo, A. P. and Quagliari, A. (2012) 'New forms of tourism in Barcelona', paper presented at the ATLAS Annual Conference, London, 12–15 September.

Salman, D. (2010) 'Rethinking of cities, culture and tourism within a creative perspective', *PASOS. Revista de Turismo y Patrimonio Cultural*, 8(3): 1–5.

Santagata, W. (2009) *Libro bianco sulla creatività*, Rome: Ministero per i Beni e le Attività culturali.

Scott, A. J. (2006) 'Entrepreneurship, innovation and industrial development: Geography and the creative field revisited', *Small Business Economics*, 26(1): 1–24.

Sepe, M. and Di Trapani, G. (2010) 'Cultural tourism and creative regeneration: Two case studies', *International Journal of Culture, Tourism and Hospitality*, 4(3): 214–27.

Stam, E., De Jong, J.P.J. and Marlet, G. (2008) 'Creative industries in the Netherlands: Structure, development, innovativeness and effects on urban growth', *Geografiska Annaler: Series B, Human Geography*, 90(2): 119–32.

Stolarick, K. and Florida, R. (2006) 'Creativity, connections and innovation: A study of linkages in the Montréal Region', *Environment and Planning A*, 38(10): 1799–1817.

Tafel-Viia, K., Viia, A., Terk, E. and Lassur, S. (2014) 'Urban policies for the creative industries: A European comparison', *European Planning Studies*, 22(4): 796–815.

UNCTAD = United Nations Conference on Trade and Development (2010) *Creative Economy Report. Creative Economy*, Geneva and New York: UNDP and UNCTAD.

UNESCO – United Nations Educational, Scientific and Cultural Organization (2013) *Creative Economy Report. Widening Local Development Pathways*, Paris: UNESCO.

Yang, Y. (2009) 'Integration of tourism and creative industries: A comparative study of industries', *Journal of Nanjing College for Population Programme Management*, 1: 67–70.

Yusuf, S. and Nabeshima, K. (2005) 'Creative industries in East Asia', *Cities*, 22(2): 109–22.

8 The experience-related economy in the UK

Rafael Boix and Lisa De Propris

1 Introduction

The post-knowledge economy debate has witnessed the emergence of a new set of concerns that have turned the attention of scholars and policy makers towards industries that so far have been neglected. With the relocation of mass production in low-cost countries, and with technological advancement transforming many industries and inventing others, the focus has now shifted to those economic activities that are producing value. The 2008 financial crisis has also triggered a widespread critique of aggressive forms of capitalism then symbolised by the financial sector. Across the European economies, the post-recession debate has pivoted around strategies that could rebalance the economy and lock them on sustainable growth paths. This means a different way of looking at local economic development, where the 'local' captures both fast growing but congested cities, and more peripheral and often rural areas. The sustainable growth of both becomes in this context part of a set of local development strategies that reconsiders the economic value of a broader set of industries.

The economic contribution of creative, cultural and experience industries has garnered the attention of scholars and especially policy makers, who were looking for alternatives to other historical sectors in demise and shrinking. Creative, cultural and experience industries coincide with economic activities that form an evolution from blue-collar manufacturing and are on the cusp between manufacturing and services.

There is a lively and ongoing debate on how to define such industries: what are the differences across them? Do they overlap? Do they behave differently? What drives them and what constrains them? What is their impact on the local economy? What policies to develop and support them?

Drawing on the American and Scandinavian literature on the experience economy, this chapter presents an in-depth analysis of the experience economy in the UK. Here the debate has focused primarily on creative industries, leaving aside sectors that the current literature has referred to as being part of the experience economy. The Department for Culture, Media and Sports (DCMS) in the UK has in particular shaped the academic and policy debate by putting forward a clear, albeit not necessarily accurate, classification of creative industries. One of the key drawbacks of the UK's economic appreciation of creative industries is that it only includes sectors relatively intensive in hard technology, such as games and digital, thereby neglecting the importance of culture and tourism industries. However, according to Deloitte (2008), in 2007 the 'Visitor economy' (this would include both cultural industries and tourism) accounted for more than 8% of the UK's GDP. A back of the envelope calculation would show that the combined creative and cultural economies could account to up to 15% of the national GDP.

This chapter presents therefore two main novelties. First, it maps the UK experience industries. This enables important reflections on the behaviour of such industries and on their juxtaposition with creative industries. An analytical framework will then be proposed where the key features of the experience industries will be identified in order to understand how they compare with creative industries. This will refine our understanding of both experience and creative economies in view of appreciating their different drivers and dynamics.

The chapter will proceed as follows: section 2 will present a critical survey of the current debate on creative, cultural and experience-related industries, so as to highlight its drivers and trends. Section 3 will discuss how the concept of 'experience economy' has been captured by the UK debate where the focus has recently been more on creative industry. Section 4 will present the methodological issues related to the mapping analysis of experience industries in the UK and sections 5 and 6 will discuss the results of the mapping exercise. In a pure deductive approach, a tentative conceptual framework to understand experience industries will be introduced in section 7 before some concluding remarks.

2 A definitional maze

Since Florida's scholarly book on the *Creative Class* (2002), both the economic and geography disciplines have translated such concept in creative activities, firms and industries: these have been extensively studied across countries with case or sector studies to unearth phenomena completely *hidden* in the economy until then. The real interest in them stems from their ability to generate economic value and innovation. We can read in European Commission (EC 2010) that 'Creative and Cultural Industries often contribute to boosting local economies in decline, contributing to the emergence of new economic activities, creating new and sustainable jobs and enhancing the attractiveness of European regions and cities' (p. 13). The reference to the 'experience economy' (p. 17), confirms that these three terms carry equal weight in the debate, contributing somehow to the current definitional maze.

Galloway and Dunlop (2007) present an overarching reflection on the distinctions between creative and cultural industries by identifying five criteria: creativity, intellectual property, symbolic meaning, use value and methods of product. Of these, the last two are probably the most enlightening in providing some clarity. Throsby (2001) suggests that culture industries should be those that *involve some form of creativity in their production*, generate and communicate *symbolic meaning*, and can be protected by *intellectual property*. Our understanding of cultural industries is complicated by the fact that culture and cultural outputs can become the inputs of other cultural and non-cultural goods (Throsby 2001). In these cases, it is very difficult to say what is a cultural good and what is not, how much cultural input qualifies to define a cultural output? From a different perspective, cultural industries are those for which the methods of production involve the creation of symbolic meaning and mass production (Galloway and Dunlop 2007). One might wonder, so what are the creative industries? The discussion above suggests that the latter are those that cannot be defined as cultural. The terminological clutter suggested by Galloway and Dunlop (2007), in reality proves something more profound characterising creative and cultural industries: that is they create value, such value can feed across the economy, the economic revenue of such value creation can be appropriated. Whether the creative or cultural output is input for another production process or consumption good is probably of minor importance, as is the fact that in both cases it contains innovative, creative value.

In this chapter, we are complicating the analysis by adding in the picture experience-related industries. Drawing on the Scandinavian academic literature, the experience economy has come to the fore over the last few years acknowledging a phenomenon that was unfolding before our very eyes.

Experiences represent an existing but previously unarticulated genre of economic output. Whereas commodities are fungible materials extracted from the natural world, goods are tangible products that companies standardise and then inventory, services are intangible activities performed for a particular client, 'experiences are events that engage individuals in a personal way' (Pine and Gilmore 1999: 12).

The definition of 'experience economy' is somewhat fuzzy. A clear definition of the term is not found in Pine and Gilmore (1998; 1999) although refers to a kind of economy in which products are differentiated through the quality of the consumer experience which adds the differential level of added value. In the Danish government report (Regeringen 2003: 8), it is defined as 'an economy that is based on an increasing demand for experiences and that builds upon the added value that creativity lends to both new and traditional products and services'. As Bille (2010) exposes, some 'experiences' are produced by the public sector with public funds (e.g. a part of the culture) so this introduces some apparent contradiction between the primary definitions of the idea that the author suggests to solve by focusing only on the commercial (business) part of the experience economy.

Even if previous definitions refer to results of the experience economy as 'products' to be consumed, another way of defining it refers to 'specific industries where the experience component is particularly strong or where the potential for developing the experience component is evident' (Smidt-Jensen, Skytt and Winther 2009). Thus, the experience economy is more evident in certain specific sectors of the economy as in cultural and creative industries, leisure and entertainment, and tourism.

The increasing relevance of the experience economy draws on the deep societal changes characterising the last decade. First, the increasing affluence of Western societies – Europe included – and the spread of marketing and advertising have created needs and thereby encouraged greater consumption of goods and services. Indeed, between 1870 and 2002, incomes in the industrialised countries have grown at an annual rate of 2.3% (Smidt-Jensen, Skytt and Winther 2009), and in particular, the share of *recreational consumption* almost doubled in the UK from 5.9% to 13.2% (Andersson and Andersson 2006: 42). Recent trends in income, work-time choice, demography and education have impacted on the way people consume cultural and leisure products and services, and this has shaped the way the respective industries have grown and strengthened over time (Lorentzen 2009). The shortening of the working time and better paid jobs have relaxed people's constraints to leisure consumption related to income and time; indeed never before have the opportunities for the consumption of leisure products and services been so great (Tofler 1970). Better educated people also have learned a more sophisticated appreciation of cultural products and are prepared to travel to experience a unique cultural event. Lorentzen (2009) also argues that especially in the advanced countries, demographic trends have also played a key role as people live longer, and have an increasing ability to command a comfortable pension.

Affluence is another important factor; however, a second recent trend has played a role. The emergence of the Asian economies having havens of low-cost manufacturing production has attracted many labour-intensive activities leaving behind large number of old-fashioned manufacturing jobs especially in advanced economies including Europe. The slow but inevitable process of *tertiarisation* has coincided with service industries growing in size in terms of both employment and GDP contribution. In this process, service industries began to absorb the talent dismissed by a shrinking manufacturing sector: this included white collars, but also retailing, entertainment, consulting, finance and hospitality – dining and drinking. In particular, some of these industries found themselves at the right place at the right time: for instance, hospitality and entertainment were able to respond to a growing public demand thanks to the ability to expand capacity by attracting the necessary skills.

The rise in demand is somewhat related to a third factor, which is that over the last two decades, the world has become flatter and smaller thanks to easy and cheaper transport, immediate communication and high worldwide *virtual* visibility on the Internet. Globalisation has indeed enabled people to discover, to access and physically to visit more places than ever. The authenticity (Kebir and Crevoisier 2008) and experience of doing something or being somewhere has become a consumption good that has permeated urban and rural scenes. Lorentzen (2009) refers to an economy whose experience product is '-ing the thing'. Such experience product can be a service or a good, think of 'wine tasting in Tuscany' which probably is able to combine the two.

The concomitance of increased affluence, the tertiarisation of the economy and 'the death of distance' (Cairncross 1997) have created economic activities that mainstream economic analysis had until recently dismissed. On the contrary, these are taking centre stage for two reasons: one is that there is a growing demand for experience goods and services, and therefore the related sectors are actually growing in terms of jobs and GDP contribution. The second one is that these industries comprise activities that tend to develop across urban and rural areas. Whilst they might make art and culture accessible to large educated audiences in, for instance, 'cities of art' such as Florence (Lazzeretti 2003) or global cities such as London, they also open up to the world heritage, natural and cultural intensive places that are in peripheral and more rural regions.

Lorentzen (2009) and Lorentzen and Hansen (2009) present a discussion of the spatial characteristics of the experience economy and compare the latter with other spatial paradigms – the industrial economy and the knowledge economy. Thus, for them the experience economy is produced and consumed both in central or peripheral locations: central places can be magnets for inhabitants and visitors and those that are bigger and more specialised can offer experiences based in variety and history. Peripheral places can offer experiences based on their environment and authenticity and engage in growth paths based on tourism, events and activities.

Despite the strong relationship between experience economy and place, the geography of the experience economy has received very little attention in empirical research. Smidt-Jensen, Skytt and Winther (2009) map the attendance-based experience products and services (AEPS) in Denmark. AEPS refers to those experience outputs that are bound to a specific place, in contrast with detachable experience products and services (DEPS) that can be accessed by consumers from all over the world. The authors used a sector-based approach based on 'Hotels and restaurants' and 'Entertainment, culture and sport'. They found that the employment in AEPS industries grew 30% in Denmark (from 1993–2006) and that the spatial patterns of distribution both AEPS sectors are slightly different, even if, in general, both tend to co-locate. 'Entertainment, culture and sports' concentrates in tourism resorts (west coast of North and South Jutland) and in the fourth largest cities in the country. 'Hotels and restaurants' tend to concentrate, in absolute and relative terms, in Copenhagen and surrounding municipalities, and in tourist destinations, but tend not to be important in peripheral places. They conclude that 'the experience economy can be a window of opportunities for small and medium-sized municipalities outside the growth centres is partly valid when it comes to the traditional tourist places with natural, cultural or entertainment amenities' (Smidt-Jensen, Skytt and Winther 2009: 858).

From an operational point of view, the experience economy has strong and understandable overlaps with the cultural economy. The Danish Ministry includes in the 'culture and experience economy' a broad range of sectors such as fashion, visual arts, music, toys and amusement, tourism, books, theatre, radio and television, architecture, sports industries, design, printed media, film and video, advertising, edutainment, content production, events and cultural institutions.

Cultural industries more broadly include museums, artisan foods/cuisine, heritage sites and festivals, and historical and natural heritage (Cooke and Lazzeretti 2008; Lorentzen 2009). The EU defines cultural sectors as those related to publishing, library and archive activities, museum activities and preservation of historical sites and buildings, audiovisual activities and other entertainment activities. UNESCO (2009) has recently produced a comparative analysis of creative and cultural industries across 14 countries, including the UK, which provides a good starting point to compare such industries in a meaningful way. However, experience economies are in this respect absorbed by cultural economies.

Overall a clear definition of experience industries has not yet been agreed on and scholars are still in the process of reaching a better understanding of what they are, especially in relation to creative and cultural industries.

3 The experience economy in the UK debate

The concept of *experience economy* is very little known in the UK. The DCMS has steered the academic and policy debate by providing a clear classification of creative industries which, however, overlooks some important cultural experience-based activities. These coincide with an ample sector of the economy that has expanded over the last decades as the UK has become more affluent and society more eager to consume leisure goods and services.

In the DCMS classification, creative industries include: Advertising, Architecture, Arts and antique markets, Computer and video games, Crafts, Design, Designer Fashion, Film and video, Music, Performing arts, Publishing, Software, Television and Radio.

Cooke and De Propris (2011) suggest that the policy agenda endorsed by the UK government has developed within a techno-scientific paradigm which privileges technology-intensive sectors against more traditional ones. This means that some of the targeted creative industries pivot around technology platforms such as digital, design, and software. As important as this will be for the innovation leaps of the country, this underestimates the innovation capacity of culture and experience-led activities, and their potential as crucial users At the same time, it concentrates the attention uniquely on urban areas neglecting rural economies. Indeed, De Propris *et al.* (2009) found that most creative industries cluster in urban areas to benefit from agglomeration and urbanisation economies. The exception was 'Arts and antiques' which not only appeared to spread quite evenly across regions, but their location was negatively correlated with all the other creative industries, which populated urban areas.

Nevertheless, the DCMS ought to be a wider remit which embraces 'cultural and sporting activities' as well as 'tourism, creative and leisure industries'. Indeed culture has centre stage in the government department website with an understanding that it encompasses all sorts of socio-economic activities that include: the arts; broadcasting; creative industries; the historic environment; Internet and international ICT; licensing and gambling; libraries; museums and galleries; sport; telecommunications and broadband; and tourism. In this almost rimless sphere of activities, it finds itself out of sync with the debate that is on the other hand developing in Northern and continental Europe, where embedded and place-based resources generate economic activities that are associated with the value of having the first-hand, authentic experience of certain phenomenon.

Deloitte (2008; 2010) looks at the contribution of the 'Visitor economy' and finds that in 2007 the visitor sector directly accounted for 3.7% of GDP and supported 1.36 million jobs, but the total – direct and indirect effect – was up to 8.2% of the UK GDP. In particular, the Visitor economy include 'Hotels', 'Camping sites', 'Restaurants', 'Bars', 'Travel agencies', 'Libraries, archives and museums', 'Sport' and 'Other recreational activities'. These sectors in reality cover a wide range of cultural and experience-centred activities that draw on the country's natural resources, historical heritage and cultural vibrancy. They include museum activities, preservation of historical sites and buildings, botanical and zoological gardens, and nature reserve activities. They also take account of all sorts of sporting activities, from horseracing to football. The classification includes ancillary hospitality activities such as hotels, camping sites, lodgings and holiday villages, together with restaurant and bars. Finally, it recognises the role of travel agencies, tour operators, as well as tourist assistance and tour guides.

Another government document relevant in this debate, is the UKTI (2010) creative industries report, which portrays UK's experience industries as attractive industries for foreign investment. The report acknowledges that 'The UK is one of the world's leaders in the aptly named "experience economy" – the creation and operation of visitor attractions such as museums, art galleries, heritage sites, gardens, zoos and leisure parks' (p. 30).

The first novelty of this chapter is identifying experience and experience-related industries whilst taking into account the well-accepted classification of creative industries endorsed by the DCMS. These include both those identified by the Deloitte report and those selected in the UKTI report, however, we have decided to add as well economic activities related to the 'Retail sale in temporary markets on stalls'. This acknowledges the boom in market craft and food fairs which UK cities and towns have experienced over the last decade. FOE (2000) reveals that there were no farmers' markets, for instance, in the UK in 1997, but 240 in 2000 and more than 500 in 2010 (data from National Farmers' Retail & Markets Association). We have also decided to include the 'Activities of other membership organisations'. These are interesting and active private organisations that mobilise people on the basis of their common interest, including environmental and ecological movements, touring clubs and associations for the pursuit of a cultural or recreational activity or hobby (e.g. historical, gardening, art, craft and collectors' clubs, social clubs and carnival clubs). This category captures the presence of various forms of collective coordination and lobbying as expressions of spontaneous, locally embedded interests and concerns.

In reality, there are two other sectors that would naturally fall within this category. These are 'Arts and antiques' and 'Visual and performing art'; however, both of them are currently classified by the DCMS as creative industries. A spatial analysis of these latter sectors can be found in De Propris *et al.* (2009).

There are two further sectors we have not considered in our study but which are worth of further investigation: food and craft. There are serious difficulties in singling out the 'experience' component from these sectors. The food sector is extremely fragmented and comprises industries that are typically mechanised and that tend to mass produce, whilst also including homemade cheese in Cheltenham. From the statistical point of view it is very difficult to discern between the two and

Table 8.1 Some relevant classifications

Visitor economy (Deloitte 2010)		UKTI 'experience economy'	
551	Hotel		
552	Camping sites		
553	Restaurants		
554	Bars		
633	Travel agencies		
925	Libraries, archives and museums	925	Museums and art galleries, zoos, gardens, heritage sites
926	Sport		
927	Other recreational activities	923	Leisure parks

Source: Our elaboration.

Table 8.2 Experience economy (ONS 2003)

Experience economy	
551	Hotel
552	Camping sites and other accommodations
553	Restaurants
554	Bars
633	Travel agencies, tour operators and tourist assistance activities
923	Other entertainment activities (artistic and literary creation and interpretation, operation of arts facilities, fair and amusement park activities)
925	Libraries, archives and museums
926	Sporting activities
927	Other recreational activities
5262	Retail sale via stalls and markets
9133	Membership organisations including pursuit of cultural and recreational activities

Source: Our elaboration.

capture quantitatively the 'gourmet', 'authentic', 'homemade' and 'slow' food that would genuinely reflect an experience activity (Arthur 2009). On the other hand, craft activities are not separately classified in the statistical database from the more traditional activities, so for instance, mass produced garments would fall under the same category as hand-knitted scarves. The same can be said for glass, furniture, jewelry or ceramic tableware.

We therefore start our mapping analysis by concentrating only on the 11 above listed (Table 8.2). We expect the spatial analysis of the experience sectors to throw some light on how appropriate it is for the two latter sectors to be classified either as creative or experience sectors.

4 Methodology

The mapping analysis is carried out by relying on firm data at the travel-to-work-areas (TTWAs). There are 232 TTWAs in 2008 across England, Wales and Scotland – data for Northern Ireland are not available. TTWAs represent self-contained local labour markets mirroring local commuting patterns. They are particularly appropriate to study firms' clustering and co-location since they embody not only an agglomeration of firms but a local labour market. TTWAs have been previously used in the analysis of clustering of the creative industries in Italy, Spain and France (see Lazzeretti, Boix and Capone 2008; Boix *et al.* 2014) as well as in the UK (De Propris *et al.* 2009). Firm data is extracted from the Annual Business Inquiry at the three and four-digit level. Sectors are defined according to the Office for National Statistics (ONS) (2003) classification and the year is 2008.

We use standard location quotients (LQs) as an indicator of industrial agglomeration in a given geographical unit of analysis. If the LQ is greater than one, this means that the agglomeration is greater than the national average, which indicates relative specialisation in that sector for that unit of geographical analysis. LQs, however, capture the relevance of an industry within the broader economy of a particular place irrespective of the absolute number of firms actually present. So, even a small number of firms might be flagged in a sector as being dominant in a particular place, depending on the make-up of that local economy. Conversely, LQs can hide agglomerations firms in a sector in areas with a larger than average number of firms from all sectors (Lazzeretti, Boix and Capone 2008).

5 Results of the mapping analysis

An initial important aspect of the experience sector – as defined in this chapter – in the UK is that between 1998 and 2008, employment grew by about 17% compared to a contraction of one-third of the manufacturing sector: this explains the increasing attentions it is receiving from policy makers. The spatial patterns will provide further insight on the potential of the sector to be a driver of local economic development.

We begin by looking into the distribution and concentration of experience industries across British regions by considering both the absolute number of firms and the LQ (Figures 8.1 and 8.2). The first novel finding is that London appears to host the largest number of firms in the experience industries – that is 46,800 out of 247,720 corresponding to about 20%. However, the weight of such industries on the economy of the capital is quite limited, as the LQ for London is below one. The high number of firms in experience industries is due primarily to the large number of 'Restaurants', 'Bars' and 'Other entertainment activities'. The LQ gives us a measure of how specialised in a sector a particular TTWA is in comparison with the country average. It is no surprise therefore that London – as a global city – does not appear to be specialised in experience industries, but rather presents a quite diversified economic make-up. On the contrary, London tends to concentrate a large number of firms in many sectors especially services. So, contrary to what was found in De Propris *et al.* (2009) where London appeared to be *the creative industry hotspot*, experience industries are present in London but they do not characterise the local urban economy. Experience industries are also secondary in the local economy of Britain's manufacturing heartland: the Midlands. Again looking at the maps in Figure 8.1 and 8.2, one can see that although TTWAs in the Midlands host a large number of experience activities, the LQs are below one. These regions tend to be dominated by manufacturing activities, some of which have high-technology content, and would fall under the creative industry category (De Propris *et al.* 2009). Our evidence shows that experience activities tend to spread across less urban areas,

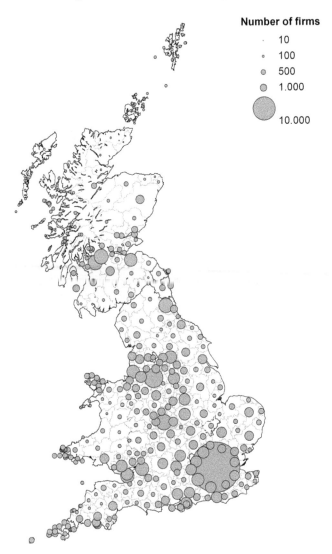

Figure 8.1 Experience industries (number of firms by TTWA), 2008

Source: Our elaboration.

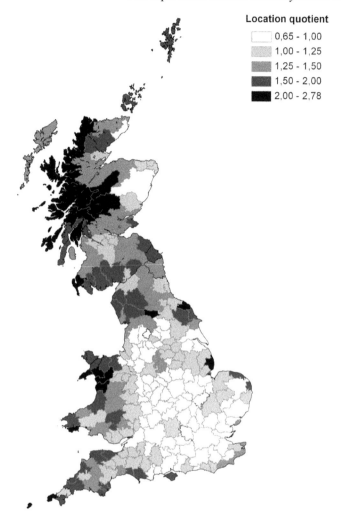

Location quotient
☐ 0,65 - 1,00
▨ 1,00 - 1,25
▨ 1,25 - 1,50
▨ 1,50 - 2,00
■ 2,00 - 2,78

Figure 8.2 Experience industries (LQs by TTWA), 2008

Source: Our elaboration.

in more rural and peripheral areas. TTWAs in Wales and Scotland, as well as in the north of England and the southwest appear to be highly specialised in experience industries.

Figures 8.3a–k shows the spatial concentration of the individual experience industries across Britain. In reality, the 11 industries considered comprise some which are strictly related to experience activities such as 'Other entertainment activities' (e.g. fair and amusement park activities), 'Libraries, archives and museums', 'Sporting activities', 'Other recreational activities', and 'Retail sale via stalls and markets'; and others that correspond to the provision of amenities, such as 'Restaurants', 'Bars', and 'Hotels'.

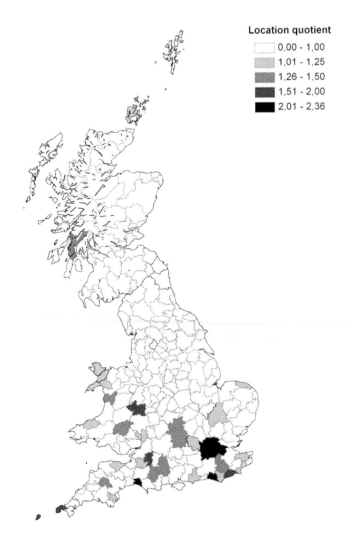

Figure 8.3a Maps of spatial concentration of the individual experience industries across the UK: Other entertainment activities, (LQs by TTWA), 2008

Source: Our elaboration.

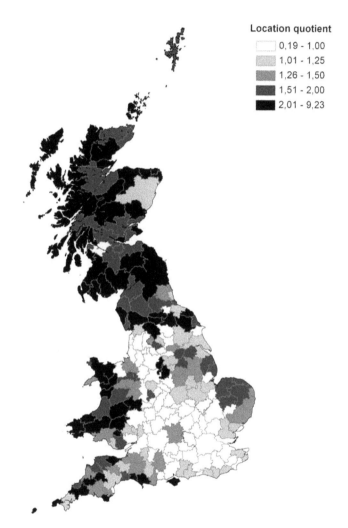

Figure 8.3b Maps of spatial concentration of the individual experience industries across the UK: Libraries, archives and museums (LQs by TTWA), 2008

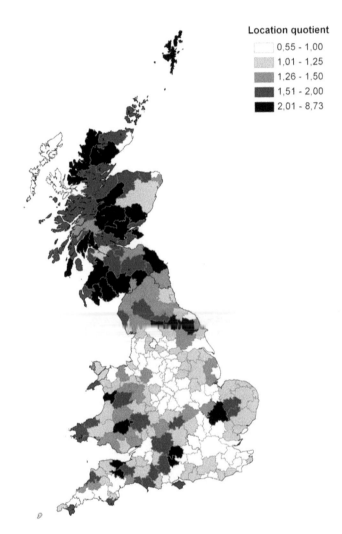

Figure 8.3c Maps of spatial concentration of the individual experience industries across the UK: Sporting activities (LQs by TTWA), 2008

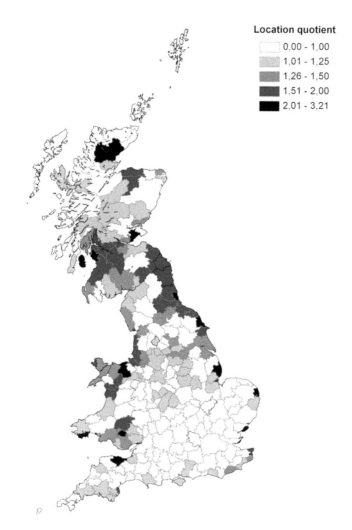

Figure 8.3d Maps of spatial concentration of the individual experience industries across the UK: Other recreational activities (LQs by TTWA), 2008

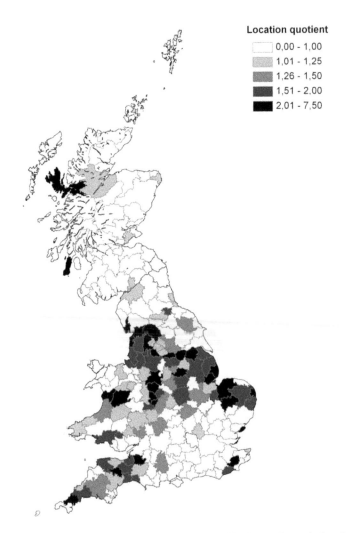

Figure 8.3e Maps of spatial concentration of the individual experience industries across the UK: Retail sale via stalls and markets (LQs by TTWA), 2008

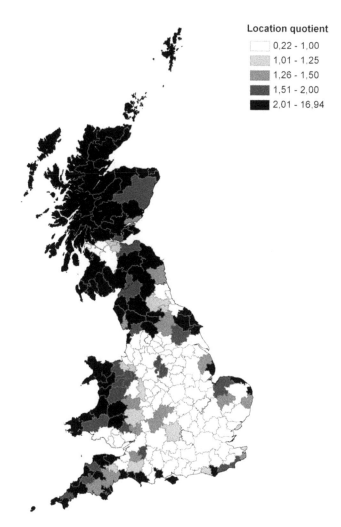

Figure 8.3f Maps of spatial concentration of the individual experience industries across the UK: Hotels (LQs by TTWA), 2008

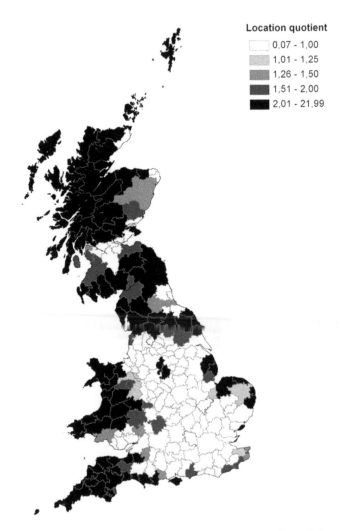

Figure 8.3g Maps of spatial concentration of the individual experience industries across the UK: Camping sites (LQs by TTWA), 2008

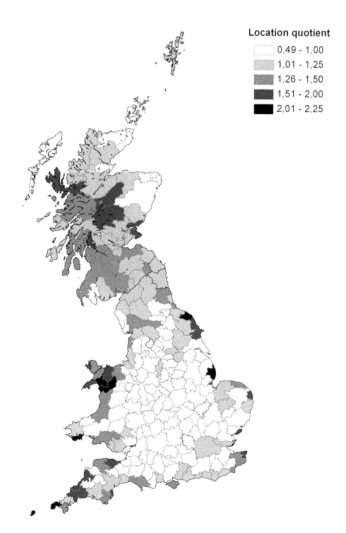

Figure 8.3h Maps of spatial concentration of the individual experience industries across the UK: Restaurants (LQs by TTWA), 2008

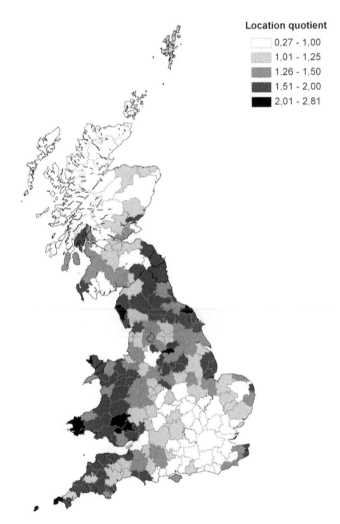

Figure 8.3i Maps of spatial concentration of the individual experience industries across the UK: Bars (LQs by TTWA), 2008

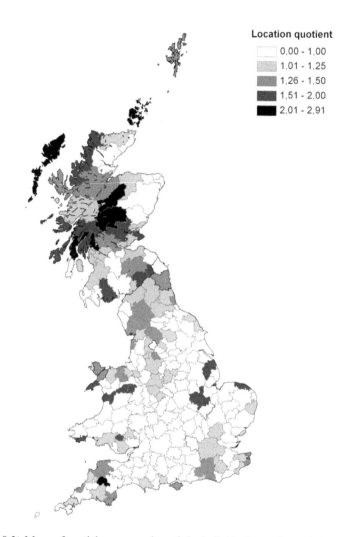

Figure 8.3j Maps of spatial concentration of the individual experience industries across the UK: Travel agencies and tour operators (LQs by TTWA), 2008

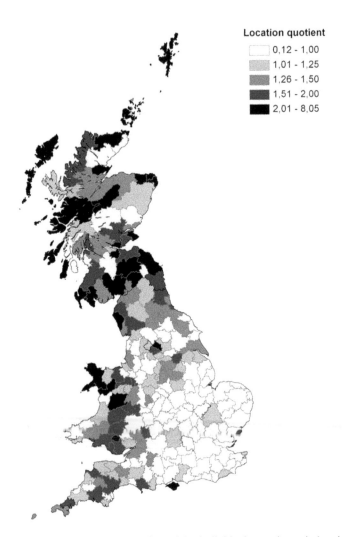

Figure 8.3k Maps of spatial concentration of the individual experience industries across the UK: Membership organisations (LQs by TTWA), 2008

The mapping analysis shows that rural and peripheral areas tend be more highly specialised in experience activities, in other words their local economy is far more reliant on these industries than more urban areas. In the latter, the presence of experience activities is dwarfed by a mix of other manufacturing and service activities. Looking at the maps for the 'Libraries, archives and museums', 'Sporting activities', and 'Other recreational activities', it can be suggested that these activities seem to characterise especially Wales, Scotland and the north and west of England where the LQ is around two. For these places, experience activities have a very important role to play as they probably constitute a sizable portion of the local economy in terms of jobs and income. The experience activities in these areas vary enormously, as some draw on natural resources – such as coastal areas or natural reserves in Scotland – others on cultural or heritage assets, such as stately homes, or National Trust countryside properties. 'Retail sale via stalls and markets' seems to be more important for some parts of the Midlands and the southwest of England, as well as being important in some peripheral coastal areas of Scotland. The only sector which presents a different spatial pattern is 'Other entertainment activities'; in fact only a few TTWAs and London seem to show a concentration of these activities above the national average. These location patterns of entertainment activities are indeed not very different from those found by Smidt-Jensen, Skytt and Winther (2009) for Denmark, where location patterns concentrate in the largest cities of the country and tourist resorts.

The other important component of the experience economy comprises ancillary hospitality activities. Our mapping analysis shows that the latter mirror the presence of experience activities; in fact, those areas that appear to specialise in experience activities also show a high concentration of 'Hotels', 'Bars' and 'Restaurants'. This means that hospitality activities again weigh heavily in the local economy in conjunction with the other experience industries. Some places in Scotland, Wales and the southeast of England appear to have above average concentrations of such amenities with LQs in many cases around two. 'Membership organisations' also show a similar spatial pattern as the latter. This does not mean that such organisations are not present elsewhere in the country, but only that the intensity of such organisations (their number) is felt more strongly in local economies where the industrial make-up is less diversified. We notice that in this case the results are different from Smidt-Jensen, Skytt and Winther (2009) in which they concentrated in Copenhagen and surrounding municipalities, and in tourist destinations, being non-important in the rest of places.

6 Correlation analysis

In mapping experience activities across Britain, we have been able to identify key spatial patterns of location. We have found that rural and peripheral places tend to be the most specialised in experience activities. Indeed, we have found evidence of such rural and peripheral places hosting a critical mass of many and varied experience activities. In other words, we have found that experience activities tend to locate close to one another. We use correlation techniques to ascertain whether these preliminary findings are statistically significant: that is, whether they provide robust evidence of underlying patterns of co-location between experience activities.

We calculate correlation coefficient between the LQs of different experience industries at the TTWA level, in order to establish to what extent the LQ of specific experience activities vary together across TTWAs. In this way, we can find whether the purpose of this exercise is to detect instances of simultaneous specialisation between the experience activities. We rely on Spearman coefficients at a 5% level of significance. Positive and significant correlation coefficients between two industries suggest they tend to co-locate in the same TTWAs; namely, places that concentrate activities of one industry also show a strong presence of the

Table 8.3 Correlation matrix. Location quotients of different experience industries at the TTWA level

	LQ Experience Economy	Retail sale via stalls and markets	Activities of other membership org.	Hotels	Camping sites	Restaurants	Bars	Travel agencies, tour operators, tourist assistance	Other entertainment activities	Library, archives, museums and other cultural activities	Sporting activities	Other recreational activities	firms Arts and antiques	firms Visual and performing arts
LQ Experience economy	1													
Retail sale via stalls and markets	−0.1489*	1												
Activities of other membership organisations not elsewhere classified	0.3349*	−0.2090*	1											
Hotels	0.8197*	−0.2280*	0.2868*	1										
Camping sites and other provision of short-stay accommodation	0.8638*	−0.1119	0.2033*	0.8018*	1									
Restaurants	0.7698*	−0.0567	0.1464*	0.5039*	0.6049*	1								
Bars	0.3419*	0.1355*	0.0877	−0.108	0.1172	0.2394*	1							
Activities of travel agencies and tour operators; tourist assistance, activities not elsewhere classified	0.4634*	−0.1262	0.1754*	0.3908*	0.4058*	0.4008*	0.0215	1						
Other entertainment activities	0.0988	−0.02	−0.2172*	−0.0118	0.0939	0.0821	−0.0232	0.0833	1					
Library, archives, museums and other cultural activities	0.7394*	−0.2360*	0.3547*	0.7329*	0.6016*	0.3751*	0.0647	0.2969*	−0.0364	1				
Sporting activities	0.5082*	−0.2237*	0.2147*	0.3750*	0.3093*	0.1773*	0.0457	0.1604*	−0.035	0.5610*	1			
Other recreational activities	0.3649*	0.1215	0.0446	0.0808	0.1333	0.5318*	0.4160*	0.1033	−0.2336*	0.1179	0.0881	1		
firms Arts and antiques	0.6340*	−0.0515	0.1055	0.4023*	0.5360*	0.6674*	0.3346*	0.3068*	0.0936	0.4166*	0.2050*	0.3034*	1	
firms Visual and performing arts	0.2447*	−0.1134	−0.1721*	0.1443*	0.2233*	0.1491*	−0.0112	0.1498*	0.9358*	0.1143	0.0864	−0.1402*	0.1547*	1

Source: Our elaboration. Note: *5% significant.

other industry. On the other hand, negative and significant correlation coefficients would indicate that two sectors tend not to co-locate.

Several interesting findings emerge from this analysis. The first finding of interest is that amenities are positively correlated with one another, as they tend to benefit from co-location even in rural areas. Indeed, we find very strong, significant and positive correlation of coefficients for 'Hotels', 'Restaurants', 'Travel agencies' and 'Membership organisations', suggesting a tendency towards spatial simultaneity.

Second, 'Libraries and museums' and 'Sporting events' are found to be very strongly correlated, which means that places tend to find them co-located; in contrast, 'Activities in market stalls' appears to have a negative correlation coefficient with all the other experience activities and tends therefore to locate in places not specialised in these activities.

Third, a very strong and positive correlation is found between strictly speaking experience activities and the amenities. For instance, all the hospitality activities are found to locate where there is a local specialisation in 'Libraries and museums' and 'Sporting events'. The causality between the two is not clear from the analysis, but we can assume that hotels and restaurants are likely to develop around pre-existing forms of natural, cultural or heritage assets.

Fourth, 'Retail sale via stalls and markets' and 'Other entertainment activities' are either insignificantly or negatively correlated with the aggregate experience economy LQ: this confirms what we found in the mapping as these two industries had quite different spatial patterns from the others.

Finally, we have also calculated the correlation coefficient between the experience industries here classified with 'Arts and antiques', currently classified as creative under the DCMS classification. Evidence suggests that this industry is significantly and positively correlated with the aggregate experience economy LQ and with the other experience activities; in particular, there is evidence of strong co-location with amenities. This is revealing of an industry that appears to be closer in nature to experience activities than to creative industries. A hint of that emerged in the NESTA report *The Geography of Creativity* (De Propris *et al.* 2009) where 'Arts and antiques' was found to be negatively and significantly correlated with all the other creative industries. On the other hand, 'Other entertainment activities' is found to be strongly positively correlated with 'Visual and performing arts' – also classified as creative industry according to the DCMS. This confirms what could be already anticipated from the maps, which is that such a sector tends to concentrate in urban areas rather than rural ones. Further analysis would help unearth further such trends.

7 A better understanding

Economic activities are never space blind. Qualifying characteristics of places have somewhat determined the type of economic development in such places, and some of such trends have shown path dependency as the anchoring factors of economic activities have changed over time. In the pre-industrial economy, economic activities started and developed around natural resources and in conjunction with point of access to production and markets, such as ports and canals. It was argued that the current urban pattern is indeed shaped by such initial endowments (Glaeser 1998). Industrialisation coincided with already existing artisan concentration in urban areas. The industrial revolution of the 1700s and 1800s in the UK overlapped with the development of cities like Birmingham, Manchester and Liverpool. In such cities, firms agglomerated in Marshallian industrial districts rather than spreading across space to benefit from external and agglomeration economies (Becattini, Bellandi and De Propris 2009). Places are therefore different and firms are attracted to some but not others: such centripetal forces have reinforced the attractiveness of some places against other. In a similar manner, the flexible specialisation model that anticipated Porter's clusters emphasised how firms' agglomeration was cumulative and path dependent driven by firms' economic advantages (Markusen 1996; Porter 2000). In other words, firms' location choices sustained the growth of some clusters as they spawned in more and more complex economic systems. The immobility of such systems in particular places is only justified by the critical mass of economic activities embedded in such place. A tight link with the place was also suggested by Florida (2002) in his work on the creative class, for talented people tend to congregate at certain locations which become places of consumption and production. Urban spaces contain a critical mass of amenities and become therefore attractive *creative places*. Again economic activities discriminate across space and studies on creative industries finds that these tend also to form creative clusters. Creative firms chose to locate close to other firms driven by the same external economies of Marshallian industrial districts. Co-locating with buyers and suppliers creates valuable economic benefits firms want to reap (De Propris *et al.* 2009). However, in the case of creative industries, evidence suggests that these tend to locate in urban areas where there are other creative industries. Although unconnected along the value chain, firms in different sectors co-locate to benefit from either cross-sectoral spinoffs or serendipitous synergies. Such urbanisation economies generate and feed creative places, and in particular creative cities, which become therefore agglomerations of many creative clusters (see Lazzeretti, Capone and Boix 2012; and Boix, Hervás and De Miguel 2014).

What about cultural or experience industries? How do they relate to places? Are they immobile and what anchors them? This chapter addresses and in part answers such questions. The subtle distinction between cultural and experience-related industries would be a separate chapter in itself, nevertheless the spatial patterns presented here suggests some quite robust reflections. The conceptual contribution of the chapter draws therefore on its findings. In particular, the uniqueness of the experience economy rests of four nested features: (a) the authenticity of the cultural asset (experience or heritage); (b) the immobility and local embeddedness of cultural assets; (c) the distinction between cultural asset and cultural capital; and finally (d) embedded and immobile cultural capital generates cultural/experience clusters.

From the current literature, we know already that the experience economy tends to be characterised by experiences that are space bound. Lorentzen (2009: 11) argues that 'the place has a role to play in the experience economy as space of consumption and production of the experience'. Indeed, the core value of this type of economic activity is that it engages people to participate in something first hand. Pine and Gilmore (1998) argue that experiences may connect to people in different ways and distinguish 'four realms of experience' (p. 304): 'passive-active participation' and 'absorption-immersion'. In other words, visiting Shakespeare's birth place is a different activity from horseracing on a country lane in the Peak District in the north of England, however, they both share the fact that they come to life when people live them as experience – whether active and immersed or not.

The definition of the experience industries underpinning this study suggests a set of activities that are typically experience-based. They reflect either the 'offer' of experiences in the form of museums, sporting events or live theatrical presentation, or the 'enabling' of such experience by making a place accessible for visitors.

A crucial aspect is that establishing a real connection with the place enables the authenticity of the experience, crucial for consumers. Indeed, the value of the experience for the consumer is somewhat related to the fact that it happens in that place. Lorentzen (2009) and Lorentzen and Hansen (2009) confirm that one of the key features of the experience economy is that it is attendance-based, and 'it needs to be consumed in situ' (p. 822). This means that experience activities are immobile and locally embedded. Whether the cultural asset is a heritage site, a summer festival or a ski slope, they cannot be separated from the place where they are or take place. This introduces an element of uniqueness in relation to experience-related economies: they are spread across urban and rural areas. In particular, as our study has found, they weigh much more in the economy of rural and peripheral places, than in the economy of urban areas.

The evidence presented in this chapter shows that places become attractive because of their immobile natural, experience or heritage assets, however, for the latter to be an engine of local economic development they must become a natural, experience or heritage capital. In other words, the asset is invested in it to have the capacity to catalyse a critical mass of economic activities. Evidence of this in our study is the co-location of museums and sporting events, for instance, with the provision of amenities to enable attendance, namely restaurants and hotels. Such supporting industries enable the asset to be accessible, livable, *experiential*, and in so doing they transform the asset into an experience that is capitalised on and becomes therefore a factor of local economic growth. In other words, as natural, experience or heritage assets become natural, experience or heritage capital – if invested in – they are able to generate socio-economic value. The co-location of a critical mass of related activities suggests that places with experience-related activities develop into complex systems of production coinciding with a form of cluster. Unlike other manufacturing or service clusters, those revolving around a natural, experience or heritage capital are truly immobile and embedded. This does not mean they will not go through a quite natural life cycle and in some cases fall out of fashion.

8 Concluding remarks and further research

This chapter sets out to explore experience-related industries in the UK by looking at their spatial patterns and co-location trends. This is inevitably a risky venture in a debate that is still in flux. The objective of the study is to challenge the current, static debate on creative industries in the UK, by intersecting it with an understanding of the experience economy. It aims to instigate it by making a tentative suggestion, by opening a conversation rather than closing it.

The starting point of the chapter was to distil from the existing literature a classification of experience industries that could have been used to map them across Britain's regions. This effort produced the first novelty of the study. We identified 11 experience industries bearing in mind the DCMS classification of creative industries.

As we mapped them across Britain's TTWAs, we were able to reach a better understanding of where and how they are spatially located. We found confirmed the argument that rural and peripheral areas tend to be more specialised in experience industries, for which their weight in the local economy is greater than in urban areas. In reality, this is also valid for a sector currently classified by the DCMS as a creative industry, but that in reality presents the same spatial characteristics as experience industries, namely 'Arts and antiques'. In fact, on the basis of this robust evidence, we suggest that 'Arts and antiques' ought to be re-grouped more appropriately as an experience industry.

The correlation analysis shows that experience industries tend to co-locate and in particular that places that show a high degree of specialisation of experience activities also host a critical mass of hospitality activities. This suggests that the various natural, cultural or sport-related attractions are supported by the provision of services for visitors, from restaurants to hotel to travel agencies. More qualitative and in-depth studies could expand the analysis of some of these places to reach a better understanding of how these function as cultural clusters.

There are valuable policy recommendations that can be derived from the findings of the present study. First, investment in natural, experience or heritage capital must mobilise local economic strategies, rather than a national one: local players have a deep understanding of the asset and are able to identify the needed investment. Second, experience-based development strategies ought to support existing and 'real' experience-related capital; indeed only the latter can attract a critical mass of related activities and become a destination for visitors on a sustainable manner. This means that not all places will have an experience-related cluster. Finally, if there is one lesson we have learned from the last recession, it is that economies must rely on a balanced set of activities; in the same way, a seasonal and somehow cyclical sector like the experience-based economy can only be part of a place's economic make-up. Regional and local resilience rests more than ever on a well-balanced and diversified economy: this not only creates opportunities for economic renewal but it provides the terrain for all sorts of serendipitous innovations, like in cities.

The chapter addresses an unexplored topic in the UK debate and some of its findings open up questions rather than providing certainties. There is no doubt that, further research is necessary to unpack some of the issues that emerge. Two are worth mentioning as a possible research agenda. First, what is the link between the experience economy and technology, in particular an ICT? In a globalised world where even remote places have become virtually accessible, how do such virtual connections impact the place's projection of offering an authentic experience? Second, how have these industries evolved over time and in particular how have they weathered the recession? Such conversation is just beginning in the UK and the advancements in other European countries offer signposts along the way.

Appendix 8.1 Sectors' definitions (SIC 2003)

SIC code	Definition	
55.1 Hotels	55.10/1	Hotels and motels, with restaurant (licensed)
	55.10/2	Hotels and motels, with restaurant (unlicensed)
	55.10/3	Hotels and motels without restaurant
55.2 Camping sites and other provision of short-stay accommodation	55.21	Youth hostels and mountain refuges
	55.22	Camping sites, including caravan sites
	55.23	Other provision of lodgings not elsewhere classified
	55.23/1	Holiday centres and holiday villages
	55.23/2	Other self-catering holiday accommodation
	55.23/9	Other tourist or short-stay accommodation
55.3 Restaurants	55.30/1	Licensed restaurants
	55.30/2	Unlicensed restaurants and cafes
	55.30/3	Take-away food shops
	55.30/4	Take-away food mobile stands
55.4 Bars	55.40/1	Licensed clubs
	55.40/2	Independent public houses and bars
	55.40/3	Tenanted public houses and bars
	55.40/4	Managed public houses and bars
63.3 Activities of travel agencies and tour operators; tourist assistance activities not elsewhere classified	63.30/1	Activities of travel agencies
	63.30/2	Activities of travel organisers
	63.30/3	Activities of tour guides
	63.30/9	Other tourist assistance activities not elsewhere classified
92.3 Other entertainment activities	92.31	Artistic and literary creation and interpretation
	92.31/1	Live theatrical presentation
	92.31/9	Other artistic and literary creation and interpretation
	92.32	Operation of arts facilities
	92.33	Fair and amusement park activities
	92.34	Other entertainment activities not elsewhere classified

(Continued)

SIC code		Definition
		92.34/1 Dance halls and dance instructor services
		92.34/9 Other entertainment activities not elsewhere classified
92.5	Libraries, archives, museums and other cultural activities	92.51 Library and archive activities
		92.52 Museum activities and preservation of historical sites and buildings
		92.52/1 Museum activities
		92.52/2 Preservation of historical sites and buildings
		92.53 Botanical and zoological gardens and nature reserve activities
92.6	Sporting activities	92.61 Operation of sports arenas and stadiums
		92.61/1 Operation of ice rinks and roller skating rinks
		92.61/9 Operation of other sports arenas and stadiums not elsewhere classified
		92.62 Other sporting activities
		92.62/1 Activities of racehorse owners
		92.62/9 Other sporting activities not elsewhere classified
92.7	Other recreational activities	92.71 Gambling and betting activities • Sale of lottery tickets • Operation (exploitation) of coin-operated gambling machines
		92.72 Other recreational activities not elsewhere classified
		92.72/1 Motion picture, television and other theatrical casting • Personal theatrical or artistic agency services cf. 74.87/9
		92.72/9 Other recreational activities not elsewhere classified • Activities of recreation parks and beaches including renting of facilities such as bath houses, lockers, chairs, etc. • Operation (exploitation) of coin-operated video games
52.62	Retail sale via stalls and markets	
91.33	Activities of other membership organisations not elsewhere classified	This class includes: • Activities of organisations related: — Citizens' initiative or protest movements — Environmental and ecological movements — Organisations supporting community and educational facilities not elsewhere classified — Organisations for the protection and betterment of special groups, e.g. ethnic and minority groups — Associations for patriotic purposes including war veterans' associations

SIC code	Definition

	• Special interest groups such as touring clubs and automobile associations and consumer associations
	• Associations for the purpose of social acquaintanceship such as rotary clubs, lodges, etc.
	• Associations of youth, young persons' associations, student associations, clubs and fraternities, etc.
	• Associations for the pursuit of a cultural or recreational activity or hobby (other than sports or games),
	   – E.g. poetry, literature clubs, historical, gardening, film and photo, music and art, craft and collectors'
	   – Clubs, social clubs, carnival clubs, etc.
	• Associations for the protection of animals

References

Andersson, A. E. and Andersson, D. E. (2006) *The Economics of Experiences, the Arts and Entertainment*, Cheltenham, UK: Edward Elgar.

Arthur, I. K. (2009) 'Investigating the prospects of experience economy in the food sector: A pilot study on Thisted Municipality', paper presented at the Regional Studies Association Annual Conference, Leuven, Belgium, 6–8 April.

Becattini, G. Bellandi, M. and De Propris, L. (2009) *The Handbook of Industrial Districts*, Cheltenham, UK: Edward Elgar.

Bille, T. (2010) *The Nordic Approach to the Experience Economy. Does it Make Sense?* Creative Encounters Working Paper no. 44, Copenhagen Business School.

Boix, R., Capone, F., De Propris, L., Lazzeretti, L. and Sánchez, D. (2014) 'Comparing creative industries in Europe', *European Urban and Regional Studies*, published online 21 August 2014.

Boix, R., Hervás, J. L. and De Miguel, B. (2014) 'Micro-geographies of creative industries clusters in Europe: from hot spots to assemblages', *Papers in Regional Science*, first published online 20 January 2014.

Cairncross, F. (1997) *The Death of Distance: How the Communications Revolution Will Change our Lives*, Boston, MA: Harvard Business School Press.

Cooke, P. and De Propris, P. (2011) 'A policy agenda for EU smart growth: The role of creative and cultural industries', *Policy Studies*, 32(4): 365–75.

Cooke, P. and Lazzeretti, L. (eds) (2008) *Creative Cities, Cultural Clusters and Local Economic Development*, Cheltenham, UK: Edward Elgar.

De Propris, L., Chapain, C., Cooke, P., MacNeill, S. and Mateos-Garcia, J. (2009) *The Geography of Creativity*, London: NESTA.

Deloitte (2008) *The Economic Case for the Visitor Economy*, London: Deloitte MCS.

Deloitte (2010) *The Economic Case for the Visitor Economy. UK and the Nations*, London: Deloitte MCS.

EC – European Commission (2010) *Green Paper on Cultural and Creative Industries: Unlocking the Potential of Cultural and Creative Industries*, COM (2010) 183, Brussels: EU Commission.

EC – European Commission (2010) *Green Paper: Unlocking the Potential of Cultural and Creative Industries*, COM (2010) 183, Brussels.

Florida, R. (2002) *The Rise of the Creative Class*, New York: Basic Books.

FOE – Friends of the Earth (2000) *The Economic Benefits of Farmers' Markets*, London: Friends of the Earth Trust.

Galloway, S., and Dunlop, S. (2007) 'A critique of definitions of the cultural and creative industries in public policy', *International Journal of Cultural Policy*, 13(1): 17–31.

Glaeser, E. L. (1998) 'Are cities dying?' *Journal of Economic Perspectives*, 12(2): 139–60.

Kebir, L. and Crevoisier, O. (2008) 'Cultural resources and regional development: The case of the cultural legacy of watchmaking', in L. Lazzeretti and P. Cooke (eds), *Creative Cities, Cultural Clusters and Local Economic Development*, Cheltenham, UK: Edward Elgar, pp. 48–69.

Lazzeretti, L. (2003) 'City of art as a high culture local system and cultural districtualization processes: The cluster of art restoration in Florence', *International Journal of Urban and Regional Research*, 27(3): 635–48.

Lazzeretti, L., Boix, R. and Capone, F. (2008) 'Do creative industries cluster? Mapping creative local production systems in Italy and Spain', *Industry and Innovation*, 15(5): 549–67.

Lazzeretti L., Capone F. and Boix R. (2012) 'Reasons for clustering of creative industries in Italy and Spain', *European Planning Studies*, 20(8): 1243–1262.

Lorentzen, A. (2009) 'Gateway: Experience economy and spatial strategies. Space and place in the experience economy. A proactive approach', paper presented at the Regional Studies Association Annual Conference, Leuven, Belgium, 6–8 April.

Lorentzen, A. and Hansen, C.J. (2009) 'The role and transformation of the city in the experience economy: Identifying and exploring research challenges', *European Planning Studies*, 17(6): 817–27.

Markusen, A. (1996) 'Sticky places in slippery space: A typology of industrial districts', *Economic Geography*, 72(3). 293–313.

Office for National Statistics (ONS) (2003), *UK Standard Industrial Classification of Economic Activities 2003*, HMSO, UK.

Pine, B. J. and Gilmore, J. H. (1998) 'Welcome to the experience economy', *Harvard Business Review*, 76(4): 97–105.

Pine, B. J. and Gilmore, J. H. (1999) *The Experience Economy*, Boston, MA: Harvard University Press.

Porter, M. E. (2000) 'Location, competition, and economic development: Local clusters in a global economy', *Economic Development Quarterly*, 14(15): 15–34.

Regeringen (2003) *Danmark i kultur- og oplevelsesøkonomien – 5 nye skridt på vejen*, Copenhagen: Schultz.

Smidt-Jensen, S., Skytt, C. B. and Winther, L. (2009) 'The geography of the experience economy in Denmark: Employment change and location dynamics in attendance-based experience industries', *European Planning Studies*, 17(6): 847–62.

Throsby, D. (2001) *Economics and Culture*, Cambridge, UK: Cambridge University Press.

Tofler, A. (1970) *Future Shock*, New York: Bentam Books.

UKTI – UK Trade and Investment (2010) *UK Creative Industries*, London: UK Trade and Investment.

UNESCO – United Nations Educational, Scientific and Cultural Organization (2009) *The 2009 UNESCO Framework for Cultural Statistics*, Montreal: UNESCO Institute for Statistics.

Index

 Taylor & Francis eBooks

Helping you to choose the right eBooks for your Library

Add Routledge titles to your library's digital collection today. Taylor and Francis ebooks contains over 50,000 titles in the Humanities, Social Sciences, Behavioural Sciences, Built Environment and Law.

Choose from a range of subject packages or create your own!

Benefits for you

- » Free MARC records
- » COUNTER-compliant usage statistics
- » Flexible purchase and pricing options
- » All titles DRM-free.

 REQUEST YOUR **FREE** INSTITUTIONAL TRIAL TODAY

Free Trials Available
We offer free trials to qualifying academic, corporate and government customers.

Benefits for your user

- » Off-site, anytime access via Athens or referring URL
- » Print or copy pages or chapters
- » Full content search
- » Bookmark, highlight and annotate text
- » Access to thousands of pages of quality research at the click of a button.

eCollections – Choose from over 30 subject eCollections, including:

Archaeology	Language Learning
Architecture	Law
Asian Studies	Literature
Business & Management	Media & Communication
Classical Studies	Middle East Studies
Construction	Music
Creative & Media Arts	Philosophy
Criminology & Criminal Justice	Planning
Economics	Politics
Education	Psychology & Mental Health
Energy	Religion
Engineering	Security
English Language & Linguistics	Social Work
Environment & Sustainability	Sociology
Geography	Sport
Health Studies	Theatre & Performance
History	Tourism, Hospitality & Events

For more information, pricing enquiries or to order a free trial, please contact your local sales team:
www.tandfebooks.com/page/sales

 Routledge
Taylor & Francis Group

The home of
Routledge books

www.tandfebooks.com

For Product Safety Concerns and Information please contact our EU
representative GPSR@taylorandfrancis.com
Taylor & Francis Verlag GmbH, Kaufingerstraße 24, 80331 München, Germany

www.ingramcontent.com/pod-product-compliance
Ingram Content Group UK Ltd.
Pitfield, Milton Keynes, MK11 3LW, UK
UKHW020953180425
457613UK00019B/652